To Margaret on her birthday

September 1 1989

From

E. Art

Charlotte, Mary E & John.

Walter J. Blackburn
A Man for All Media

Walter Juxon Blackburn
1914 — 1983

Walter J. Blackburn

A Man for All Media

Michael Nolan

Macmillan of Canada
A Division of Canada Publishing Corporation
Toronto, Ontario, Canada

Canadian Cataloguing in Publication Data

Nolan, Michael, 1940–
  Walter J. Blackburn, a man for all media

Includes bibliographical references and index.
ISBN 0-7715-9200-0

1. Blackburn, Walter Juxon, 1914– . 2. London free press
— History. 3. London Free Press Holdings Limited —
Biography. 4. Publishers and publishing — Ontario —
London — Biography. 5. Broadcasting — Ontario —
Biography. I. Title.

PN4913.B58N64 1989   070.5′092′4   C89–093113–5

Jacket and Text design: David Montle
Frontispiece: Photo courtesy of the Blackburn Family

MACMILLAN OF CANADA
A Division of Canada Publishing Corporation
Toronto, Ontario, Canada

Printed by T.H. Best Company Ltd.

FOREWORD

◇ ———————————————— ◇

IT IS MOST APPROPRIATE that Walter Blackburn's many and varied contributions to journalism, both print and electronic, should thus be set down and preserved for this and future generations. It was the family's happy inspiration to invite Michael Nolan to undertake the task and to give him their full co-operation, plus access to both the papers and people he needed to see. As an experienced, practicing journalist himself, Mr. Nolan knows the field and knows whereof he speaks. As a professor of journalism, he also enjoys the advantages that scholarly detachment confers.

The book, then, consists primarily of the inside story of Walter's life and his long list of achievements as "a man for all media" — a title well deserved. The building of *The London Free Press* from a small local to large regional daily is one part of the story. The early ventures into radio, the risks he ran trying to overcome the timidity of print-oriented advertisers is another, as is the development of private ownership in television. Then the weaving together of all these autonomous media into a broad family enterprise that preserved their independence while cementing their fundamental unity is a story to be read with mounting excitement.

And all of this had to be done while maintaining cordial relations with government on the one hand, the public on the other, and his growing number of employees in the middle. None of it was easy. All of it was innovative, calling for vision and high imagination, coupled with a ferocious devotion to the mastery of technological detail — a combination rare enough in a management team, let alone a single individual. Yet Walter did possess all these attributes, along with the confidence in his own judgment to take the risks involved.

This entrepreneurial journalism of his had, as one of its principal policies, service to the people of London and its surroundings. As a citizen he pursued that same ideal in his personal service to the London Symphony, Theatre London, The YM-YWCA, the Salvation Army and the Board of The University of Western Ontario and of the London Health Association. In this latter capacity, he was a tower of strength in the building of University Hospital — perhaps his greatest single civic accomplishment.

But what about the man behind all this? Well, we can see he must be a man of courage, self-confidence, vision, and concern for the welfare of others, to name but a few of his attributes. The memories of family, friends and associates also help illuminate his character. But perhaps a further word is in order.

David Riesman, in his book *The Lonely Crowd*, sees us all as either "inner-directed" or "outer-directed". The former are equipped with an internal moral compass which, regardless of the changing sentiments of the crowd, sets the moral course they steer by. The latter group, by contrast, are equipped with sensitive social radar antennae, quick to detect changes in the public mood and eager to adjust their course to "go with the flow".

Walter was, of course, an inner-directed man. His morals, values and standards were learned early and he steered his life's course accordingly. If that meant going against the majority, anything from prolonging a board meeting to clarify a detail, to standing up for an unpopular moral principle, so be it. I suspect that nowhere was that moral compass more severely tested than when, on the outbreak of World War II, this twenty-five-year-old youth, longing to join up with his friends in that dangerous adventure, put it all behind him and accepted his less glamorous but heavily demanding obligations as the third-generation publisher of the family paper, hoping that people would understand.

It is not without interest either, to ponder the fact that this quiet, self-contained, inner-directed man made his great contribution to canadian media; of all fields surely the one that must depend for its existence on outer directedness, on sensitivity to changes in public feelings, on the need to "hold the mirror up to nature" as Hamlet put it. But by that very token, media owner-ship should have the high social standards, the moral clarity and the sense of *noblesse oblige* that the inner-directed bring to it. Only thus do the media earn public trust and confidence. These matters were to Walter the essence of his being, his raison d'être and the core of his philosophy.

Of course it is possible to publish trash and thrive on it. Many do. For them, Walter had nothing but contempt. He would agree with Hilaire Belloc when he said, "Rock endures, mud washes away." Walter's particular "rock" has endured now for four generations. He would, I suspect, be greatly pleased but not in the least surprised to see how well his daughter applies the things he taught her to the new challenges of today.

D. Carlton Williams
President and Vice-Chancellor
The University of Western Ontario 1967-1977

CONTENTS

Preface xii

Acknowledgements xiii

ONE: Born to the Job *1849–1936* 1

TWO: "Mister Blackburn" *1936–1945* 31

THREE: A Broadcast Innovator *1945-1950* 55

FOUR: A Multi-media Owner *1950-1958* 77

FIVE: A Publisher's Hopes Dashed *1958-1970* 105

SIX: The House that Walter Built *1970-1974* 133

SEVEN: A Lifetime Ambition Fulfilled *1974-1976* . . . 153

EIGHT: The Final Years *1976-1984* 169

NINE: The Fourth Generation *1984-1988* 201

Epilogue 229

Endnotes 233

Note on Sources 250

Index 251

PREFACE

◇ ——————————————— ◇

WALTER JUXON BLACKBURN had a permanent impact on the newspaper and broadcasting industries in Canada. During his lifetime as a multi-media owner in London, Ontario, Blackburn combined a uniquely humanitarian approach toward employees with a far-sighted belief in the need for technological innovation and adaptation.

This book examines the Blackburn family's historic connection to London and western Ontario and assesses Walter Blackburn's performance and contribution as a media owner, publisher, businessman, and public citizen. Throughout his fifty-odd years as a third-generation newspaperman, Blackburn modernized *The London Free Press*, redesigned CFPL-AM radio, introduced FM broadcasting and later television to London.

As a member of the Canadian Press, Blackburn was instrumental in the development of Broadcast News, the CP subsidiary that now serves several hundred Canadian radio stations. He was a strong believer in CP and the need for readers to be able to enjoy a free flow of information across the country. He defended the need for a free press and reiterated this belief repeatedly before federal inquiries into the media. He was exceedingly skeptical of any initiative that presented a potential threat of government interference in the mass media's day-to-day operations.

This biography was commissioned by the Blackburn family as a tribute, and an objective evaluation of Walter Blackburn and his career as a media owner. The subject of Canadian media history remains largely unexplored; scholars have tended to focus on institutional subjects such as the evolution of the Canadian Broadcasting Corporation, so an important story remains to be told about the essential role and growth of private ownership of the media in Canada. I hope this book will serve as a model and an inspiration for others to explore this fascinating area of Canadian history.

———————

WHILE UNDERTAKING THIS STUDY I have had the full support and encouragement of the Blackburn family. To enable a thorough history of Walter Blackburn's life and times to be written, I was granted access to private family documents and financial records of The Blackburn Group Inc. A letter from Martha Grace Blackburn, chairman and president of The Blackburn Group Inc., showing the family's support for the project opened many doors that led to both interviews and documents within the print and broadcast industries. Both she, her older sister, Susan Marjorie Toledo, and Marjorie Ludwell Blackburn, sat through many interviews and patiently answered questions relating to Walter Blackburn's career and family life.

Many other individuals helped in the research and writing of thie book. At *The London Free Press*, columnist L.N. Bronson was extremely helpful with his thorough knowledge of the newspaper's and London's history. Helen Daly, Walter Blackburn's corporate secretary for many years, gave of her time generously; and Ken Lemon, the Blackburn family's financial adviser, patiently took me through the financial history of the various media companies.

I also received kind assistance from Ed Phelps, librarian-in-charge of the Regional Collection, and from John Lutman, librarian-in-charge of Special Collections, at the D.B. Weldon Library at the University of Western Ontario. W. Glen Curnoe, London Room librarian, and Alastair Neely at the central branch of London Public Libraries were of considerable help. At the Public Archives of Canada, Ian McClymont, chief of political and public affairs archives, and archivist Brian Murphy also provided assistance.

Acknowledgements also to the following, who helped with photo research: Edythe Cusack, librarian, Michael Pittana and

Mike Hensen, both lab technicians/photographers, and Paul Gartlan, chief photographer, all at *The London Free Press*; Leslie McIntosh, editor, *The Fourth Estate*; the Blackburn Media Employees' Association; Margaret Stokesberry-Leeson, Special Collection, and Theresa Regnier, Regional Collection, D.B. Weldon Library, University of Western Ontario.

Sheldon Fischer, a skilled and sensitive editor at Macmillan of Canada, was of great help. My wife, Carole, provided her usual wise counsel. To all these and those who helped in lesser ways, my thanks.

◇————————◇

CHAPTER ONE

Born to the Job
1849 — 1936

*T*HE YOUNG, INTENSE and somewhat shy graduate, who on 3 June 1936 received an honours B.A. in Business Administration at the University of Western Ontario, knew the challenges that lay ahead. In January 1936 following his father's death, he had become president and manager of *The London Free Press* at the age of 21 — the youngest publisher of a daily newspaper in Canada. His annual salary was $3,500.

Tomorrow he would begin to devote his full energies to the southwestern Ontario newspaper whose origins and tradition dated back to 1849, preceding by five years the incorporation of the city of London. The evolution of *The Free Press*, owned successively by three generations of the Blackburn family, had paralleled closely the growth and development of the city and region. It would fall to Walter Juxon Blackburn to bring the mass circulation daily into the mid-twentieth century and to expand the family's regional media dynasty.

Early in life the notions of family commitment and individual responsibility were impressed upon Blackburn. His three aunts, Susan, Margaret and Eleanor, and two sisters, Constance and Miriam, relied heavily on his performance as head of the family-owned business. On graduation day he received several reminders of their expectations. His aunts sent him a congratulatory message on his academic achievement. They expressed a collective hope that "the years to come [would] bring . . . peace, joy and further success."[1] His sister, Constance, also told him that he had upheld the Blackburn name "in noble style." Recalling her late father's diabetic condition and the difficulties the family had faced through her brother's university days, she noted that "the past few years have been difficult ones. . . . Perhaps more for you than for [sister] Miriam or me as you have shared more of the responsibility." She praised him for his "staunchness and courage" and quoted Walpole in her graduation note: "It is not life that matters but the courage that you bring to it." Their father would be pleased, she said, because "he had the utmost faith in his only lad."[2]

Walter's father and aunts had made the third-generation publisher acutely aware, as a youngster, of his family's history and the sense of responsibility that inevitably accompanied ownership of a community newspaper. Each Blackburn had managed to assume control of the newspaper at a relatively young age, enabling him to put his own stamp on the enterprise. That successive generations of Blackburns had nurtured the family-owned business, without selling to a larger or richer buyer and simply living off the family inheritance, was evidence of a corporate individualism that had its roots set deeply and firmly in the nineteenth century.

Walter's grandfather, Josiah Blackburn, who had been born in England, had come to Canada in 1850 after a European tour to join his brother, John, at the *Star* in Paris, Ontario, near London. A couple of years later, Josiah purchased *The Canadian Free Press* from James Daniell, the holder of a $500 mortgage against William Sutherland, founder of the weekly newspaper.[3] Blackburn's takeover on 1 January 1853 marked the beginning of the Blackburn media dynasty in London.

Josiah Blackburn's remote ancestry on the paternal side had its novel aspects. He was descended from North Country folk in England, the Blackburns of Lancaster and Yorkshire. Several of his ancestors had been "men of the cloth," including one of a different stripe, a legendary Blackburn of York who at one time had been a pirate. After forsaking his past, he was consecrated a prelate of the Church of England. He had a keen interest in the violin and was eventually nicknamed the "Fiddling Bishop of York," a character in which he was later sculptured at York Minster.

Josiah's grandmother on his father's side had her ancestral roots in the Juxon family of Suffolk, whose most distinguished member probably was the renowned Bishop Juxon who died in 1663 at the age of 81. He served as Bishop of London and Lord High Treasurer of England under Charles I and as Archbishop of Canterbury under Charles II. Bishop Juxon was involved in a somewhat curious incident at the time of the execution of Charles I on 30 January 1649. The condemned Stuart king had requested the Bishop to stand with him upon the scaffold. In the midst of the mild confusion prior to the beheading of Charles, the King passed to the Bishop a ring with the word *Memento* engraved upon it. The ring later was placed in the British Museum as an historic relic.[4] Many generations later Josiah Blackburn's grandson, who was born in St. Joseph's Hospital in London on 18 March 1914, was christened Walter Juxon Blackburn.

On the maternal side Josiah's grandfather was Robert Smith, Squire of Beslyns, a manor in Essex, England. His daughter, Sarah, married the Reverend John Blackburn who had been born in 1792. Reverend Blackburn eventually became an eminent Congregationalist theologian. He participated in the formation of the Congregational Union of England and Wales and acted as Home Secretary. As editor of the *Congregational Calendar* between 1840 and 1848, his efforts were devoted largely to the literary side of Congregationalism. In his work, *The Congregational Two Hundred*, Albert Peel described Reverend Blackburn's extensive career and concluded that "Congregationalism had few better minds."[5]

A year after arriving in Canada, Josiah married his first wife, Emma Jane Delamore, on 29 May 1851. She was the daughter of an Englishman who had settled in the Don Valley area of what is now Toronto. The Blackburns had eight children, six daughters and two sons. The two oldest children, Sarah Emma (born on 18 June 1853) and Mary Charlotte, had no direct involvement with their father's publishing business. Both married and moved from London. However, the other four sisters, Margaret Rose, Eleanor Lucy, Victoria Grace, and the youngest, Susan May (born 20 August 1871), all held shares in the company.

These four aunts, especially Grace and Susan, had considerable influence on Walter Juxon as boy and man. They placed importance on the notions of excellence and personal responsibility. Their code of conduct was strict. Slang was to be avoided in spoken English; their nephew was always to be properly attired. Their literary and cultural interests also impressed him. They were art enthusiasts and early purchasers of Group of Seven works. Susan and her nephew occasionally attended concerts and opera in New York. "W.J." considered it a unique achievement that these four sisters "who were unmarried lived together . . . in harmony. . . . I was frequently in that house. It was a nice house to be in."[6]

The "aunts," as they were affectionately referred to in family circles, were typical mid-Victorian ladies. Their London home at 652 Talbot Street was a house that had been originally designed as a cottage and later remodelled. Two of the four spinster sisters, Susan and Grace, actively served the newspaper in the editorial department, while Eleanor and Margaret were preoccupied with household duties.

Grace's nom de plume was "Fan-fan." Her column appeared regularly as a weekend feature providing readers with both literary and drama criticism. An extensive traveller, Grace was frequently in New York for Broadway openings. Her reviews were considered highly informed, among the best of Canadian journalism. Her creative writing also extended to poetry and fiction. Most of her poetry appeared in the four-year period from 1898 to 1902 and during the early years of World War I when she seldom travelled. Her sole novel, *The Man Child*, was published shortly after her death in 1928 and was well received by reviewers.[7]

Susan, who lived somewhat in the shadow of Grace's dominating personality, spent considerable time travelling in the Far East. A series of articles she wrote on the Orient for *The Free Press* attracted wide attention. Susan became Western University's second female graduate upon receipt of her degree from the

4

Faculty of Arts in 1900. She was fluent in German and taught school in both Germany and Japan. Like her sister Grace, Susan was keenly interested in the cultural development of London and southwestern Ontario.

The two sons born to Josiah, Walter Josiah on 4 August 1862 and Arthur Stephen on 27 November 1869, eventually succeeded their father as owners of the company. It would be their responsibility to bring the newspaper into the early-twentieth century, the era dominated by the publisher capitalist. Changes in technology would ultimately usher in the age of the mass-circulation daily. For the time being, however, their father struggled to turn a near bankrupt weekly into a profitable enterprise.

London, Ontario, experienced considerable economic growth throughout the early and mid-1850s. However, the town had not yet emerged from the frontier stage when the decade began. The market square on King Street was the hub of activity when farmers from the region came to London to sell produce and purchase supplies. A garrison town, London was the home of the 32nd Regiment of the British regulars. The military had arrived following the Upper Canada rebellions of 1837-38; the presence of the regulars had a lasting effect on the town situated at the forks of the Thames River, which the Indians called *Askunesippi*, meaning "antlered one."[8]

When Josiah Blackburn assumed official control of *The Canadian Free Press* on 1 January 1853, the London newspaper was in its third location on the east side of Talbot Street, just a few doors north of Dundas Street. Although London was on the verge of economic expansion with the advent of the railway, publishing a newspaper was still an arduous undertaking. Transportation throughout the city and Middlesex County was difficult given the poor condition of streets and roads. The county contained only about 150 miles of proper roads. Telegraph communication, that would soon become all important to the newspaper business, was relatively new in Canada West when Blackburn took over the newspaper. The problems presented by the social conditions of the day, as well as the actual printing of the four-page *Canadian Free Press*, made for a time-consuming struggle. Each letter in every word of the weekly was set by hand. This requirement meant that compositors spent a good portion of their time setting copy in type. They had to redistribute the type to the proper places in the type cases after the paper had been printed. Until the invention of the linotype machine at the beginning of the twentieth century, many hours were spent in what was clearly mundane, repetitive labour. In his reminiscences on the pioneer days of the newspaper, Harry Gorman, an early employee, described Josiah Blackburn as "editor, reporter, proof-reader, book-keeper, collector and canvassing agent," someone who knew "what it . . . [was] like to run a country newspaper when money . . . [was] scarce and roads bad."[9]

Spurred on by the interest and enthusiasm which the Crimean War had nurtured in the minds of the reading public, Blackburn launched a daily newspaper. *The London Free Press and Daily Western Advertiser* made its appearance on 5 May 1855. Except for a brief period in 1857, the daily has been available to Londoners ever since. The weekly *Canadian Free Press*, which initially served as the financial underpinning of the daily, lasted until the 1880s.[10]

Some twenty years later, on 10 May 1875 amidst a world depression, Blackburn started an evening edition of *The London Free Press*. The evening edition, which sold for two cents a copy, one cent less than the morning paper, enabled advertisers to get double exposure for their products free of any extra charge. This edition was introduced to counter *The London Evening Advertiser* started by John Cameron twelve years earlier when he was just 19 years old. The 1872 circulation figures show that *The Advertiser* had considerable impact. It had a daily circulation of 10,600 subscribers compared to just 2,540 for the *The Free Press*.[11]

Josiah's younger brother, Stephen, had joined him after *The Free Press* became a daily. "J. and S. Blackburn, printers and publishers" was born in 1856. Stephen Blackburn had entered the printing and publishing business in London, England, before immigrating to Canada. His wife was Susanna Whitaker, the second daughter of Henry Whitaker, solicitor of Chancery Lane in London and founder of the noted publication, *Whitaker's Almanac*. John Cameron, who published *The London*

Evening Advertiser, found the younger Blackburn to be "energetic, quick, impetuous and, like most impetuous men, warm hearted and ready to do a good turn."

The arrival of his brother meant that Josiah could relieve himself of some of the newspaper's financial responsibilities. He preferred to focus on the editorial department, the aspect of journalism that seemed to delight him most. The result was that Blackburn eventually was successful in turning his newspaper into the most influential journal west of Toronto.

As was the case with other early newspaper proprietors, Blackburn became a central figure in the political controversies surrounding the Reform Party and its leader George Brown, publisher of the *Toronto Globe*. In the process, Blackburn's trenchant pen moved *The Free Press* editorially from the Reform Party, which it had supported between 1849 and 1858, to John A. Macdonald and the Conservatives by the time of Confederation. The London journal continued to give its editorial support to the Conservative Party until Walter Blackburn, Josiah's grandson, broke with Arthur Ford, his editor-in-chief of the day, and endorsed the Liberals in the early 1960s, a hundred years later.

Josiah Blackburn himself ran unsuccessfully as a Reform candidate in East Middlesex during the 1857 election, and blamed his defeat on Brown. He felt that Brown, through his preoccupation with the concerns of Canada West and his antipathy toward French Canadians, had hurt the party's chances at the polls and had kept the Reformers in opposition. Under Blackburn's guidance *The Free Press* played a significant role in the party debates on Reform policies and Brown's leadership throughout the late 1850s and early 1860s.[12]

During the decade before Confederation, stable government in the Canadas proved to be elusive; ministries lasted for relatively short periods. Within the Reform Party, there was discord. Blackburn broke with Brown over the noted "Double Shuffle" incident, terminology used by Brown's *Globe* to describe the manner in which the Liberal-Conservative government of Macdonald and Cartier regained office after the Brown-Dorion government was defeated in 1858. A technicality had allowed the Liberal-Conservatives to form a government once again

7

without having to face the electorate. *The Free Press* opposed the "Double Shuffle," claiming the move was against the spirit of the law; still, the newspaper cautioned that the action could be seen as valid from a strictly legal standpoint.

Brown at first favoured dissolution and then proposed a federation of the Canadas to break the political deadlock that had prevented stable government. In contrast, *The Free Press* favoured the double majority principle, a concept whereby the country would be governed by voting majorities in Canada West and Canada East. Later *The Free Press* supported the Great Coalition that led to Confederation and the Conservative Party under John A. Macdonald.[13]

Politics fascinated Blackburn. One of the highlights of his career was in the summer of 1864 when he managed to obtain an interview with President Abraham Lincoln who was then in the middle of the Civil War. Blackburn wrote: "I at once placed in the hands of a messenger my card and letters (previously procured from friends in New York and Cincinnati), to deliver to the President and with scarcely a moment's delay I was ushered into his presence, when he arose and stepped forward in a stooping position . . . 'I am glad to see you sir; be seated.'" Blackburn explained that London was near Detroit and said, "Your position must indeed be responsible and trying, President." To this comment Lincoln replied, "Yes, to think of it, it is very strange that I, a boy brought up in the woods, and seeing, as it were, but little of the world, should be drifted into the very apex of this great event." Blackburn included a description of Lincoln's private room in his story and quoted the President as saying "there was never anything in history to equal . . . [the Civil War]." The brief conversation with the President, which was written down by Blackburn immediately after the interview, appeared in the *Sacramento Daily Union* on 23 August 1864.[14]

During the immediate post-Confederation years when *The Free Press* shifted its political orientation, the newspaper also underwent personnel changes. In 1871 the earlier partnership between Josiah and Stephen Blackburn was dissolved and replaced by a joint stock company prior to incorporation seven years later. Stephen did not appear to have Josiah's keen interest in the editorial aspect of the newspaper business nor his passion for political writing. But he did possess a sharp business sense. He also had shown an interest in the oil discoveries at nearby Petrolia.

In 1871 Stephen was appointed Registrar of Titles for West Middlesex in the town of Glencoe. *The Free Press* informed its readers that he had decided to leave the newspaper to devote more attention to the oil business. Several opponents of the location of the registry office in Glencoe, especially those in the town of Strathroy, saw the newspaper's announcement as something of a smokescreen to hide what was perceived as blatant political patronage on the part of Sandfield Macdonald, Ontario's first premier, who had made the appointment. The Premier and Josiah Blackburn had been on close terms when they opposed George Brown as head of the Reform Party. Strathroy had wanted the registry office, claiming that "its enterprise, wealth, rapid growth, prospective advancement and railway facilities offer advantages, far superior to any other place in the riding."[15]

The dissolving of the partnership between the Blackburn brothers saw Stephen's interest in the company pass to William Southam, later founder of the newspaper dynasty, and to Henry Mathewson, a former confectioner, and John Kingsley Clare who became secretary-treasurer of the newspaper. When Josiah Blackburn had started his daily newspaper in 1855, Southam, then 12 years old, left school to become a *Free Press* paper boy. Four years later, he became an indentured apprentice to the printing trade with the newspaper. When the London Free Press Printing and Publishing Company was formed in 1871, Southam donned a leather apron and took charge of the job printing department which supplemented the two dailies and the weekly that the firm published. Starting with a salary of $1,200 annually, he stayed with the newspaper for six more years before selling his interest. He then took control of the *Hamilton Spectator* and later established a national newspaper empire.[16]

In a fiftieth anniversary issue of *The Free Press*, Southam recalled that one of his most valued possessions was "a handsome volume of Scott's poetical works with the following inscription on the fly leaf in the handwriting of Stephen Blackburn: 'To William Southam as a token of regard and esteem on the completion of his five years' apprenticeship at the Free Press office, from J. & S. Blackburn, London, Canada West, 7 January 1864.'"[17]

The Free Press continued to evolve. After Southam left for Hamilton, the company became incorporated on 8 October 1878, with capital stock to the value of $60,000. A decade later the job printing and lithographic departments of the newspaper were sold, underlining the shift in emphasis that had occurred in Canadian journalism since the early days of *The Free Press*. Whereas Josiah Blackburn had to support his newspaper enterprise with the operating capital from these two sources of income, his sons Walter Josiah and Arthur Stephen, were to concentrate their efforts on increasing readership and building advertising revenue. Job printing could be profitable but demanded both time and production space. On 1 January 1890 the company accepted the offer of Thomas Orr, an old-time *Free Press* employee, and John Weld, publisher of the *Farmers Advocate* newspaper, to purchase the job printing and lithographic departments and "the stock in trade for the sum of twenty five thousand dollars."[18]

Five months later on 10 May Josiah Blackburn attended his last shareholders' meeting. In ill health at the time, the managing director urged that the utmost economy be observed in the future operation of the newspaper. His death on 11 November 1890 at the age of 68 in Hot Springs, Arkansas, where he had gone hoping to improve his health, truly represented the passing of the early era of journalism for *The Free Press*.

During the final decade of his life, Blackburn had served as census commissioner in Western Ontario. The federal government also appointed him to oversee the organization of a printing bureau at Ottawa.[19] Blackburn's recommendations following visits to Washington and various state capitals resulted in the formation of the Department of Public Printing and Stationery in 1886, forerunner of the printing section of the Department of Supply and Services.

Josiah was a man seemingly given to considerable soul searching about both public and private matters which in his day invariably touched upon the areas of politics and religion. He had shown an independent side in political journalism. He broke with the past when he moved his paper from the Reform Party to the Conservative side. In his religion he was no less given to thoughtful examination. Though raised as a Congregationalist, Blackburn along with his first wife and six of their eight children had been rebaptized as Anglicans in St. Paul's Cathedral in London, Ontario. J. Lambert Payne, an early journalist with *The Free Press*, wrote that Josiah "was scarcely a brilliant writer as that term is understood, but he was marvellously forceful. He gave *The Free Press* a soul."[20]

Blackburn's estate had real and personal assets that totalled nearly $20,000. The shares he held in The London Free Press Printing Company and Carling Brewing and Malting Company had a value of approximately $35,000.[21] In his will, he handed down his 601 shares of common stock in the printing company to Walter Josiah, his son, and to his nephew, Henry Stephen Blackburn, his executors and trustees.

The will stipulated that any sale of the stock must be done "en bloc but not otherwise" and that five thousand dollars from the sale was to be invested for his second wife Marion Billington, whom he had married in 1886, after the death of his first wife; the interest on that investment was to be paid to her during her lifetime. The remainder of the proceeds from selling of the stock was to be divided among the children of his first wife, with one quarter going to each of his sons, Walter Josiah and Arthur Stephen, and the remainder to be divided among his daughters. According to the will, "pending the sale of the said stock," it was not lawful "for any of my said children to dispose of their beneficial interest therein or any part thereof to any person or persons other than to his or her brother or sister."[22] Josiah was determined to keep it in the family.

Between Josiah's death and the start of the First World War, *The Free Press*, with its Conservative orientation, continued in keen competition with the Liberal *Advertiser*. Walter Josiah

11

and Arthur Stephen Blackburn, who became president and secretary treasurer, respectively, of the company in 1900, continued to raise advertising revenue; from $84,158 in 1907 to $155,481 in 1914. *The Advertiser* had its best year in 1911 when it accumulated $74,292.32 in advertising revenue, but still well short of the $117,022.64 taken in by *The Free Press*.[23] Arthur succeeded his brother as president following Walter Josiah's death in 1920.

In 1902 Arthur Blackburn had married Etta Irene Henderson of Wardsville near London. Arthur and his wife had two girls and a boy; the oldest, Constance Margaret, was born on 14 August 1904, the younger, Miriam Irene, on 18 December 1909. The couple gave birth to their only son, Walter Juxon, on 18 March 1914. The arrival of a new male in the Blackburn family, the heir apparent to Arthur, was a much heralded event. The ordained successor later hinted that he would have preferred to be a mechanical engineer or an astronomer, but as he explained, "I had been born into the job."[24]

Walter Blackburn was a quiet and unassuming young man, almost solemn in his demeanour. His aunt Grace occasionally predicted that he would become a bishop. John Ralph, a classics professor at the University of Western Ontario and a father figure to the young Walter, remembered that Arthur Blackburn gave his son steady support and encouragement. A sometimes strained atmosphere in the household prompted Walter to spend a considerable amount of time during his youthful years with his four aunts in their house at 652 Talbot Street. They were well travelled and read and taught him much. The aunt's adoration of their nephew was matched by his fondness for them.

Walter's father, Arthur, was an austere individual who suffered from diabetes. He would leave London occasionally for medical treatment at the Stenben Sanitarium in Hornell, New York, leaving much of the responsibility for the day-to-day operation of the newspaper to Charles Thomas who was appointed secretary-treasurer of the company in January 1921, later becoming general manager. Thomas, who had been born at Cold Stream near London, had joined the newspaper in 1900 as a bookkeeper. A hard-driving individual, he would later have a personal clash with the third generation publisher when he succeeded his father.

Arthur was a member of the London Hunt and Country Club which he joined in December 1920 when the entrance and annual subscription fees were $50 and $75 respectively; however his socializing was generally confined to business friends. In the early 1920s he held 23 shares of capital stock in the Carling Brewery and Malting Company of London and was also a director of Big Creek Muskrat Farms Limited, a Port Rowan, Ontario, company specializing in the sale of live muskrats for breeding purposes.

Blackburn removed himself largely from London's social life and spent endless hours as a recluse on the third floor of the family's Richmond Street home to which they had moved in the 1920s, with a remarkable collection of radio apparatus and equipment. Despite this reclusive nature, his personality was not without contradictions; he enjoyed luxurious automobiles and loved speed. On an occasional afternoon, he would turn to Ernie Agnew, a member of the newspaper's advertising department, and ask to be taken for a drive in his Stearns-Knight. "Could you take me out and give me the air for a little while?" was a frequent request.[25]

Perhaps the notable achievement of Arthur's presidency was the company's expansion of its media operations. CJGC radio, a new form of communication, was introduced to London on 30 September 1922. Arthur Blackburn's hobby interest in radio made him eager to introduce the medium to London as early as possible. He saw that radio could supplement but not necessarily supplant the form of service provided by *The London Free Press*. At a time when numerous newspaper owners throughout Canada saw this new electronic medium as a threat to their advertising revenue, Blackburn saw it as an alternative that could not be forestalled, and so should be absorbed.

CJGC was born at a time when the radio "studio" was in the early stages of its evolution. Initially the station's studio was situated in the executive offices of the newspaper; the studio consisted of not much more than a large, old-fashioned microphone on a tripod, a home-made transmitter constructed by a local gunsmith and an upright piano for whatever programming could be provided. Later the station was moved to its own separate quarters on the third floor of the newspaper building on Richmond Street.

During the first broadcast over CJGC on 30 September 1922, listeners heard the voice of Sir Adam Beck, the father of Ontario Hydro. Beck noted that the medium had been considered a fad just a year earlier but now was perceived as a supplement to newspapers. On 18 August 1925, CJGC provided a remote broadcast of Beck's funeral, following his death three days earlier.

The personality of Arthur contrasted with that of his wife, who was an attractive, fun-loving twenty-three-year old at the time of the marriage. On the other hand, he was thirty-two. She enjoyed travel, parties and was something of a free spirit. Her husband, on the other hand, had little time for that kind of social activity. He would retire after dinner to his radio room, source of endless fascination for him, just as the medium was for many Canadians in the 1920s, the era of the ukelele, the coonskin coat and bootleggers. Moreover, his diabetic problem was always a cause of concern for the family, especially in his later years when the Blackburns kept a resident nurse full time to attend to him. On her travels to such places as Florida, Bermuda and Cuba, Blackburn's wife always maintained regular contact with the family in London. The family had moments of enjoyment but did not always seem to pull together.

Although Arthur as president of *The Free Press* was prominent in business circles, the family tended to be removed from London society. Both he and his wife kept a low profile just as Josiah, Arthur's father, had done. The only major community project in which Etta Irene Blackburn became involved was with Anna Burgess Shaw-Wood, a prominent figure in church and social work during and following the First World War. The two women directed a Red Cross committee which established a clothing supply depot for civic relief in London.

Like many other young Londoners of his day, Irene's son, Walter, made the transitions from Ryerson Public School to the

London Central Collegiate Institute and then to the University of Western Ontario. Throughout his elementary, high school and university days, Blackburn remained a steady and conscientious student. In his final year at Ryerson, he finished fifth in a class of 31 students.

The year of Canada's Diamond Jubilee, 1927, Blackburn entered Central Collegiate Institute. He graduated four years later in 1931 with a junior matriculation. He missed a year of high school following an attack of scarlet fever and therefore did not complete the usual five-year stay. Central was a high school with a long tradition dating back to its founding in 1878. The high school tended to stress the fundamental Anglo-Saxon qualities of stability, hard work and class loyalty.

In few ways was Blackburn a conspicuous student at Central. He remained aloof from the crowd and played virtually no sports with one exception: he joined the school's track team. Surprisingly, he did not appear to show any interest in the school newspaper. His fellow students remembered Blackburn as being quiet, reserved and seldom a party-goer. "He always seemed to have a low profile," said Cedric Tanner, a fellow student, "although he had a nice car."[26] The luxurious automobiles he drove made Blackburn the envy of students during his Central days. Another long-time friend who also attended the school remembered that Arthur Blackburn "always had great, big cars . . . he always supplied Walter with the most beautiful, expensive convertibles that you have ever seen, big Buicks and Chryslers. While the rest of us were driving Fords, Walter always had the great, big cars."[27]

Perhaps his extra-curricular interests help to explain why Blackburn was not more active in the school's social life. In the late 1920s he became a radio amateur, a ham operator, which involved learning Morse code, a considerable amount of radio theory and passing examinations in both of these categories. "Walter's amateur station in those days was . . . a good one," said Cedric Tanner. "It takes quite a bit of study to become a ham and he operated mostly on morse. You [could] have contact with places all over the world." He also had "an elaborate electric train in his basement [where] he was always rigging up motors and gadgets. On one occasion he gave me about 15,000 volts in the seat of the pants."

Even at the age of thirteen, Blackburn had shown he had inherited the mechanical interests of his father. He was a camera enthusiast and later joined the London Camera Club. "My father had, at my request, bought a motion picture camera for me as a birthday gift in the 1920s," Blackburn recalled. "I was fascinated with motion pictures and producing them." Perhaps it was those early interests in radio and photography that helped to nurture his later interest in broadcasting, particularly television.

Blackburn's ham radio station, which was reasonably sophisticated for the 1920s, the medium's pioneer age, consisted of a transmitter and receiver along with a phone device capable of communicating by voice as well as code. "My phone rig required 190 volts," said Blackburn. "In my second year at high school . . . I began to spend so much time on radio, my amateur hobby, that I wasn't doing quite as well as my father thought I should do in school. So he turned off the money for the [batteries]." Blackburn later sold his phone equipment and began to concentrate on his studies to prepare for university. "The man who bought the phone rig . . . [wanted] to see if he could transmit pictures. He had heard about some of the work . . . by [J.L.] Baird who was transmitting pictures over the air." Blackburn maintained contact with the purchaser of the phone apparatus and later watched some of his experiments. "He never did make it work, but I did a bit of reading as a result of that," he recalled. "This was in 1929 . . . [my] first introduction to sending pictures by air. I maintained an interest in it."

His interest in science and mechanics helps to explain why Blackburn received a first-class standing in physics during his final year at Central. Throughout his last two years of high school, he seemed to excel in mathematics and sciences, whereas earlier some of his highest achievements had been in English literature and composition. But as high school drew to a close, his father encouraged him to pursue business administration at the University of Western Ontario, recognizing that a new newspaper age demanded an educational background encompassing marketing, sales and finance.

Blackburn's undergraduate years at Western proved to be an academic training ground for his future position as *The Free Press* publisher. He pursued the arts program with an honours in business administration, received his first introduction to Canadian journalism as a reporter with *The Gazette*, the student newspaper, and wrote a thesis entitled "The Merchandising Activities of a Typical Canadian Daily Newspaper."

If his five-year stay at Western was preparation for his subsequent professional life, it was no less so on a personal level. During his first year at Western, he met a popular and fun-loving co-ed, Marjorie Ludwell Dampier, the daughter of a Strathroy bank manager. A member of the 1934 university badminton team and first president of Pi Beta Phi fraternity, the pioneer national fraternity for women, she graduated in arts with an honours in English and French the following year. The pair were later married in 1938, two years after Blackburn officially had assumed the publisher's chair at *The Free Press*.

All was not favourable in the Blackburn household during Walter's stay at Western. The year he had entered university his mother died and his father's diabetic condition continued to worsen throughout the early 1930s. The state of his father's health was one reason why the son attended Western rather than leave London for some other university. "I didn't go to school as I might well have," Walter recalled. "I was needed at home to help my father. . . . During my high school and university days until [the] time of his death . . . I was on the job to help look after him." He remembered organizing his father's financial books and preparing his income tax returns. On at least two occasions he helped to save his father, whose life had been extended by the discovery of insulin in 1922, after he had lapsed into a coma.

An instructor at Western, Mark Inman, who taught Blackburn economics, remembered his somewhat reserved nature in the classroom: "It was very surprising to me that here was a young man who came from a well-to-do family who seemed to be interested in not so much the maintenance of wealth, but rather in the broad social problems which were becoming quite promi-

17

nent during the Depression." Inman remembered that Blackburn was not one for small talk, either as a student or as an adult
later in life: "I think he felt at times that some members of the
class were a bit frivolous and didn't take their opportunities
seriously. Sometimes students would ask . . . questions to get the
professors going but Walter didn't like that type of thing. He
wanted to stay on . . . the topic."[28]

Blackburn assumed an active part in university life throughout his five years as a student. In 1932 he served as arts editor of
The Gazette. The following year he became secretary of the Delta
Upsilon fraternity and a member of the Macdonald-Cartier
political club on campus. He was also executive treasurer of the
Badminton Club, director of publications for the University
Student's Council and a member of the golf team. "I was to have
been editor of *The Gazette*," Blackburn recalled, "but because of
the problems of my father . . . I decided to turn down being
editor . . . and I went into the politics of the university and
became what they called Director of [Publications]," his first
experience as a publisher. He was responsible to the student
council for the newspaper.

As a reporter with *The Gazette*, Blackburn avoided one particular story sensing that it could cause embarrassment to K.P.R.
Neville, the Registrar and Dean of Arts and Science. Blackburn
was assigned to interview him on Remembrance Day, later
recalling that "Doctor Neville was always interested in a cute
quip." He said to the young student-reporter, "Walter, I have to
say that it's not really a matter of remembrance; it's a matter of
forgetting." Blackburn decided not to quote him: "That
[remark] would have caused him immense difficulty. I think I
was a responsible reporter in that case. That quip, if published,
could easily have destroyed him. The veterans would have, quite
rightly, hated him. Emotions then ran silent and deep."

Membership in a university fraternity during the early
1930s was considered an important social step for any young
man seeking a future place of prominence in society. Not surprisingly, Blackburn joined Delta Upsilon (ΔΥ), a fraternity originally located just a block or so from his family home on
Richmond Street. DU, which was the first fraternity to be estab-

lished at Western and the sixth organized in North America, tended to see itself as exclusive and tried deliberately to pledge members from prosperous families. Another important criteria for membership was athletic prowess. Blackburn fitted the former category but not the latter, having refrained from participation in physical contact sports. But he was an enthusiastic golfer and badminton player. Like private schools, fraternities such as DU focused on the character side. They were expected to help individuals acquire the social skills for making the right contacts and sensing opportunities later in life. During these years, Blackburn formed lasting relationships with his fellow members.

A DU member who remained a long-time friend, Mel Pryce, maintained that Blackburn, who approached him initially to join the fraternity, had numerous friends at university but was not "a hail fellow well met." Still he was an active member of the group and fitted into the casual atmosphere easily. By now he was more of a party-goer and was "a very friendly chap but . . . not the glad-handing, back-slapping type."[29] At Western, Blackburn appeared to be closest to students in a position similar to his own, such as James McConnell, Jr., whose father owned an advertising agency. These students were prepared to take over the operation of their family businesses. Their peers, who often read newspaper headlines telling of lengthy breadlines during a time of high unemployment, naturally envied them. Heirs to family companies had no need to undertake the painful exercise of job hunting during a stagnant economy.

The business program at Western was based on the case method modelled after the Harvard Business School. Students dealt with the case histories of businesses, their triumphs and shortcomings. The recollection of fellow student, Larry Dampier, whose sister Blackburn later married, was that class discussions frequently involved those individuals whose career paths were charted for them. Blackburn was an enthusiastic participant in class. When a business subject that might involve newspapers or advertising was the topic, he was central to the discussion. As Dampier explained, "We all knew what Walter was going to do because his father owned *The Free Press*, just like we knew Jim McConnell was going to go into advertising. . . . There was never any immodesty or hiding it. . . . These guys had it made."[30]

The study of one business case dealing with American railroads had a lasting impact on Blackburn and helped to explain his reasons for later expanding the print business developed by his ancestors to include other forms of media. It was the railways' failure "to recognize that they were in transportation [generally] rather than transportation by rail" as well as the reasons why management had avoided involvement in other forms of transport such as trucking and aircraft that caught his attention. "That gave me an awareness and a conviction," said Blackburn, that "we were in the communication business legitimately . . . [and] any development . . . should be . . . [one] which we were interested in and we shouldn't miss it by failing to recognize that it was a form of communication."

Especially in his latter years at university, Blackburn undertook research assignments directly related to the operation of a daily newspaper. He wrote a paper entitled "A History of the London Free Press" in which he traced the growth and evolution of the newspaper from the days of his grandfather, noting the difficulties Josiah Blackburn had faced when he established the daily edition in May 1855. Blackburn seemed fascinated by the technological changes introduced at the various stages of the newspaper's development: "Realizing that the old Washington hand press would be unable to turn out the work in a short enough period of time, [Josiah], before launching the daily, installed a Northrup stop-cylinder press. Operated by steam, it was the first power press to be erected in the city of London. . . . The press had the almost unbelievable capacity of 600 papers per hour."[31]

Blackburn cited a number of reasons why he felt the newspaper had survived successfully compared to other journals. Most important of all, in his eyes, was the learning acquired through successive generations of publishers: "The continuity of management which The Free Press has enjoyed from the time of its being acquired by Josiah Blackburn in 1852 has been another contributing factor. Since 1852, the control of the paper has been in the hands of the Blackburn family, and the policies have been built up from experience obtained over a long period of time and handed down from one generation to the next." He concluded that the newspaper had always been provided with the latest machinery and equipment and had commanded a high measure of loyalty and zeal from its staff.

But Blackburn was not solely preoccupied with the newspaper's past and his family heritage. In his university thesis on the merchandising aspects of the newspaper business, he looked to the future, underlining the challenges the print medium faced in servicing local and national advertisers. His thesis showed how most newspapers in Canada had been slow to sense the impact a well-organized merchandising department could have in dealing with advertising agencies and clients. While newspapers were heavily involved in advertising during the early twentieth century, "merchandising," which went beyond straight selling and advertising to include the preparation of reader surveys, solicitation of national advertising through ad-agencies, and other numerous services to clients, was largely an unexplored area. "It was only during the war," he wrote, "that men really became aware of the possibilities lying behind merchandising goods to customers and began to study the problem in a businesslike manner." He drew attention to the volume and value of the work performed by the merchandising department: "At least ninety-five per cent of the local retail accounts require continual service, while, in the national field, more than seventy-five per cent of the clients request merchandising information and services either before or after the publication of the first advertisements." Looking to the future, Blackburn foresaw "the circulation of the newspaper [being] analysed more thoroughly, showing its total volume . . . the exact areas reached by the paper . . . the number of men and women readers, their attitude toward the publication . . . and other information designed for the use of space buyers." He concluded that "the future of the newspaper merchandising department is very great indeed, but no greater than the future for men with ability in this work. . . . The future is there. Only its realization remains."[32]

Blackburn admitted he thought of virtually no other career

during university days besides becoming the successor to his father whose advice he sought regularly: "I was raised [as successor] so I guess I naturally hitched myself to his star." As in high school, he spent considerable time with his aunts, whose advice he soon came to rely on as a twenty-one-year-old publisher. They had instilled in him at an early age a pride in the family's heritage and a sense of responsibility: "My father and his sisters used to talk about the family quite a bit . . . deliberately."

Throughout Blackburn's high school and university days, notable developments pertaining to the family business occurred, some with a direct influence on the young publisher. These included his father's purchase of *The London Advertiser*; the sale of radio station CJGC to a Windsor, Ontario, company; the Southam Company's overtures to purchase *The Free Press*; and a bitter printers' strike at the newspaper.

Unlike Thomas Purdom, owner of *The Advertiser*, who believed that the city of London could remain a multi-newspaper city, Arthur Blackburn felt that only a single daily could survive. The competition between the two London newspapers following the First World War produced a keen rivalry. Even as a youth, W.J. realized the importance of *The Free Press* to his family's economic future: "I was aware that it was a battle for survival because my father had told me in his view it was." Still, after his father purchased the *Advertiser* in 1926, he continued it as an individual newspaper with a Liberal orientation. A former editor, Melville Rossie, was reappointed and remained in that position until the paper ceased publication in the mid-1930s. His resolution to stop publishing the paper was the first major decision Walter Blackburn made after he succeeded his father.

The Advertiser never recovered from its steadfast support of the Laurier Liberals during the First World War and its vigorous criticism of Borden's Union government. The newspaper did not oppose conscription during the 1917 election campaign. While its support of Laurier won some backers in places such as Toronto and Windsor, the paper alienated Unionist Liberals in London, its main circulation area. After the war, Purdom began a concentrated effort to sell the newspaper as circulation dropped and revenues declined.

Thomas Purdom was an arch rival of the Blackburns. As solicitor for the Bank of Canada, he had been involved in various business transactions in London. When he decided to sell the paper, his initial asking price was $500,000. Moreover Purdom held that a continuation of the paper's editorial policy should be a condition of the sale. As he explained, "A Liberal paper should adhere to sound liberal principles, as closely as a judge adheres to a principle of Justice."

A year before his death, Purdom sold the paper on 22 September 1922 to W.F. Herman of Saskatoon, publisher of the *Saskatoon Phoenix* and the *Border Cities Star* in Windsor, for $175,000, a far cry from his original asking price. In December of that same year, Herman in turn sold *The Advertiser* to Joseph Atkinson, publisher of the *Toronto Star*, for $180,000. Under Atkinson's direction the paper remained in the Liberal camp, endorsing party candidates and poking fun at the federal Conservative Party's leadership problems. But its circulation continued to decline. During the three years that Atkinson owned the newspaper, *The Advertiser* experienced a loss of "$292,214.82 on operations" and "$189,839.09 on surplus account," for "a total book loss of $482,053.91". But if the various forms of free service the *Star* gave *The Advertiser*, such as the use of advertising and circulation experts whose salaries the *Star* paid, were counted, the loss was about half a million dollars.[33]

When Atkinson decided to get rid of the paper, the Blackburn family was the only party interested in the purchase. Accordingly on 15 February 1926, *The Free Press* owners decided to buy the competing newspaper for $112,500, an amount that was $67,500 less than Atkinson had paid for the paper three years earlier. Why Arthur Blackburn had decided to embark on such a risky venture is evident from the minutes of the 15 February 1926 meeting of the company's shareholders. *The Free Press* had suffered "large and unprofitable expense in combatting the competition of the London Advertiser Company Limited by way of contests for subscribers to the newspapers of both companies . . . large amounts of money [had] been paid in prizes all of which contests were advanced and carried out by the London Advertiser Company Limited to the injury of this Company." By purchasing the newspaper, *The Free Press* would put an end "to unnecessary expense in continuing such contests for subscribers and also . . . avoid unreasonable competition in cutting rates for advertising and for subscriptions in . . . the Free Press."[34] The sale of the paper to the Blackburns involved the three thousand shares of *The Advertiser's* stock and all the assets of the newspaper.

The competition had been bought out. Within the next decade when Walter Blackburn became head of *The Free Press*, London would follow the pattern of many North American communities and become a one newspaper city. Wartime had accelerated a trend in London that had become apparent in the newspaper industry throughout Canada during the twentieth century. The country witnessed the evolution from the multi-newspaper to the single newspaper city. [35]

The decision taken by The London Free Press Printing Company to sell its radio station, CJGC, to Essex Broadcasters Limited of Windsor, Ontario, never sat well with Blackburn even though his father had endorsed the sale. Only brief mention was made of the transaction in the minutes of the board of directors' meeting on 13 April 1933, a meeting attended by Arthur Blackburn, his two sisters Margaret and Susan, and Charles Thomas, the company's secretary-treasurer. The agreement between station CKOK in Windsor, owned by Essex Broadcasters, and CJGC called for the sale of the London station and the amalgamation of both broadcast outlets to form a new station based in Windsor, CKLW, the last two letters of the station's designation standing for London and Windsor.

The Canadian Radio Broadcasting Commission, then the broadcast regulator, had recommended the merger of the stations hoping that CKLW would provide a powerful, 5,000 watt, private affiliate to carry network programs. CJGC had originated the first national program, the band of the Royal Canadian Regiment, heard coast to coast over the CRBC network, consisting of both publicly and privately owned stations. Essex Broadcasters Limited paid *The Free Press* $90,000 in the form of cash and stock when CKLW came into being.[36] Significantly, the decision marked the only occasion throughout four generations that the Blackburn family chose to sell a communications entity related to the conventional media of print or broadcasting.

The sale of the station to Essex Broadcasters irritated a number of *Free Press* employees, in particular, Charles G. Hunter, CJGC's chief engineer. The loss of the London station also brought an irate reaction from local listeners accustomed to their own station. Within London a heated competition soon ensued between a coterie of Hunter's supporters acting independently and *The Free Press* management to see who would obtain a new broadcasting licence for the city.

When CJGC was sold, the station's staff had been released, and Hunter was incensed with the amalgamation of CJGC and CKOK for this reason. He also claimed the arrangement had resulted in a handsome bargain for *The Free Press*. Hunter maintained that Charles Thomas, the newspaper's general manager, had let it be known that *The Free Press* did not desire to own and operate another London station after the sale of CJGC. However, *The Free Press* management apparently had a change of heart upon learning of other applications for a new London station; they suspected that the Windsor *Border Cities Star*, a *Free Press* rival, might be involved in a licence application. In the end, a new radio licence was awarded to *The Free Press* which received support in its application from Tory partisans including the Western Ontario Conservative Association. Indeed, the competition for the London station occurred at a time when many Conservative supporters throughout the country lobbied the government of R.B. Bennett for broadcast licences. The new *Free Press* station, CFPL-AM, opened on 25 September 1933 and continues to serve London and southwestern Ontario.

During Blackburn's high school and university days, his family turned down overtures by the Southam Company, which held a twenty-five per cent interest in the newspaper (which Southam had re-purchased in 1907), to purchase *The Free Press*. F.I. Ker, manager of the *Hamilton Spectator*, had held discussions with Arthur Blackburn in the fall of 1927 at Port Stanley near London where Blackburn rented a cottage. On 23 September 1927 in a brief letter, Blackburn responded to Ker's invitation to sell: "Regarding our conversation at Port Stanley, I have talked the matter over with my sisters and have concluded we do not care to sell at the present time, however you may assure the Messrs. Southam they will be offered an opportunity to purchase [the newspaper] before it is sold to anyone else."[37]

At the end of September, Ker responded expressing his disappointment at the Blackburns' reluctance to sell: "I am sorry that you and your sisters do not care to join forces with us at the present time," he wrote. "But [I] wish to thank you for the consideration which you have given the matter, and for the kindly assurance that the Messrs Southam would be offered an opportunity to purchase before the property is disposed of to anyone else."

Another exchange of letters, this time between Fred Southam, president of the Southam Publishing Company, and Arthur Blackburn occurred in the summer of 1932. Blackburn had obviously inquired about a possible sale of the quarter interest Southam's father, William, had acquired from Josiah Blackburn. Fred Southam responded: "With reference to our interest in the Free Press, I don't think I would care to set down any specific price or terms in connection with a possible sale of our stock, at least, not before discussing the matter further with you."

However, Southam was eager to explore the possibility of purchasing *The Free Press*. In July 1932 he wrote to Blackburn: "I am still hoping that you may be interested in a 'sale' rather than 'buy', in either event I think a frank talk would be more helpful than trying to deal by correspondence with the matter we have been discussing." Southam promised that on his next trip to Hamilton, in early August, he would contact Blackburn and "run up to London for an informal chat."

Discussions between both sides during the next two years produced no agreement on either a purchase of the Southam stock or a sale of *The Free Press*. In November 1934 Fred Southam informed an associate in Toronto, J.F. MacKay, that he had "nothing new to add . . . with regard to our relations with the London

Free Press. Now, as in the past, they run their own show and, on the whole, have made a rather satisfactory job of it." The purchase of the Southam shares was to be left to Arthur's son Walter some four decades later.

Probably the most memorable event at *The London Free Press* during Blackburn's years at university was a strike by members of the International Typographical Union (ITU). The walkout left him with a bitter feeling towards unions. This labour strife later prompted Blackburn to form The London Free Press Employees' Association, an organization designed to allow regular dialogue between employees and management. "While I was in university, I drove my father to the office every night to see how things were going," he recalled. "That strike really killed [him]. . . . Worry and diabetes don't mix well."

Feuds between the printers and *The Free Press* management had occurred as far back as 1856, just after Josiah Blackburn had begun to publish a daily newspaper. The printing trade had been in the vanguard of the union movement in Canada since the 1830s. The ITU was a powerful organization with locals in New York, Boston, Chicago and St. Louis. Eventually the union established locals in Canada. Local 133 of the ITU had been formed in London on 22 November 1869 with seven members.

The printers' strike occurred at *The Free Press* over management's refusal to sign a new contract with the typographers. Previously the union had been able to secure written agreements. In the midst of the Depression, the newspaper's management now was willing to offer only a verbal agreement with the printers. Grievances involving wages, shorter hours or fringe benefits were not issues in the dispute. The company argued that its other employees worked without a signed contract, and the printers should do likewise.

The walkout over the right of the workers to a signed contract began on 1 March 1934 after the union had voted 58-8 in favour of strike action. The strike lasted nearly 14 months. Charles Thomas, the general manager of the newspaper, was in the forefront of negotiations and was determined to stay the course after refusing the union a contract. With Arthur Blackburn ill at the time, he was largely responsible for day-to-day management of the newspaper. Thomas, who had a favourite expression, "I fear neither God, man, nor devil," saw the strike as a challenge.[38] He insisted the newspaper would continue to publish.

The union turned its wrath on Thomas, especially after *The Free Press* general manager brought in outside workers from both Toronto and Montreal. When the strikers clashed with them during picket line crossings, Thomas took corrective action. To keep the "outsiders" free from attacks, he would stay overnight with the workers at the newspaper after arranging for food supplies and bedding to be provided. Annoyed at this development, the union charged that "rats" had been brought in from elsewhere "to displace citizens and taxpayers of London."[39]

The strike had its nasty side. Blackburn, who was near completion of his university days when the strike ended in 1935, remembered that nitric acid was found on the clothing of the workers on the job and that "steel pipes [were] used to try to beat our men off. . . . [They] carried their own steel pipe for protection." He also recalled "driving one of [the] men to hospital with a broken collar bone after being in a fight. The strikers used to try to run our men down with motor cars."

In May 1935 the strike was brought to a conclusion when the union accepted an agreement from the management to re-employ some strikers immediately, and the others as soon as possible. Wages and hours of work were to remain as before the strike. But no signed agreement was involved in the settlement.[40] Blackburn recalled that his father, Arthur, never lived to see the pickets withdrawn from *The Free Press*. Although he was determined "to see [the strike] through. . . . His health suffered and he was having difficulty maintaining a good balance of insulin. Finally, he just seemed to lose control of the situation and he . . . died in a diabetic coma."

Thus his son inherited the publisher's chair immediately after the company had gone through a painful labour dispute. The London Free Press Printing Company had yet to consolidate its position amidst the lingering Depression. A fledgling radio station, CFPL, now had to win a faithful audience. Despite the growth of *The Free Press*, the company's second newspaper, *The Advertiser*, which had also been struck by printers, was losing money steadily. Still, within the next three decades Blackburn was to build a multi-million dollar communications' empire. "W.J.," as he preferred to sign his memos, was about to become a man for all media.

CHAPTER TWO

"Mr. Blackburn"
1936 — 1945

BEFORE HE BECAME PUBLISHER, Walter Blackburn's closest working connection with the newspaper had been as a youth filling delivery trucks with gas on Saturdays at the company's Wellington Street garage to earn pocket money. He had never worked for the paper, but at his father's insistence he had studied earnestly to learn the management aspects of the newspaper business. Now his time had come, and he admitted to some anxiety and fear, "I had never thought of doing anything else because of the manner in which I was brought up by my father and his four sisters; still I wasn't trained for the job when I had to assume it."[1] When Blackburn took over as publisher, The London Free Press Printing Company was located at 442 Richmond Street, formerly the headquarters of Huron and Erie Mortgage Corporation and the Canada Trust Company. The company had paid $75,000 for the property that became the sixth location for the newspaper since its inception.

Blackburn's first major challenge as publisher was to restore unity to the company. In this, as in his overall approach as a business manager, the young publisher soon displayed a style that was a curious blend of the old and the new. "He was," as William Heine, a former editor-in-chief of *The Free Press*, observed, "an unusual mixture of 19th century paternalism and 20th century technological vision."[2] Blackburn was a staunch defender of the monarchy and was strong on property rights.

But it was his genuine concern for employees, and the manner in which he attempted to modernize the family business through extensive social benefit reforms that showed his sense of paternalism, a quality characteristic of most successful family corporations. His electronic media innovations, especially the introduction of television to southwestern Ontario, were manifestations of his desire to harness new forms of communications technology. A conservative ethos, that combined a sense of noblesse oblige and benevolence towards employees with an accompanying belief in the need for individual responsibility, characterized his business outlook.

Blackburn demonstrated an acute awareness of his family's business tradition. The notion of generational continuity weighed heavily upon him. "Heads of [family] companies fully realize that they have inherited a business judged by a criterion that does not apply to companies lacking the continued leadership of blood relatives," Thomas Goldwasser has explained in *Family Pride*, a study of leading family businesses in the United States. "The family name and reputation are at stake."[3] Blackburn was determined to nurture this special legacy as he sought to ensure that the company prospered.

Blackburn's managerial approach embodied many of the nineteenth-century attitudes that Josiah Blackburn's daughters had imbued in him at a young age. Blackburn had been influenced by a heritage based on such notions as self-help and the need for harmony among individuals. His business outlook, as it pertained to people, reflected this earlier age. He stressed harmonious relations, freedom of discussion and reasonableness, all recognized as virtues in the Victorian age: "We believe that there is no fundamental conflict between the corporation and those who work for it, that in fact their interests are the same, and that the differences of opinion which exist can be worked out to the general satisfaction of all by free discussion conducted by reasonable men in the atmosphere of goodwill, faith and trust."[4]

Clearly co-operation within the organization, not confrontation was the desired goal. Self-help and personal discipline were cherished qualities in Blackburn's business creed: "We believe that people should be secure but that most security in the final analysis comes from within the individual and his personal efforts." He was prepared to be a benevolent manager but he qualified this notion: "We believe in lending a helping hand to those in need for the purpose of getting a person back on his own feet — not of extending charity."

Above all, this business philosophy upheld the central tenets of nineteenth-century liberalism: "We believe in the fundamental rights of man, freedom of worship, freedom to speak, freedom to be heard, [and] freedom of association." Blackburn compared the corporation to "a family . . . working together in a common purpose, prospering and suffering together, each dependent on the skills of the other."

Blackburn, the young business graduate, brought essentially an expansive management philosophy to the business when he succeeded his father. "If we . . . [were] going to sell our product, it . . . [had] to be worth buying, and if it . . .[were] going to be worth buying, it . . . [had] to serve the people who . . . [were] purchasing it." This included "both the readers . . . and the advertisers." Blackburn saw the need for considerable expenditures to meet his twin objectives of better service and greater advertising revenue.

Blackburn, of course, was the embodiment of the company's philosophy through his public behaviour. Less visible were his private demonstrations of generosity towards employees. As George Hutchison, a former *Free Press* reporter, has written, Blackburn's benevolence was evident in a number of ways: "In good times, he . . . provided bonuses to supplement incomes, and [doted] over plans for annual Christmas parties, picnics and dinner dances. There [were] little gestures of support for the bereaved widow of a staff member, and quiet offerings of assistance to those in personal crisis: payment of an uninsured medical bill, a house painted for a pensioner, little gifts when least expected."[5]

When Jack Schenck was a twenty-three-year-old member of *The Free Press* photography department, Blackburn came to his aid. Schenck required a loan of three hundred dollars to purchase a Ford Roadster automobile. When he learned that

Schenck had approached a finance company for the money, Blackburn called him to the office: "I don't like to see my employees get tied into finance companies," said Blackburn. To Schenck's surprise, the publisher inquired, "How would it be if I loan you the 300 bucks?" Schenck agreed to the arrangement that called for the loan to be paid back through payroll deductions on whatever terms he wished to make. If the loan were not paid in full within a year, three per cent interest was to be charged on the unpaid balance. Blackburn promptly wrote out a personal check. The loan was repaid completely within ten months. Schenck recalled: "It was a good lesson in finance at a very impressionable, young age. . . . He had my undying loyalty from that point on. It was sort of a judgement call on his part [because] he didn't know me."[6]

Blackburn's major innovation in management-employee relations during the war years was the establishment of The London Free Press Employees' Benefit Society, now known as The Blackburn Media Employees' Association. (The roots of the Association date back to the formation of The Free Press Sick and Funeral Benefit Society on 3 July 1886. The Employees' Benefit Society was formed on 8 February 1943; the Employees' Association on 14 March 1950. The Blackburn Media Employees' Association came into being on 18 April 1986). This initiative typified his business philosophy which emphasized the need for a harmonious relationship between the company and employees.

Still, this new structure, which was perceived as giving employees a greater voice in company decision making, was also self-serving. After his bitter experience with the printers' strike in 1934-35, Blackburn had no time for unions. He maintained that the labour strife at *The Free Press* was a contributing factor to his father's death. The employees' organization was a positive response to a situation that had left him with personal antagonistic feelings. He saw this new structure as a vehicle to discourage union organizers. It largely achieved his objectives.

There were no certified unions in the company after Blackburn became publisher. The printers had suffered a setback after their recent strike and failed to obtain a written agreement with *The Free Press*. The stereotypers and pressmen were unionized and paid dues; both unions had no signed contracts with the company. For the most part, workers remained content with the working arrangements and conditions Blackburn established after he took over. The editorial and reporting staffs in both print and broadcast divisions were paid salaries at least to match, and in some cases surpass, other leading Canadian daily newspapers and broadcasters.

Blackburn supplemented these economic measures with a number of social benefits for employees including pension, dental and drug insurance plans, the five-day week, night differential pay for editors and more attractive holiday packages. Such innovations in the newspaper and broadcast industries were by no means commonplace during the Second World War. Blackburn's management style clearly was aimed at modernizing The London Free Press Printing Company. He was prepared to break with outdated established practices and set his sights on bringing the company into the mid-twentieth century.

"I hate unions," Blackburn once remarked. "And yet one realizes that there must be mechanisms established through which staff and management must communicate because staff isn't all wrong." He stressed co-operation and communication between both sides. Throughout his career as publisher, he steadfastly served as the company's representative on the General Committee, the group that managed the affairs of the Employees' Association. Bruce Pearson, a member of the board of directors of The Blackburn Group Inc., explained: "He was a man who had a dynastic sense as many people in family business do have. But he also had a tremendous concern for the other constituents that were involved in the business, namely, his employees and the public. . . . You can call it benevolence, paternalism, you can call it good business."[7]

Blackburn was successful in getting his employees to organize themselves using a familiar structure of the corporate world as their model. The General Committee (GC), which had representatives from the various company divisions elected annually by the employees through secret ballot, was similar to a board of directors. With Blackburn present at GC meetings, there was opportunity for the elected representatives to speak directly to him and voice their concerns over virtually any aspect of the company's operations. All members who were elected to the General Committee were below the supervisory level. Department supervisors provided yet another outlet for employees' grievances. Membership in the Employees' Association was voluntary and open to full and part-time workers for a small fee which was tax deductible. Freelance employees were eligible for social memberships entitling them to participate in the Association's recreational activities.

Blackburn insisted that "people who are working should have a say in the terms . . . of employment and the other working conditions that affect them." The Employees' Association was "a means of giving people an opportunity to talk with management and influence management's decisions but without unions as such. It's a company union. The unions would call it that." Blackburn preferred to describe the structure he had introduced as a staff association with staff council. While he was of the opinion that in some industries unions were necessary, Blackburn dismissed as speculation the notion that they had enhanced workers' quality of life. He was disturbed when he saw financial decisions related to the cost of operating companies made under pressure from unions who threatened strike action: unions, he said, ultimately would have to think in terms other than how much money they got. They would have to think about whether the public can afford to pay the price increases that would be necessary if they got what they wanted. The Employees' Association, whose motto was "mutual understanding brings mutual benefits," exemplified Blackburn's sense of noblesse oblige. But he was also an intensely pragmatic, conventional businessman who saw that this structural change, if implemented successfully, would serve the company well in the long run and keep it free of labour strife.

Since 4 March 1944 the Employees' Benefit Society and later the Association have published a newspaper, *The Fourth Estate*, which serves as a communication link between management and workers. Its main function, as the official publication of the Association, is to report to the membership the work of their elected General Committee representatives. In the first edition of the internal newspaper Blackburn explained that the idea of having a newspaper within a newspaper was a positive move and predicted that the Association's newspaper would play an essential role in the life and work of *The Free Press*.

Blackburn would bristle at the criticisms of some employees that the Association and his approach were needlessly paternalistic. But Russ Waide, whom Blackburn chose to head the company's newly created personnel department in the 1940s, argued that the notion of paternalism, in the strictest sense, was "not in tune with [Blackburn's] philosophy. . . . He believed in individuals and that they got their strength from within themselves [but also] that you should have an atmosphere in which they work that is going to take care of people."[8] Blackburn frowned on the narrow interpretation of "paternalism" which tended to divorce its meaning from individual responsibility. But he strongly endorsed the notion of "the boss listening to and acting on views expressed by the staff." As he explained, "I guess I don't feel a paternal father to staff but rather as a brother, sharing the same risks and . . . the same responsibilities . . . the same objectives and . . . joys of being involved in a rather fascinating business." By paying close attention to the affairs of the General Committee, Blackburn could remain sensitive to the grass-roots feeling among employees throughout the company. He was obviously convinced that steady dialogue could prevent employees' disenchantment from building up over a period of time into grievances that could lead to a disruption in the smooth operation of the company. The Employees' Association, a properly functioning supervisory chain of command, and a sensitive personnel department — these mechanisms, he believed, provided ready outlets for any discontent among staff.

In addition to introducing progressive social measures for employees, Blackburn was, from the beginning, also unusually single-minded about a more personal economic objective that he seldom enunciated publicly. By 1938, the Blackburn family held 889 of the 1,200 shares of common stock in the Free Press Printing Company. George Mathewson, the son of Henry Mathewson, one of the original stock holders, and the estate of

George's wife, Philippa, held eleven shares. William Southam and Sons Limited had the remaining 300 shares of the company's stock. But Blackburn looked to the day when he would control the total common stock of the company, especially the one-quarter interest held by the Southam family. It would take some forty years for that to happen, but it was a constant obsession that never wavered.

When Walter Blackburn became publisher, The London Free Press Printing Company consisted of *The Free Press* and *The Advertiser* newspapers and radio station CFPL, the successor to CJGC. *The Advertiser* undoubtedly was the weakest of the company's three wings and ceased publication in 1936. Economic forces proved Arthur Blackburn to be correct in his prediction that London could support only one newspaper. The high costs involved in publishing a mass-circulation daily inevitably meant that the newspaper able to gather the widest circulation base would be the ultimate survivor in virtually any competitive newspaper market.

Another Londoner, George McCullagh, also reflected this new newspaper age. He had formed the *Globe and Mail* following his purchase of the *Globe* and the *Mail and Empire* in 1936. Blackburn recalled that McCullagh's paper provided tough competition for *The Free Press* in southwestern Ontario, especially under Bob Farquharson, "one of the best editors the *Globe* ever had." Clearly businessmen-publishers had replaced the partisan editors of the late nineteenth century. The journalistic age that greeted Blackburn as publisher dictated that a huge readership was required to support a high level of expenditures for improved printing presses and other technological advances in the newspaper industry.

The Advertiser had never recovered from its support of the Laurier Liberals in the 1917 federal election. In 1926 when the Blackburns purchased *The Advertiser*, it carried only 14 pages during the week. Three years later some editions consisted of only 12 pages. When advertising declined, the newspaper resorted to razzle-dazzle journalism, hoping to recover lost ground. The London readers who stayed with the newspaper were treated to some spectacular journalism. It was common to see headlines such as NORFOLK MAN SLAYS FATHER WITH AXE or, in the same vein, BLOOD-STAINED RAZOR HINTS AT TRAGEDY.[9] For a while *The Advertiser* seemed to lose interest in politics. Later the newspaper returned to its traditional role of supporting Liberal policies and attacked the government of R.B. Bennett for failing to cope with the changed economic circumstances created by the Depression. But clearly *The Advertiser*'s days were numbered.

The Dirty Thirties had a sharp impact on both London newspapers. *The Advertiser*'s daily circulation dropped to 15,030 in 1934, while the corresponding figure for *The Free Press* was 35,140, a decline from 39,248 three years earlier.[10] The economic figures tell the true story and the predicament that the new publisher faced. In the five-year period between 1928 and 1932, *The Advertiser* had operated at an annual loss ranging from $51,894 to $77,793. By contrast, the five-year net profit of *The Free Press* for the same period had been $873,961 for a yearly average of $174,792. During the same five-year period, the radio station's net profit averaged $14,820.[11] Advertisers in Canada were relatively slow to adopt the electronic medium as a vehicle to sell their products. The crunch for *The Advertiser* came in 1935 when it lost $90,000 and the company was obviously finding it a liability.

The decision to stop publication of the paper was taken at a meeting of the board of directors on 20 October 1936. The publisher's aunt, Margaret Blackburn, made a motion, seconded by her sister, Susan, that the paper discontinue publication on 30 October 1936. Blackburn's aunts had urged him to stop publishing the paper, given the economic difficulties which now seemed insurmountable. Some members of *The Advertiser*'s staff joined *The Free Press*. These included Randolph Churchill, who later held the post of executive editor, and John Elliott, who eventually succeeded Arthur Ford as editor-in-chief of *The Free Press*. Blackburn recalled that his aunts were very concerned that no staff of *The Advertiser* get into trouble financially during the Depression. The company decided to amalgamate some staff members of the defunct newspaper with *The Free Press*. Others were carried on the payroll until they subsequently obtained employment.

The final editon of *The Advertiser* explained to its readers the reasons for the newspaper's demise. "For the past twelve years, and particularly during the last five, *The Advertiser* has been struggling against adverse economic circumstances which have brought about the discontinuance of dozens of daily papers, in even much more populous centres, all over the continent. The closing of *The Advertiser* today leaves only two Ontario cities, Ottawa and Toronto, with more than one daily newspaper." While noting that the deficits for the past several years had been almost as large as the payroll, this message informed readers that *The Free Press* would assume all subscription obligations of *The Advertiser*. An editorial in the final edition underlined the need for tolerance to help avert a disastrous international crisis which could lead to a major war. The editorial entitled "The Need for Liberalism" was not optimistic about the future: "It is difficult to derive much satisfaction from a contemplation of the world today. Violence and force seem dominant in many parts of the world." The newspaper concluded that liberalism "and the theory of giving the other nation an even break" were the only ways in which war could be avoided: "More and more it becomes evident to those with even a scintilla of perception that the liberal way is, in the last analysis, the only way."[12]

The closing of *The Advertiser* was a somewhat inauspicious start for Walter Blackburn. In fact, he found his first decade as publisher burdensome. Power struggles within the company which pitted him against the newspaper's general manager, Charles Thomas, the need for personnel changes to improve the newspaper, and the heavy expenses involved when he introduced technological improvements amidst an uncertain economy gave the youthful publisher many sleepless nights.

After the closure of *The Advertiser* Blackburn moved quickly to better working conditions and upgrade technology. The lighting in the newspaper's composing room was improved; a new printing press was installed to replace the old Hoe press which had been acquired during World War I. "My father had told me when Hitler became chancellor, in his opinion, there would be war [and] I believed him," Blackburn recalled. "So I felt that my job, once I got in full time, was to prepare for that war." The old printing press, which had been installed in 1915, "wouldn't have carried us through ... a period of war with the circulation increase that we would experience. It wouldn't do the job [because] it wouldn't permit us to run fast enough." He was prepared to incur expenditures, because he felt that the newspaper, now London's sole daily, had to be improved to meet that challenge. Furthermore, steady profit would be more readily achieved through an improved product rather than by severe cost cutting.

Throughout the years when Blackburn attempted to consolidate his position as publisher, he either fired for cause, or retired early, numerous individuals. He admitted to "a lot of blood on [his] hands" during this turbulent period of structural reorganization. The dismissal of personnel, for whatever reason, never came easily to him: "Usually after sleepless nights I would make the decision, balancing the situation as best I could in the interests of the newspaper and I suppose to a degree in my own interests of survival." He hoped he would never be described as ruthless. Still he was intensely pragmatic and ultimately reached decisions relating to personnel based on the overall good of the company. He seemed to have placed a strong belief in the business school dictate that "there is no pat answer to any problem or question" and that business decisions should be taken not hastily but only after careful analysis of the possible consequences. During these early years, Walter Gunn, the newspaper's advertising manager, editor-in-chief Arthur Ford, and Mel Parkinson, the composing room superintendant, were important allies for Blackburn. Gunn had left the McConnell Advertising Agency to join *The Free Press*. Ford joined the newspaper in 1920 after serving as correspondent for the *Winnipeg Telegram* in the Parliamentary Press Gallery. Parkinson was the second generation of his family to work for *The Free Press*; his father had been head of composing for twenty years. Parkinson's son, Bob, later also worked for the newspaper, a generational continuity Blackburn seemed to encourage. But the publisher's

41

management style and expansive approach brought him into sharp conflict with Charles Thomas, the newspaper's general manager, who had seen *The Free Press* through the difficult Depression days and whose first inclination was to limit costs.

Charles Thomas, who had enjoyed considerable autonomy in operating *The Free Press* under Arthur Blackburn's tenure as publisher, was skeptical of the son's methods of operation. Thomas had proved himself a vigorous manager, having been responsible for breaking the printers' strike in 1935. *The Free Press* was "the only newspaper in Canada who [sic] ever had gumption enough to carry this through for fifteen months and win."[13] Blackburn realized that he had a great deal to learn from Thomas about the operation of the daily newspaper. But in their business practices, the new publisher and Thomas were diametrically opposed. A bitter and lengthy struggle ensued until Thomas was finally given early retirement in 1944.

The enmity that developed between Thomas and Blackburn was hardly surprising. "I think he hated me and I hated him," said Blackburn. Both men represented different generations. Thomas took an accountant's approach to the operation of the company, especially after he was named to the board of directors in 1930 and became general manager. As befitting an accountant, Thomas seemed to measure his performance by the balance sheet, the amount of money he could make and save. Throughout the early 1930s Thomas saw the need for economic restraint. Blackburn, on the other hand, wanted to develop and expand the business and was prepared to incur sizeable expenditures in the process.

Thomas claimed to have inquired from Blackburn on more than one occasion, "if he could point to any mistake . . . [Thomas] had made that cost or might cost the company money and his answer was 'No.'" The general manager took credit for "having the happy faculty of being able to pick good men" such as Walter Gunn, Mel Parkinson and Arthur Ford, the three individuals whom Blackburn eventually came to rely upon heavily as publisher.

Thomas also claimed responsibility for getting the company

involved in radio. In this venture, he argued that "[Arthur] Blackburn gave . . . [him] a free hand to spend and do what . . . [he] considered necessary." Thomas realized that the new publisher thought it had been a mistake to sell the company's radio station to Windsor interests, but maintained that he and the elder Blackburn had agreed it was the best thing to do at that time.

But along with their generational differences, the styles and approaches of the two men were fundamentally different. Thomas had shown himself to be a forceful, hard-driving and at times intransigent manager. Given the responsibility that Arthur Blackburn had placed upon him, Thomas seemingly had come to look upon the newspaper as his own. Blackburn's personality and style, which stressed a sympathetic, quietly purposeful approach, was a picture in contrast to Thomas's assertive and aggressive manner. Thomas had prided himself on past accomplishments. Blackburn wanted to look to the future.

The struggle between the two men created an uneasy working environment for the employees of the newspaper, who were uncertain where their loyalties should lie. Blackburn recalled: "The staff of *The London Free Press* was in a difficult position. He was sort of boss while I was a learner."

The first major disagreement between the pair revolved around Blackburn's decision to improve the composing-room lighting and to purchase a more efficient printing press. In November 1936 the board of directors had authorized the new publisher to purchase a new press and any additional equipment necessary and also to make any necessary alterations in the buildings. Thomas hesitated at these expenditures. With the printers' strike and labour strife fresh in his mind, Blackburn wanted to appear sensitive to the composing-room staff. These employees were forced to work with old-fashioned incandescent lights that had to be adjusted by long cords hanging down from the ceiling. Fluorescent lighting had not yet been invented, but the best incandescent illumination was installed. "I had to fight the general manager on that decision and many others," said Blackburn. "[He] didn't believe in spending any money." Thomas also resisted introduction of the new press, because he felt it unnecessary. "I put it in," said Blackburn, "practically over his dead body."

Perhaps another irritant for Thomas was the deference shown by middle management and employees towards the youthful publisher who from the beginning was addressed as "Mr. Blackburn," an appellation that was to stay with him throughout his professional career. Blackburn maintained that he was never comfortable when addressed in this manner. He would have preferred the less formal Walter or W.J. But that was not to be. His aunts wanted to ensure that he had the respect of all *the Free Press* employees. "My aunts, who were on the board and were the dominating influence after my father's death, insisted that I be called 'Mr. Blackburn,'" he remembered, "and that . . . carried on. . . . They were old fashioned." Despite his dignified, austere demeanour, Blackburn insisted that he had never sought deference deliberately: "I may [have been] old fashioned in some respects, but I don't really know. . . . In so far as deference [was] concerned, I [didn't] seek it. I never [thought] much of it. My memos to my senior executives [were signed] . . . 'W.J.' and I [got] 'Mr. Blackburn' back."

The eight-year rivalry between Blackburn and Thomas ended towards the end of the war when Thomas was given early retirement in November 1944, and well compensated. Blackburn realized he either had to get rid of Charles Thomas or get out himself. The tension between the two men had reached a breaking point. Four months before leaving the company, Thomas had written to Susan Blackburn, the publisher's aunt, a letter in which he defended his contribution to the company. "Taking everything into consideration," Thomas explained, "the recent outburst was most unfair to say the least." When Thomas left the newspaper, *The Fourth Estate* overlooked the management struggles that had occurred and emphasized Thomas's forty-four years of service: "During his long years with the company he was affectionately known as C.T., to whom [employees] could turn when the going was a 'little rough.'"[14] But an era was over; Blackburn now had undisputed control.

Given the influence that his aunts had had on him during his early life and formative years as publisher, their approval of the woman he chose to marry was a matter of high priority for Blackburn. He abandoned his single status on 9 November 1938 when he married Marjorie Ludwell Dampier, whom he had met while attending the University of Western Ontario. He had no difficulty in convincing his aunts that his choice was a wise one.

His wife's father, Lawrence Henry Dampier, was a Strathroy bank manager who died in 1930. The Ludwells were English folk whose ancestry dated back to at least the eighteenth century in the Dampier family. A branch of the Dampier family came to the new world via Williamsburg, Virginia. Lawrence Dampier's first wife had two daughters, one of whom died from diptheria. The second daughter, Helen, married Harold Bucke, the son of the noted physician Richard Maurice Bucke, who was the first super-intendent of Ontario Hospital; Dr. Bucke had arrived in the London region during the mid-nineteenth century. Dampier's second wife was Edith Isabella English, a friend of the daughter from his first marriage. He was in his fifties at his second mar-riage, she was twenty-eight. The couple had two boys and two girls: Marjorie, Lawrence, Edward and Mary.

Blackburn never knew either of his wife's parents. Both had died by the time he and Marjorie met at Western. Their first encounter came as seventeen year-olds during initiation week at university in 1931, the year Blackburn's mother died. His wife remembered the occasion: "I was bright-eyed and bushy-tailed. . . . Walter spotted me . . . and was interested in me so it seemed right away." The serious young man seemed drawn to her more carefree personality: "I always loved fun and Walter liked nothing better than to be part of it but he was not quite so good at generating it."[15]

Not surprisingly, their first date was a family gathering with Walter's aunts who were anxious that he marry what they consid-ered to be the proper woman. As his wife recalled, the occasion was on a Saturday afternoon at 652 Talbot Street: "They were lovely women. They all came out and greeted me and they were soft-spoken. . . . The aunts I think liked me right away, because I was at home with older people from my own experience . . . and it didn't take them long to sense what you were like. . . . I had enormous respect for them as well as affection." Even on these casual occasions, she recognized early Blackburn's intense personality: "You couldn't help but be affected by a person like that because his attentions were flattering and yet they were frightening at the same time. . . . But you did have this feeling that he was really serious."

It was not a steady romance from the beginning. "These were the depression days," Marjorie recalled. "The business of [finding] a husband was the furthest from my thoughts." The pair found time for university parties and played badminton at the London Club: "[Walter] loved to get me at the back line and make me hit long shots and I would try and just drop them over the net. If he got me at the back line, I was sunk."

The couple was officially engaged while Marjorie worked at the Bell Telephone Company. The sun shone brightly on 9 November 1938 when the young couple was married at the Anglican Church of St. John the Evangelist in London. As on all wedding occasions, it was a day filled with hope and promise. Following the church ceremony, the entourage made its way to the Hunt Club where classics professor, Doctor John Ralph, a fatherly adviser to the groom, and Canon Quinton Warner proposed humorous toasts. The couple travelled to Miami Beach by train for their honeymoon before returning to London to reside at 401 Huron Street where Blackburn and his new bride rented a house. Before the couple was married a year, Canada joined the war effort in September 1939. Their first child, Susan Marjorie, was born on 28 November 1939.

Blackburn had joined the C squadron of the First Hussars, an army militia regiment, in February 1938. He held the rank of second lieutenant until September 1940 when he resigned from the militia. When the Hussars were recruiting, he did not join up for active service, a decision that prompted occasional private criticism in London. His reasons for failing to enlist revolved around both his personal and professional circumstances at the time.

Blackburn saw his first responsibility to the family newspaper business which he had managed for only three years when war broke out. Two of his closest aunts were still living and relied on the family business for income, as did his two sisters. Forever proud of his heritage and the newspaper tradition established by his grandfather, Josiah, he felt keenly about building the family enterprise. With no other male family member present to head the business, and after considerable discussion with his wife, he concluded that he would not serve. Moreover, he felt that all Canadian newspapers had an important role to play in the war effort, a belief that helped influence his action.[16] Still, with London's military tradition dating back to the Upper Canada Rebellion when British regulars occupied the town in the late 1830s, it was a difficult choice for Blackburn, and he certainly had his critics.

Tom Lawson, his friend since boyhood days, who served with the Canadian Fusiliers taking part in operations in the Aleutian Islands in 1943 and 1944, understood Blackburn's decision. Lawson, an honorary colonel of the Royal Canadian Regiment, recognized that *The Free Press* publisher was influenced by family circumstances and his responsibilities following his father's death. "I can completely understand that," he said. "It would have been a very difficult decision for Walter ... [when] one incurs an obligation to serve." Lawson felt that "had he not been in the militia then there would have been no feeling about it, because people understood the great responsibility he had of heading up *The London Free Press*."[17]

Douglas Trowell, who joined CFPL radio following the Second World War and later became station manager, recalled the haughty social climate of London. He maintained that "it would be far harder to sit in London, Ontario. . . . and not go to war, not to wear the colours and whatever. It would have been a very much easier thing to do [go to war] than to stick with that [business] and go with it. I think that showed great courage."[18] Captain Joseph Jeffery, a former naval officer who headed the London Life Insurance Company founded by his grandfather, echoed that perspective: "I always felt badly that Walter was put in such a difficult position, because I'm sure he would have liked to have been in the show just like anybody else.... He didn't decide that. His family decided it for him."[19]

Two other children were born to the Blackburns before the war ended. The birth of their son, Walter Juxon, Junior, on 31 May 1941 was greeted with the customary applause afforded new males in the Blackburn household. His father naturally saw him as the heir apparent who would sustain the patriarchal succession of family publishers into the fourth generation. He could not know then that it was not to be. The couple's second daughter, Martha Grace, who was born on 9 October 1944, would eventually succeed her father as publisher of the newspaper forty-eight years to the day after Walter Juxon had first assumed responsibility.

In 1940 Blackburn purchased a farm northeast of London where the family enjoyed some of their most memorable moments. His original idea had been to build a year-round house at the farm, but those intentions were abandoned during the war, and a small bungalow was constructed from plans contained in a catalogue. The first summer at the farm was in 1942. For the next fifteen years or so the family would leave their home in London about the middle of June, returning in early September. Blackburn's wife, Marjorie, recalled that "most of the people who came out to the farm. . . . [with] their children to swim were war wives whose husbands were overseas. . . . We all had victory gardens. . . . We all planted vegetables like mad."[20]

Throughout his years at the farm and away from the family business, Blackburn was a more relaxed father, although he was still reluctant to break with the strict rules of decorum and conduct he had established for the children, a legacy from his own upbringing. His son and two daughters were expected to behave "as the children of the publisher of a local newspaper with roots in the community." Any kind of human quarrelling, even among children, Blackburn found upsetting. His reaction seemed uncontrollable. At the farm he enjoyed the children one at a time rather than together for this reason. His wife explained: "Children are always competing with each other and having to decide to settle the quarrel was something he couldn't emotionally cope with."[21]

Recalling her early childhood, his daughter, Martha, explained: "I can remember being somewhat in awe of [Dad]. . . . [It was] a household in which there were very specific rules of deportment and behaviour. . . . I think that some very strict rules were placed on [father] by his great aunts . . . [and] part of it was a very specific carryover from that." She felt her father was basically a shy person: "Other people . . . held back from him because he had some sort of awesomeness about him or unapproachability which I didn't find at all on the personal level. . . . I think a lot of his past was very painful to him."[22] Both she and her sister remember the time spent at the family's farm as some of the more enjoyable moments with their father, because he enjoyed country living.

Susan, the couple's first child, felt her father sought to control the lives of his children. His bad temper was evident on more than one occasion: "He could really terrify you, but if you had a good argument he would listen. He wanted us to have strong values and good principles. . . . [Sometimes] he blew his cool when he came home. As a grandfather he was best. He softened in his later years [but] his principles stayed the same."[23]

While he accompanied his children as youngsters to St. John the Evangelist Church, Blackburn never professed to be a deeply religious or devout person. In his later years he remarked, "I believe in the principles which Christ teaches very deeply, but as far as going to church and being seen to be a religious person . . . I don't do that."

The city of London was a relatively small community during the war and without a vibrant social life. "I remember . . . [making] dresses for the children and [doing] that kind of thing because it got difficult to buy things," Marjorie Blackburn recalled. "There wasn't the sort of glut of consumer products then that there is now. Shopping was a relatively simple matter." Other than an occasional game of badminton at the London Armories or at the London Club, the city offered little entertainment for young couples and "if you partied at all, you always brought your own bottle with you." Her husband remembered that "there wasn't much fun [because] nobody played golf." He made up for the days lost to that sport in his subsequent summers at the Hunt Club.

As a social outlet, Blackburn took great delight in his private gatherings with members of the Investors' Club whose title seemed to belie their capacity to have a rollicking good time. The Investors came together in 1939 when sixteen members met regularly at the Hunt Club, each investing a monthly fee of ten dollars. Blackburn was among the founding members who also included Fred Jenkins and George Robinson, two Londoners who were to remain his close friends. The group was disbanded in 1939 when nine members joined the armed forces. It was reorganized following the war. The fee was raised to $300 monthly and the membership eventually to forty. The club devoted most of its energy to the planning of exotic dinners, European and Las Vegas forays. Blackburn obviously enjoyed his cronies in the club which often provided him with a healthy respite. On one occasion, Blackburn persuaded the Hotel London to cook haggis, a traditional Scottish dish. To the skirl of bagpipes, the meal was ushered in for the Investors in attendance. Blackburn's friend Fred Jenkins recalled: "It was the most terrible . . . stuff I ever tasted in all my bloody life."

Blackburn's basically cautious nature meant that he always preferred to have backup systems he could rely upon in his business life. Besides the purchase of a new printing press in preparation for war, he had stockpiled newsprint and a supply of tin. Materials such as tin would be difficult to obtain in wartime to meet the company's metal requirements. With a threatened shortage of gasoline which could affect delivering the newspaper by truck, he had horses at his farm ready, if needed, to pull delivery carts to distribute *The Free Press*. The horses were never required during the war.

Throughout his first decade as publisher, he concentrated on the business aspect of the newspaper and left the editorial side to Arthur Ford. Though he was publisher, Blackburn's old-fashioned upbringing dictated from the beginning that he

should show deference to Ford, who ran the editorial department with quiet competence.

One of Blackburn's proudest moments during the early part
of the war was when *The Free Press* beat the *Globe and Mail* on
Germany's invasion of Holland and Belgium on 10 May 1940.
He credited the scoop to a newsroom cleaning woman who
heard the bulletin bell on the Canadian Press wire service that
brought word of the new development. She then alerted the
staff. The papers already printed were thrown away and page
one replated with the major news development telling of the
invasion. *The Free Press* publisher considered the coverage of
that single international story to be an important watershed in
the circulation battle between his newspaper and the *Globe*,
which had proved to be a strong competitor in southwestern
Ontario. "From that moment on our circulation grew and the
Globe's declined," Blackburn recalled. "We beat them on that big
story thanks to our cleaning woman who knew enough to get the
staff going."

Just as his father's death from diabetes following the labour
strife at the newspaper had a bearing on Blackburn's economic
outlook towards the union movement, so too did it enhance his
social commitment towards the community. His father's illness
nurtured an interest in medicine. In 1938 Blackburn became a
director of the London Health Association (LHA) and was to
hold every post in the community organization during the next
forty-two years. The LHA had been formed in 1909 under the
leadership of Sir Adam Beck to erect and operate a sanitarium
for tuberculosis patients. Blackburn was to nurture and financially support the organization throughout his career. His greatest contribution was during the several years when he served as
chairman of the Planning and Building Committee for London's University Hospital which opened in 1972. The hospital
today ranks among the world's leading health-care institutions.

In the late 1930s Blackburn was undeniably a protégé of
London's old guard. The London community closed in around
him and the major business leaders took him under their wing.
He came under the influence of establishment figures such as
Colonel Ibbotson Leonard, then president of the Health Associ-

ation, E.V. Buchanan, honorary secretary, and directors V.P. Cronyn, John S. Labatt, Ray Lawson, F.E. Parnell and D.B. Weldon. The group was devoted to the growth and development of aspects of the city they considered to be important, such as health care and the University of Western Ontario. Blackburn recognized early the interdependence his business had with various community groups. Most successful family companies have seen the need to cultivate this relationship with the community. "I guess I became one of the old guard," he said. "They asked me to join the board. . . . Nobody questioned it, [because] we were very happy to give our time to it." His work with the London Health Association was a manifestation of Blackburn's eagerness to offer time and money towards social causes in which he believed.

Years later he was disenchanted when dutifully minded citizens on Western's board of governors were criticized by the university community. Faculty and students demanded a greater role in the university's decision making during the 1960s. His "old school" upbringing enabled Blackburn to relate readily to old guard individuals he had encountered as a young publisher; he generally frowned upon any criticism directed toward such individuals who, in his eyes, were prepared to look out for London's best interests.

Even with his extensive media holdings, Blackburn never considered himself to be a highly influential public figure. He often preferred to remain a backstage presence, a posture that was characteristic of the privacy his ancestors chose to protect in the community. Despite his austere manner and at times remote personality, Blackburn insisted that he enjoyed the print and broadcast media mainly because they were people oriented. "We're people first, professionals second," he once remarked.[24]

With the demise of *The Advertiser* in 1936, Blackburn felt that *The Free Press* would eventually have to reorient itself and become more independent in its editorial positions. However, there was little evidence of this shift throughout the war years. Blackburn had put his stamp on the administrative side of the company. But the hand of Arthur Ford, whom Blackburn described as "the writing mouthpiece of the national and

Ontario Tory party," was obviously guiding the editorial page.

In his early years as publisher, Blackburn was clearly deferential towards Ford, and *The Free Press* continued to espouse an essentially Tory position. Thus in the 1940 and 1945 federal elections, *The Free Press* supported the Progressive Conservatives, holding to its established practice. Nonetheless as publisher, Blackburn insisted that he was not prepared to support any party leader simply because he was a Tory. For Blackburn, a politician's stand on issues was more important than blind party loyalty. So, for example, *The Free Press* supported King and the Liberals throughout the conscription crisis when the party was showing signs of moving closer to the war position advocated by Arthur Meighen and the Conservatives. Blackburn's undogmatic outlook would lead eventually to a rift between him and Ford, during the Diefenbaker-Pearson era, when *The Free Press* broke with its editorial practice and supported the Liberals.

During the conscription crisis *The Free Press* argued strenuously for the yes side and maintained that a negative vote, which would prevent the government from furthering the war effort, was unpatriotic. Except in Quebec, the yes vote won a clear victory. On the day of the plebiscite, the London newspaper, in a front page editorial, had this message: "Vote Yes Today."[25] The following day *The Free Press* noted that King had been given a free hand and that London had sustained the British tradition. The danger the Quebec vote had presented to national unity received only passing comment in an editorial that same day: "We are not sure if the plebiscite benefitted national unity but if Quebec considers itself a good Canadian, it will submit gracefully."[26]

In December 1944 Blackburn was able to report to the company's shareholders that for the fiscal year ending 31 October of that year "advertising revenues of the Company reached an all-time high at $680,605.70. This [was] an increase of $121,904.84 over 1943." He praised the efforts of Walter Gunn, the company's advertising manager who also had become a shareholder and director of the company, for this accomplishment: "He has left no stone unturned to bring revenue to the company."[27]

53

Both the newspaper circulation and radio revenues had increased from the preceding year. *The Free Press* had shown a circulation revenue increase of $21,627, bringing it to $382,547. CFPL radio's revenue was $97,068, an increase of $25,883 over the previous year. However, Blackburn informed the directors that in almost all departments of the company — with the exception of the pressroom — costs had also increased. Increases in wages were mainly responsible for this. The Regional War Labour Board in 1943 had granted a ten per cent increase in the basic wages of employees following the submission of a joint application by the company and The Free Press Employees' Benefit Society. The decrease in the pressroom costs was attributed to the armed forces enlistments during the war. The year before the war ended the current investments of the company totalled $750,200 of which $675,200 was in Dominion of Canada bonds.[28]

Blackburn had experienced a somewhat turbulent decade as publisher since he had taken over in the mid–1930s. His youth and inexperience were obviously early handicaps. Much of his time was spent trying to build credibility with employees who had become accustomed to a more rigid style of management during Arthur Blackburn's era. Now thirty-one years old, "W.J." had managed to consolidate his role and could see that the company had emerged from the war years in a favourable economic position. The London Free Press Printing Company clearly enjoyed a media monopoly in London, then still a relatively small southwestern Ontario community. His next challenge would be to keep pace with the post-war growth of the electronic media including frequency modulation (FM) radio and television. But first his energies had to be devoted to CFPL-AM radio. The station was about to undergo a face lift and become thoroughly modernized. Wartime had ushered in the golden age of Canadian radio.

CHAPTER THREE

◇————————————◇

A Broadcast Innovator
1945 — 1950

As HEAD OF The London Free Press Printing Company since 1936, Walter Blackburn had devoted most of his time and energy to the new technical requirements and improvements demanded by the newspaper he owned. After World War II, he shifted the emphasis to broadcasting. New personnel were brought to CFPL-AM radio and its broadcast facilities greatly expanded. Blackburn introduced Frequency Modulation (FM) broadcasting to London in 1948. Five years later he brought television to southwestern Ontario.

The times had created the man. Blackburn's belief that the company should be involved in the many facets of electronic communications prompted him to introduce these broadcasting innovations at the earliest opportunity. This outlook helps to explain the reason why The Blackburn Group Inc. remains one of Canada's most notable media dynasties. The growth of the Blackburn communications empire in London has paralleled the region's evolution from a rural backwater to a modern, urbanized Ontario centre.

Just as his father, Arthur, had seen radio providing a service distinct from but related to that of the newspaper, "W.J." perceived FM radio and television to be additional alternative services. Since the three forms of media, newspaper, radio and television were seen to be different services to the community, each was placed under separate management. In effect, his newspaper and broadcasting holdings operated on a day-to-day basis as competitors, each maintaining its own news and sales staffs. For a number of years, the CFPL radio news organization relied on the resources of the newspaper for local coverage. But eventually the tie between the two media was severed with the radio station then developing its own news-gathering team to supplement on-air personnel. Only the accounting, personnel services, data processing and engineering departments were shared by the three London media.

This decentralized organizational structure has supported the independent and separate editorial judgements of the three media. Since the three news-gathering staffs were under separate management, the possibility of deliberate uniformity in news coverage, newspaper editorials and radio commentaries was virtually eliminated. Blackburn's later media acquisitions in Wingham, Ontario, also remained under separate management.

On the face of it, Blackburn came to enjoy a media monopoly in London and southwestern Ontario. However, he emphasized time and again, before various broadcasting regulators and government inquiries, that his holdings were essentially independent entities within London and faced considerable competition from outside the city. His argument, which was always buttressed by extensive figures to show the number of external print and broadcast media with access to the London region, met with success because of his attitude towards service and profit. From his earliest days as publisher, Blackburn insisted that profits would come only from a high level of service. He showed regulators his willingness to spend to obtain his objectives.

After he had established himself as publisher, Blackburn made no secret of the fact that he was unhappy with the service provided by CFPL radio. He was also aware that the Canadian Broadcasting Corporation (CBC), the regulator of the industry at the time, was disturbed at the performance of private broadcasters generally, including CFPL, then a CBC affiliate. The need for more inspired programming was considered essential if CFPL were to avoid threats of licence cancellation.

CJGC, the forerunner to CFPL, had been a founding member of the Canadian Association of Broadcasters (CAB) in 1926. However, Blackburn pursued an independent position within this organization representing the interests of private broadcasters. In particular, he did not endorse the CAB's argument throughout the 1940s and early 1950s that the CBC should abandon its regulatory role over private stations. Many private broadcasters insisted that the CBC should not be both their broadcasting competitor and regulator. They argued for a separate regulatory body comparable to the Federal Communications Commission in the United States.

However, Blackburn saw advantages to a closer relationship with the CBC, perhaps a reason why he was successful in preserving his favourable position in southwestern Ontario. He argued that a separate regulator for broadcasting could have the potential to be even more interventionist than the corporation. As Murray Brown, who was to become president of CFPL Broadcasting Limited, explained," he felt . . . that it [was] better to live with the devil you know than the devil you don't."[1]

Blackburn wanted to improve the local and regional service of CFPL, both in news and entertainment, to allow the station to have a more recognizable identity in the community. To divert listeners away from the Detroit stations which attracted a sizable London audience, a more distinctive sound for CFPL was imperative.

Canadians had huddled beside their radios to learn of the principal international developments relating to the war. Advertisers soon recognized that radio was perceived not only as an entertainment medium but also as a new form of communication to transmit news and information. Companies abandoned their earlier reticence towards the spoken word and fully embraced the medium to sell their products.

Private radio broadcasters in Canada naturally welcomed these new, good times. The continued sale of industrial products was vital to Canada following the war, if the country were to make a smooth economic transition to peace time. The private stations were an important means of advertising such products to stimulate consumer demand. In August 1944 the broadcast regulator had agreed that the private operators could raise the power output of their radio stations to a maximum of 5,000 watts. This new ruling replaced the 1,000 watt ceiling, an out-growth of the North American Regional Broadcasting Agree-ment (Havana Treaty) in 1937 at Havana, where radio frequency allocations had been decided. Even with this more favourable broadcasting environment, Blackburn saw that better ser-vice meant greater expenditures of money.

As a cross-owner of a newspaper and radio station, Black-burn occasionally faced criticism over his level of media control. Recognizing his sensitive position, he steadfastly cultivated a favourable working relationship with CBC officials. His appear-ances before the CBC board of governors were always preceded by his own preliminary soundings in Ottawa to assess the gover-nors' views of the issues at hand. He paid scrupulous attention to detail in the briefs he presented before regulatory bodies, aware that the Blackburn name was at stake.

The chairman of the CBC board of governors for a brief period between 1944 and 1945 was Howard B. Chase, president of the Canadian Brotherhood of Locomotive Engineers. "With my views about unions," Blackburn recalled, "I didn't cherish that ... [but] he accepted me at face value. I ran into a lot of assistance I didn't expect to find both from ... the chairman of the CBC, members of the board ... and the then General Man-ager, Dr. [Augustin] Frigon."[2] The CBC remained the regulator of the private broadcasters until 1958 when its successor, the Board of Broadcast Governors (BBG), an independent regula-tory agency, was established.

Blackburn was an eager participant in a 1944 hearing before the CBC board that dealt with an application by Horace Stovin, a Calgary broadcaster, to establish a second radio station in London. This appearance, early in his career, set the tone for his later presentations to subsequent government inquiries into the media. Blackburn argued against the Calgary broadcaster's pro-posal, claiming that London simply could not support a second station. CFPL would suffer greatly, he contended, if the application were approved. He buttressed his arguments with copious facts and statistics that appeared to impress the board of governors who denied the application by the Calgary broadcaster.

Stovin had applied for a station that would operate during the daytime on 990 kilocycles, a more advantageous radio frequency than CFPL's 1570 on the dial. CFPL had begun broadcasting on 25 September 1933 using the 730 frequency, and was later assigned 1570, with a power of 1,000 watts. Generally speaking, a higher frequency required a greater power output to provide a radio signal comparable in strength to one provided on a lower frequency. In the case of CFPL, as Blackburn explained to the board of governors, the station was often not heard.

Unlike many owners of private stations, Blackburn had a clear understanding of the radio band and the strengths and limitations of radio frequencies. He argued that approval of Stovin's application would mean a steep daytime revenue loss for CFPL: "The calibration of Canadian-made receiving sets, except those of the most modern design, varies from that of American-made sets and we quickly found that a greater proportion of receiving sets than we had anticipated was unable to tune our station in at the new frequency. Their tuning-in abilities stopped short at 1500."[3]

Blackburn left no doubt with the board of governors that the 1570 frequency placed CFPL in a precarious position with WJR Detroit as a competitor in the London market: "Before we went to 1570 on 1000 watts, we had 45.52% of the daytime audience, while WJR had 34.22. In March 1941 we had 35% of the evening audience while WJR had 43%. By April 1944 our proportion of daytime audience had shrunk from 45.52% to 33.1% and our proportion of evening time audience had declined from 35% to 29.6%."

In the politely self-congratulatory manner he was to demonstrate before successive regulatory bodies, Blackburn reminded the board of governors that his family had pioneered the electronic media in London. His ancestors' achievements were cited to bolster his economic arguments: "As a station that has been in operation almost from the beginning of radio broadcasting in Canada, as a station that has a very large investment in its equip-ment and in goodwill with its listeners, its advertisers and their agents, *we must lodge the strongest protest at the possibility of such preferential treatment being accorded a new competitor in the field."* Blackburn drew the board's attention to the programming ser-vices originated by CFPL, ranging from school choirs and local orchestras to the network broadcast of the royal visit to London of the King and Queen in June 1939. He maintained that "no second station . . . be allowed to operate either in London *or* as a London and district station regardless of location at least until the licencing authority can grant the existing station CFPL a frequency as favourable as that to be enjoyed by the newcomer."

On 23 October 1944, Blackburn wrote to Walter Rush, con-troller of radio for the Department of Transport on the question of a new frequency. He explained that daytime operation of CFPL on 990 kilocycles or perhaps 1010 would provide "several important advantages both for our listeners, and for the origina-tors of the programs."[4]

Blackburn followed up by lobbying Davidson Dunton who had become chairman of the CBC board of governors in 1945: "If the 1010 frequency should become available and you should favourably consider our application . . . I feel that we should then be in a position to compete on an equal basis." Blackburn insisted that it seemed only right," as long as it [was] in the public interest," that the older stations including his own should receive prior consideration in the allocation of more desirable frequencies: "I am trying to point out that we have no desire whatsoever to be what might be termed 'dogs in the manger.' Competition, as long as it is fair competition, as a rule tends to improve rather than to injure service to the public and we are quite willing to take our chances in competing on a fair basis with any nearby stations which may be established."[5] Despite his efforts, another pioneer station, CFRB Toronto, eventually won the 1010 frequency.

Murray Brown, who became commercial manager of CFPL in 1945, reinforced Blackburn's continual efforts at the Depart-ment of Transport and at the CBC to get the station's frequency moved from 1570 kilocycles to a frequency nearer the middle of the band: "It was difficult to find a new frequency and he went to an international convention in Cuba ... found out this 980 existed and he was the one who spearheaded the change. . . . It was all his doing."[6] The international radio conference Blackburn attended in the fall of 1947 at Havana included delegates from Canada, the United States and Mexico, the signatories to the Havana Treaty in 1937. Blackburn hoped that Canadian representatives could arrange for better radio frequencies to be made available in Canada for private stations including his own.

Blackburn remained vigilant towards competitors. He boasted to Dunton that, as a Dominion network affiliate, CFPL operating at 1570 on the dial was "a loyal and enthusiastic member of the CBC family" and remained under "alert and progressive management." But the cost of improving CFPL's service was a vital consideration: "We are finding . . . as you have undoubtedly found in the operation of the CBC, that adequate revenue must be available if adequate service to the public is to be provided. The competition of another station in this area on a lower frequency would vitiate the efforts which we are making to improve our programming, to develop local talent and to provide a service of high quality to our listeners."[7]

Blackburn did not necessarily want to keep broadcasting newcomers out of London and southwestern Ontario indefinitely. Still, in the short term he was prepared to deny them equality of opportunity in the allocation of radio frequencies which were public property. He felt the CBC should limit competition until the interests of the established pioneer stations which had laid the foundation for broadcasting in Canada were satisfied. This notion he had described as competition "on a fair basis."

In the summer of 1947 Blackburn informed Dunton that he had gone over "the broadcast spectrum frequency by frequency" with Department of Transport and CBC engineering staff. No alternative frequency could be found "which did not have a higher than technically desirable night time limitation."[8] Fearful of losing the 990 frequency to a competitor in Woodstock, just east of London, Blackburn applied in late July for

980. He recognized that CFPL would lose "quite a bit of coverage night-time on this frequency."[9] He also faced future competition from operators of a new radio station in St. Thomas, a potential rival for the 980 frequency. At last Blackburn's efforts paid off; CFPL-AM radio was awarded this new frequency and began broadcasting at 980 on 20 February 1949.

While Blackburn pursued a better AM frequency, he never lost sight of developments relating to FM radio following the war. As early as 1944, Blackburn had explored FM possibilities. A representative of RCA Victor Company Limited, H.S. Walker, informed him in 1945 that he was "the first private Broadcaster that [sic] has actually placed an order . . . for an FM transmitter."[10] Frequency modulation radio as opposed to amplitude modulation (AM) was pioneered in 1933 by Major Edwin Armstrong of Columbia University. The intensity of the FM signal and its higher frequency allows it to be almost immune to interference. With its higher fidelity, FM could provide listeners with sharper reproductions of musical instruments than could be heard on the AM dial. Blackburn saw this radio innovation able to provide alternative programming in the form of pleasurable listening music to complement the news and information heard on AM radio.

In September 1947 Blackburn reiterated his desire to be in the forefront of FM broadcasting in Canada. He wrote to Davidson Dunton explaining that Fred Howes, a consulting engineer from Montreal whom he had hired, had taken ill: "As a result, he was unable to prepare our FM brief for presentation at [the current] meeting of the Board. Our site survey has been completed and we shall have our brief in for consideration at the next Board meeting. We are prepared to do everything we can to encourage FM in this area, . . ."[11] This application met fewer obstacles, and CFPL-FM began operation in 1948.

During its early years the FM station operated only for brief periods each day and carried much the same programming as was heard on the AM station. It wasn't until the fall of 1958 that some separate programming was introduced on the FM station to serve the more specialized audience of fine music and high fidelity enthusiasts. Two hours of classical music were initially provided Monday through Friday. The following year Sunday evening was added to the FM service and weekday programming was extended from 6:00 to 10:00 p.m. Like other Canadian broadcasters who started FM radio in their communities, Blackburn realized that this new service would have to be supported by the AM operation for many years. He would have to wait until his twilight years before FM could draw a sufficient audience to bring in any sizable revenue for the company. On 6 January 1979, FM-96 introduced a new, successful format featuring contemporary music and expanded newscasts; this fresh sound replaced the earlier stereo 96 format with its classical music.

Blackburn was often torn between the need to make a profit and his wish to provide on FM radio a higher level of programming than the contemporary fare heard on the AM station. His elitist, cultural outlook held that FM radio should be able to program the classics and provide a true alternate service. (Blackburn often preferred to listen to CBC-AM and FM radio; he was critical of the music heard on his own AM station.) But his economic sense inevitably persuaded him that the marketplace was the ultimate determinant of the style of programming. An FM station tailored to a minority audience could not be a financial success. For most of his career, CFPL-FM hardly turned a profit. In the immediate post-war years, AM radio in Canada had pride of place.

Following the war Blackburn made several personnel changes in the company's radio division. In December 1945 Don Wright, the director of music for London schools, was hired to replace Philip Morris as station manager. Wright's appointment marked "the inauguration of a new era for CFPL involving complete conversion of the station." The radio studios in the newspaper building on Richmond Street were redesigned by L.G. Bridgman, a local architect, and D.G. McKinstry, the chief architect for the CBC. The studio's acoustics were greatly improved and the facilities were enlarged so that they were capable of providing a variety of different programming, "from an informal interview to broadcasting a full symphony orchestra. New Western Electric studio control equipment [was] ...

installed, and . . . CFPL [would soon] have a new R.C.A. transmitter of 5,000 watts power on its clear channel frequency of 1570 kilocycles."[12] The additional radio equipment and improvement of studios to allow CFPL to operate with a greater power output involved a capital expenditure of close to $75,000.[13]

Murry Brown, who eventually became president of the company's broadcasting operations, and Blackburn quickly developed a smooth working relationship. Both men were of the same generation, Blackburn being three years older. They possessed the same demeanour and preferred to project a controlled and reserved public posture. Before regulatory bodies, their sonorous, resonant voices tended to lend an air of authority to their presentations. They could be charmingly argumentative on the sensitive issue of media monopoly. As they grew older and the company became more successful, the gentlemanly, white-haired Messrs. Blackburn and Brown epitomized the favourable position many private broadcasters came to enjoy in the prosperity of mid-twentieth century Canada. In Canadian broadcasting circles and in London society they could be perceived as a reflection of Roy Thomson's notion that a television broadcasting permit was "like having a licence to print your own money."[14] But it was a while after the war before the good times began to roll.

Blackburn felt he was fortunate to find Brown, because he recognized that the sales department and marketing of CFPL had to be improved. "I was constantly listening to the station so I could judge the work being done," said Blackburn. "One evening, a Sunday, I heard a voice on the station that somehow sounded like the kind of voice that belonged to a person worth thinking about." Blackburn left the dinner table with his wife and family: "I [wanted] to have a look at what was behind that voice. It was Murray Brown." Brown, who was employed with Moore Business Forms, had been working weekends for the station as a part-time announcer. At Blackburn's invitation he joined CFPL on a permanent basis and eventually replaced Don Wright as manager in 1948.

The hiring of Wright, the former director of music for London schools, could be seen as one of Blackburn's more questionable appointments. Wright was a talented individual and well recognized in the community. Still he did not appear to possess the business skills required for the job. Moreover, he was interested primarily in musical productions, not management. Wright was an excellent musician, and he did substantially improve the image of the station. But it became obvious to Blackburn that Wright could not manage the station from a commercial point of view. After a couple of years, Wright was given full authority over musical productions, and Brown was made manager.

By 1949, when CFPL-AM began operating on its 980 frequency, the station was on its way towards building up a much closer identification with its local audience. The station came to rely less on the CBC network and concentrated on the promotion of radio personalities and programs aimed at London to build closer identification with the local audience. Although Detroit's WJR had held the bulk of the London audience during the war, CFPL soon became the number one station with its new community programming. The station provided a range of local programs including live orchestras and drama shows.

Blackburn instilled in his staff the notion that private broadcasters, who had been licensed to operate on assigned frequencies, had a concomitant responsibility to the public, because they had a monopoly on their frequencies for the duration of their licences. "He talked about that responsibility to the people", said Douglas Trowell, who was later to become manager of CFPL. "He decided . . . to make [CFPL] into a super radio station and he devoted all kinds of money to it and all kinds of effort and energy at every level."[15]

After the war Douglas Trowell teamed up with another young broadcaster in London by the name of Max Ferguson, who later would gain fame with his popular character called "Rawhide" on the CBC. Trowell and Ferguson were popular with the teenaged CFPL audience in London during the mid-1940s. They were also devilish pranksters around *The Free Press* building on Richmond Street. As Ferguson explained in his book *And Now Here's Max*, they liked to play what was called the "Elevator Game." The pair of fun seekers soon realized that the tiny, antiquated elevator was not without its idiosyncrasies. "Whereas all other elevators unswervingly deliver passengers to any desig-nated floor and disgorge them before responding to a call from another floor," wrote Ferguson, "this senile old brute could eas-ily be distracted from its duty to its passengers. At the very moment of debarkation, a buzz from any other floor would send it scurrying off like a woman of easy virtue — eager to service a newly found customer before the old one was decently dis-missed." The incarceration of unwary travellers soon became a favourite pastime; but on one occasion their victim was Walter J. Blackburn. After the elevator descended for about the sixtieth time, the door finally opened on the ground floor and out stepped *The Free Press* publisher. Ferguson remembered Black-burn's controlled fury: "His lips began working in an ashen face. Words were being formed but, as yet, there was no sound — just a small, throbbing paroxysm of suppressed fury working on one cheek. . . . In a controlled and only slightly strangulated voice he said, 'I don't want you to fool with this elevator again,' and then walked off."[16] That was the end of the Elevator Game. Afterwards Blackburn remarked that he maintained his composure because "the best retaliation was to play it cool. If I had blown up, it would have been exactly like they wanted. They were quite a group [and] full of fun."

Despite Blackburn's characteristic reserve and formality, which could have been misinterpreted as disinterest in outside affairs, he continued his behind-the-scenes support for commu-nity projects and individuals. Illustrative of the latter was his early financial support to the founders of Bowes Publishers Limited, a Canadian newspaper chain started after the war. Jim Bowes, chairman of the publishing firm, was a 17-dollar-a-week reporter with *The London Free Press* in 1942 when he first spoke with Blackburn. Eighteen years old at the time, he was in the newsroom on a Saturday night when Blackburn walked in. The publisher had a few words with the night copy editor and then passed by the typewriter where Bowes was working. "Good after-noon," said Blackburn. Bowes replied, "Good afternoon, sir."[17] That was to be their total conversation for more than three years.

Bowes joined the army and following the war returned to *The Free Press*.

Shortly afterwards Bowes was interested in purchasing a weekly newspaper and began to search for one in southwestern Ontario. He and his brother Bill, a wartime navigator with the Royal Canadian Air Force, discovered that the *Times* in the tiny community of Dresden near Chatham was for sale. The price was $5,500 with a $3,000 down payment. The total assets of the two brothers at the time were $1,000 cash, a camera and a type-writer, the latter provided by their veterans' re-establishment credit. They could arrange a bank loan for $1,000 provided $2,000 in cash could be obtained. With their existing cash, they were $1,000 short of the required amount. A close friend, Rex McInnes, then *The Free Press* police reporter, loaned the pair $400 he had won at an outdoor bingo. The two brothers now needed $600. Jim Bowes thought he had exhausted all possibili-ties. Then he considered approaching Blackburn whom he hardly knew.

Blackburn listened to Bowes' request and agreed to the loan. He remarked: "Jim, I think you and your brother might just make it." The two brothers agreed to put up their camera and typewriter as collateral. Blackburn wrote out a cheque for $600 on his personal savings account at the Bank of Montreal across the street from the newspaper. When the teller brought Black-burn's ledger card to the counter, it was upside down. However Bowes managed to read it. "With a reporter's cultivated eye for reading carelessly displayed documents from the other side of a desk," explained Bowes, "may God forgive me, the bottom line figure popped up at me. It was $28,000. I didn't know there was that much money in the world." He and his brother bought the *Dresden Times*. The first loan they repaid was to Blackburn. His note in response read, "Now I'm sure you'll make it." In 1950 Bowes Publishers Limited was formed. The Dresden weekly was sold and the brothers bought newspapers in the developing Peace River country of northwestern Alberta. The company's growth has continued. Today it is one of the larger privately owned newspaper groups in Canada, with sixteen newspaper operations in the provinces of British Columbia, Alberta and

Ontario. The Toronto Sun Publishing Company acquired a sixty per cent interest in Bowes in April, 1988, and planned to assume complete control by 1994. Bowes recalled that "one of the crucial building blocks so many years ago was that loan from W.J. I have never forgotten. . . . I also discovered a warmth in the man that cracked the austere facade he sometimes turned towards the world."

Not surprisingly, Blackburn's support for community projects and institutions included the University of Western Ontario, his alma mater. He eagerly backed the establishment of the School of Journalism. Arthur Ford, editor-in-chief at *The Free Press*, and chancellor of UWO from 1947 to 1955, played an important role in fund-raising for the journalism program. In September 1945 *The Free Press* board of directors donated $3,000 to the school, a fifth of the outside money pledged for start-up costs. At the same time, the board provided a donation of $1,000 to the physics department to develop a new course in radio communications, a project that would have appealed to Blackburn's interest in electronics. The close relationship between *The Free Press* and the university, particularly through the School of Journalism, has continued down to the present day.[18]

The Free Press has provided to the school both money and professional journalists serving as adjunct professors. A number of the company's senior editorial executive positions have been or are still filled by Western grads — Bill Heine, Norm Ibsen, Jack Briglia and Nev LeCapelain — underlining the historic rapport that has developed between the newspaper and the university.

While Blackburn concentrated his attention on the electronic media after the war, he continued to streamline *The London Free Press*. His efforts to improve the newspaper did not go unnoticed by other executives in the industry including the Thomson organization. St. Clair McCabe, a member of the Thomson's "Galt Gang," who had begun his newspaper career with the *Galt Evening Reporter*, was credited with building the group's North American newspaper chain. He was impressed with the continual improvement in *The Free Press*. McCabe cred-

its this to Blackburn's appointment to the advertising department of Charles Fenn and Gordon Quick, who were highly
sales-oriented. Fenn, Quick and the other staff modernized both
the look of the paper and its business office efficiency. McCabe
explained: "*The London Free Press* was a pretty neat looking newspaper and a very readable newspaper and I think their circulation gains testified to that."[19]

Shortly after the war, Blackburn also purchased for $15,000
The London Echo from Alfred Talbot, the owner of a printing
company in the city and publisher of the weekly newspaper
since 1885. *The Echo*, which first made its appearance in 1879
when London's population was about 20,000, was a weekly
advertising paper distributed free throughout the city through
the postal service. The newspaper, which was known in the
industry as a shopper, allowed businesses to advertise at lower
rates than were available in *The Advertiser*, until 1936, and *The
Free Press*. The sale of the newspaper to *The Free Press* received
little public attention. Blackburn had explained simply to the
company's board of directors on 24 August 1946 that "it was
desirable that [*The Echo*] should be acquired."[20] His decision was
probably dictated by the fact that *The Echo* had boasted that it
could produce results for advertisers comparable to any other
newspaper of equal circulation. The newspaper was published
until 20 March 1957. The final issue of the paper noted that "the
publication [had] been carried on for a considerable period
with a record of steadily mounting losses due to rising costs. The
present trend indicates costs are continuing to rise and duration of the suspension is indefinite."[21]

Reflecting upon the newspaper industry's early days in
southwestern Ontario, St. Clair McCabe recalled that "the old
London Echo used to give *The Advertiser* and *The Free Press* a lot of
kicks back in those days. I guess Walter sort of cut his teeth on
the shopper as a competitor."[22] Towards the end of Blackburn's
career, *The Free Press* was to form Netmar Inc., a highly profitable
network of shopper publications known as Pennysavers that
stretched from Victoria, British Columbia, to St. John, New
Brunswick.

Amidst the unpredictable political climate throughout the

world following the war, Blackburn encouraged his editor-in-chief Arthur Ford to provide readers with first-hand accounts of new developments. *The Free Press* thus contained an international editorial perspective. In January 1948 Blackburn explained to the board of directors that Ford planned to travel abroad to prepare a series of articles upon conditions in England and the continent. Every attempt was to be made to syndicate the stories to other newspapers in the hopes of reducing the expenses incurred. During these post-war years, Ford was able to provide readers in southwestern Ontario with a personalized account of changing world events. His column, "As the World Wags On," often went beyond regional and national happenings to provide thoughtful insights into developments during the Cold War era.

Ford travelled to England in the spring of 1948, a trip that delighted him because he enjoyed close contact with the politically powerful. He explained to his friend General Victor Odlum, Canadian Ambassador in Ankara, Turkey, that he had attended the Geneva Conference on World Information as a delegate from Canada and also the Congress of Europe at The Hague. As well, Ford visited Rome and Paris, in all "a most interesting trip." He explained to Odlum that "the ambassadors in Rome and Paris, also The Hague, were very good to [him]. The highlight of the trip was a luncheon at The Hague for Churchill at which Paul Renaud was present. It was the first time they had met since 1940. . . . [Ford] really sat in on an historic occasion." He was also pleased that the federal Liberal government had offered him the high commissionership in Australia following the retirement of T.C. Davis: "Considering my politics, it was rather flattering. As I had just been made Chancellor of the University of Western Ontario . . . I felt I could not very well pull up my roots."[23]

Ford, who was the company's vice-president and editor-in-chief at the time, was at his public relations best in planning the activities for *The London Free Press* centennial year in 1949. Blackburn, of course, was eager to mark the historic occasion and threw his full support behind Ford's efforts. The company formed a special centennial committee with Blackburn as hon-

orary chairman, Ford as chairman and W.G. "Bill" Trestain as
secretary. Trestain had started his career with *The Free Press* in
December 1936 and was soon to become assistant to the president. Throughout the war years, he had been the newspaper's
"roving reporter" providing readers with regional feature material that dealt with a variety of human interest areas. The money
and time spent on organizing the various projects surrounding
the centennial year was illustrative of how Blackburn was
inclined to fuss over the plans for such occasions.

A special centenary edition of *The Free Press* published on 11
June 1949 contained a record 232 pages. Blackburn boasted that
it was "the largest single edition of standard-size pages
published to date by any Canadian newspaper." That same evening the company held a banquet in the London arena attended
by some nine hundred staff and guests. As Blackburn explained
to the shareholders, "the warmth of our hospitality apparently
matched well the weather of the day, for reports which came to
hand following the banquet indicated beyond a doubt that all
present thoroughly enjoyed themselves in spite of the terrific
heat, which was on into the nineties and the high humidity.
Although the weather was beyond our control, the amenities
were not, and seemed to have been used effectively."[24]

The company also commissioned historian Orlo Miller to
write a history of the newspaper to commemorate its centennial.
*A Century of Western Ontario: The Story of London, The Free Press, and
Western Ontario, 1849–1949* outlined the newspaper's evolution
from the days of William Sutherland and Josiah Blackburn. This
work described the historical role in communications played by
the newspaper in the growth of London as the centre of western
Ontario. The company's centennial year celebration cost
$9,645. Blackburn reassured the shareholders it was money
worth spending: "Although it is not possible to calculate in
dollars and cents the benefits which accrued to the Company
through the publicity derived across Canada from the celebra-
tions, the improvement in employee pride in his Company,
additions to public goodwill, etc., etc., I think that it may be
properly assumed that the $9,645 was money well spent."[25]

Other aspects of the centennial year were also satisfying for the company. It ended the fiscal year with a net profit after taxes of $236,273, an increase of $40,975 over the previous year. A major reason for this rise in revenue was the success of the company in placing the electronics division or radio operations on a paying basis. CFPL made an operating profit of $23,471 compared with an operating loss of $3,864 for the previous year. Blackburn attributed this turnaround in the fortunes of the radio wing of the company to the appointment of Murray Brown in January 1949 as electronics division manager replacing Don Wright. He also reported to the shareholders that *The London Echo*, the company's subsidiary, had recorded a small operating profit of $900 for the year compared to a loss of $8,761 for the previous twelve months.[26]

By the end of 1949 Blackburn had also made a number of changes in the administration of the company as well as in the editorial department. Russell Waide, formerly office manager, was appointed the company's personnel services officer. Blackburn maintained that *The Free Press* was the first newspaper in Canada to have a personnel department whose purpose was to serve the company by serving the staff. This innovation in the years immediately after the war reflected Blackburn's desire to modernize management and to maintain an harmonious working environment. Waide's duties in his new role included "the development of policies for the constant improvement of ... personnel relations, the granting and supervision of Company loans to employees and the providing to ... employees of the many small services, including making out income tax forms, which go a long way toward cementing employer-employee relationships."[27] Arthur Blahout was appointed chief accountant to relieve the company's treasurer, Nora Foulds, of the growing burden of supervising the operations of the accounting department. On the editorial side, Robert Needham was appointed as the first full-time correspondent in the Parliamentary Press Gallery. The company purchased a house, which Needham leased, in Ottawa where it was felt there was a need for a full-time *Free Press* correspondent.

There had been a considerable increase in the size of the staff of the newspaper following the war. The number of male employees far outnumbered females. In October 1949 The London Free Press Printing Company employed 395 people — 306 males and 89 females. The rise in the number of employees together with salary increases had cost the company an additional $105,000 in operating expenses compared to corresponding figures for 1948. Still, as Blackburn explained, "prospects for business [looked] quite good" in 1950. "Stocks of merchandise [were] increasing in size, buying [had] become more selective and selling, therefore, more competitive. Newspapers and radio stations [would] undoubtedly benefit from these conditions through increased linage and time sales."[28]

As the company celebrated its centennial year, Blackburn had to be in a self-congratulatory mood. His thirteen years as president had seen The London Free Press Printing Company grow from 184 employees to nearly 400. At the same time, the circulation of the newspaper almost doubled from 38,721 to 72,556. The rebuilding of the AM station CFPL, the shift in frequency to 980, and the introduction of FM were obvious accomplishments in an uncertain electronic media era.

By 1949 Blackburn had also attempted to introduce a higher level of technical organizational efficiency into the day-to-day management of the company. But perhaps his most tangible accomplishments were to be found in his insistence that the company's social benefits be improved to bring it into the modern age. Like a number of other Ontario centres, London had faced bitter labour strife during the Dirty Thirties. The printers' strike at *The Free Press* had strained relations between the company and workers. After assuming the presidency of the company, Blackburn steadfastly maintained that the betterment of employer-employee relations was a matter of the highest priority.

The greatest single employee benefit during his thirteen years as president was the introduction of the five-day week in the spring of 1946, an innovation that found *The Free Press* ahead of a number of other major industries. In September 1947 a group plan for hospitalization and surgical insurance was announced. By November 1947 a pension plan for employees was introduced. Pensions began at ages sixty-five for men and sixty for women. The General Committee (GC) of The Free Press Employees' Benefit Society had endorsed the pension plan and recommended it to all employees for approval. The GC had been actively involved in the discussion of all aspects relating to the company's benefits package for employees. On 14 March 1950, when the society changed its name to The London Free Press Employees' Association, the employees' group and the company decided to survey all social security issues. This action was taken with a view to the establishment of additional benefits in the areas of sickness, disability, maternity leave and funeral expenses.[29]

During its hundred-year history, *The Free Press* had evolved from a small mid-nineteenth century weekly to a leading mass circulation daily. However, none of Blackburn's aunts, to whom he had so frequently turned for advice after assuming the presidency, had lived to see the centennial year. Eleanor Lucy had died on 13 February 1941 and Susan, the last surviving child of Josiah Blackburn, passed away on 5 October 1946.

As The London Free Press Printing Company entered another decade, its financial position seemed secure. But Blackburn did not simply adopt a wait-and-see attitude in the face of new technological advances.

In 1949 the federal government appointed Vincent Massey to head the Royal Commission on National Development in the Arts, Letters and Sciences. The new electronic medium of television would be a focus of the Massey Commission's inquiry. Blackburn soon showed an eagerness to embrace this form of communication.

Blackburn was a camera buff and had been fascinated by home movies ever since his father had bought him his first motion picture camera back in the 1920s. The notion of providing a service whereby pictures would be transmitted over the air proved to be irresistible. If the company were in communications, he reasoned that it must embrace this new medium. Television could provide a supplementary service to radio, just as that medium had offered listeners an alternative service that complemented the newspaper.

The Blackburn empire was growing and so too was southwestern Ontario. Television, perhaps the most powerful communications medium ever invented, would provide the company with its most formidable challenge both financially and technologically. It would also bring the region into the new electronic age, the global village as the famous Canadian thinker Marshall McLuhan would call it.

CHAPTER FOUR

A Multi-Media Owner
1950 – 1958

W ALTER BLACKBURN was an unusual mixture of extreme shyness and high ego, probably as rare a combination as his nineteenth-century, paternalistic attitudes and his very modern vision of the electronic media. He struggled with his shy side throughout his life and only partially overcame it. In his view, this trait was a handicap: "It makes life very difficult for someone who suffers from [shyness]. . . . It's very difficult for a young man as I was to have the responsibilities of running a business and being where the buck stops and being aware that what you say is the law. It sometimes makes you draw into yourself a bit."[1] Blackburn did not laugh at himself easily. His shyness dictated that he was a better conversationalist in one-on-one situations than in large gatherings.

On the other hand, Blackburn became enormously satisfied with his position as a reputable and influential media owner who was envied in other parts of the country. He had been born into the job and felt he was suited to the challenge. He truly enjoyed the perks and privileges that went with his position, especially the ready access to prominent businessmen and politicians. His dignified manner tended to conceal his belief that he was owed a standard of respect by virtue of his position. He felt keenly his place in the London community. When he returned to *The London Free Press* after holidays, a trip abroad or a business foray, he expected the presidential mantle to be waiting for him.

Titles impressed him. He insisted that if an individual wore a certain title, a standard of performance and behaviour could be expected. William Heine, a former *Free Press* editor-in-chief, observed that "equating rank or position with intelligence was an assumption which led more than once to disappointment. He'd grumble and grouse that the man had this position or that responsibility . . . how could he be so uninformed?"[2] His character had several curious idiosyncrasies that manifested themselves in a variety of ways.

Blackburn was a hands-on manager for most of his career as third-generation publisher. But his office management was something short of technical organizational efficiency. He dreaded the task of processing mail. Helen Daly, his personal secretary for more than twenty years, remembered this dislike for handling paper: "Mr. Blackburn would stare at a piece of paper and then he would turn it over. Then I would watch him do it again and I would say, 'Well what are you going to do with that?' He would say, 'Well I want time to read it.'"[3] He kept most of his mail in briefcases and used as many as seven at a time. His favourite was a large rectangular brown case with W.J.B. in gold letters engraved on the top. He enjoyed this one because at a meeting he could reach down and locate several file folders easily if needed. His secretary eventually got to know the contents of the briefcases but might not see them for months, if he chose to take them home. If he rearranged any material, she had to begin over again. Another system for handling the volume of mail was tried. This one involved three separate file folders marked "decisions," "discussion" and "dictation." In time, it too had its limitations.

Simply put, Blackburn found it difficult to adhere to a regimented office routine. A standing order was that family matters received top priority. If he arrived for work and was noticeably moody, it was generally because of his preoccupation with a current family situation he found unsettling.

As befitting his background, Blackburn was a dutiful husband and father. His personality and that of his wife Marjorie complemented each other; he was intense while she was carefree. Both were tidy, meticulous individuals especially around home with the children. When any kind of family pressure arose, Marjorie often relieved the stress with a superb dinner that involved the whole family, a gala occasion.

At Christmas time Blackburn enjoyed snapping photos of the family around the dining room table and, in the process, frequently held up the carving of the turkey. The entire meal would be ready on the sideboard in the dining room while Blackburn went looking for a camera; the family would wait patiently for dinner to begin. His daughter Martha remembered how he enjoyed carving, and his mastery of that particular culinary art. He enjoyed good food generally but did not seem to delight in any special dishes; he often had a drink or cocktail before dinner and insisted that the meal be on time. He enjoyed both red and white wine; still he never considered himself to be a wine connoisseur. Blackburn was an avowed lover of white bread, especially with eggs, much to the chagrin of his wife who preached the virtues of brown bread. As for desserts, his chief dislike was strawberry ice cream or strawberries with ice cream.

He was strict with his children and expected proper behaviour; he chose not to intrude on the lives of his grandchildren in their early years but later, when they were of a learning age, he introduced them to the Pac-Man video and taught them waterskiing. Blackburn perceived this kind of recreational activity to be a form of learning for children.

Blackburn was a regular handyman at home. On one occasion his wife mentioned that it was time for a new vacuum cleaner. On cue, he dismantled the household device and repaired it. He gladly tackled small chores; heavier household tasks he left to others more qualified.

His shopping day was Saturday, generally at Canadian Tire. He would return home with bags filled with an assortment of hardware that at times baffled his wife. He was an early purchaser of mobile telephones and he had coffee-makers galore; his favourite was the one that allowed for the timer to be set at night to allow the coffee to be ready in the morning. In general, he appreciated good equipment both at home and at work.

His attitude towards women in the workplace was clearly old-fashioned by today's standards, and he probably knew it.

Nevertheless, although he recognized the talents of women at work, he believed that the important pay cheque was the man's earnings. He steadfastly clung to this notion though recognizing that some women in his company had the capacity to assume greater responsibilities.

Blackburn did not generate humour readily but could be amusing without intending to be. Such an occasion occurred with C.N. "Bud" Knight, a former general manager of CFPL radio who travelled with the publisher to a hearing before the Canadian Radio Television and Telecommunications Commission. Both stayed at the Château Laurier Hotel in Ottawa. One evening after dinner, Blackburn inquired from Knight if he would like to join him: "Would you like to go out and have a little fun?" Knight agreed and expected to have a drink or two at a suitable night spot. The pair left the lobby of the hotel on a most miserable winter evening, walked across Confederation Square, then travelled Spark, Bank and Wellington streets, past the Parliament buildings and back to the hotel. On their return Blackburn said to Knight, "Thanks Bud. Have a good evening." The walk in the snow took about a half hour, Blackburn's night on the town.

Blackburn also insisted that his executives number the paragraphs in any major documents that he was to review. The publisher could then get on the phone and confer with the author of a particular report by referring to the paragraph number rather than reading the paragraph's opening words. This he considered a great time saver.

That he was a perfectionist who strove for excellence was undeniable. It was, therefore, inevitable that he paid close attention to detail at all times. He would quibble unexpectedly over issues of seemingly minor importance. An example was his disenchantment in 1950 when The London Free Press Printing Company underwent a structural reorganization largely for tax purposes. He was perturbed that his enterprise would have to break with the company name that his grandfather had used since the late nineteenth century.

Back in the days of Josiah Blackburn, the newspaper had been incorporated as The London Free Press Printing Company on 8 October 1878. The word *Limited* had been left from the name, because corporation law at the time did not require it; however it was a limited company, with limited shareholder liability, not withstanding its title. Under the reorganization in 1950 the shareholders of the printing company approved the sale of its business and operating assets to the London Free Press Printing Company Limited, a new wholly owned subsidiary. The capital of this new operating company consisted of $60,000 divided into 600 shares of $100 each. At the same time, the name of the old company incorporated in 1878 was changed to The London Free Press Holdings Limited.[4]

This corporate restructure had no effect on ownership. The move was undertaken to allow the payment of dividends to shareholders who would not be subject to income tax. The federal government had introduced new tax legislation following the recommendations of a Royal Commission (Ives Commission) which presented its report on 29 March 1945. As Blackburn explained to Davidson Dunton in 1950, "The reorganization of The London Free Press Printing Company (Limited) has been designed to facilitate the distribution to shareholders of tax-paid undistributed income as permitted by ... [legislation], as and when funds not required in the daily operation of the business become available."[5]

The reorganization of the company was clearly undertaken with the sisters' interests in mind. Ken Lemon, a senior partner with Clarkson Gordon and financial adviser to the Blackburn family, explained: "It permitted the payment of dividends primarily to the two sisters who were still shareholders ... which would not be subject to income tax in their hands."[6] Blackburn's two sisters, Constance Orr and Miriam Smith, benefited from this new arrangement. Constance's first marriage to Ed Macdonald, a University of Toronto professor, had ended in divorce. Her second husband, Alexander Orr, was a member of the British diplomatic service. For a period the couple lived in Jerusalem. Orr later became solicitor-general for the British West Indies stationed in Nassau. Unfortunately, Constance died on 11 December 1953, just three years after Blackburn inaugurated the restructuring. Miriam's marriage to Desmond Smith, a major–general in the Canadian army, also experienced a break-down. However, Miriam lived to see the company's growth throughout the prosperous post-war decades, until her death on 12 February 1969.

The company reorganization was the first of a series of initiatives that occurred during a busy decade for Blackburn. In April 1951 he became a board member of the American News-paper Publishers Association (ANPA), succeeding F.I. Ker of the *Hamilton Spectator*. He was re-elected secretary of the ANPA in 1956. Later he was elected vice-chairman of the Canadian section of the Commonwealth Press Union.

As chairman of the radio relations committee of the Canadian Press in 1952, Blackburn had a lasting impact on the growth of radio news in Canada. He was instrumental in the establishment of Broadcast News, the CP subsidiary that has served private broadcasting stations in Canada for more than 30 years. But his next quantum leap in media ownership would be the introduction, in November 1953, of television to southwestern Ontario.

Blackburn's initiatives as chairman of CP's radio relations committee were undertaken at a time when considerable tension existed between the broadcast and print industries. He had been a member of CP since 1939 and supported the notion that the co-operative news gathering organization must provide a strong domestic service in Canada. Since he owned both print and broadcast operations, his sensitivity towards both groups did not go unnoticed by other CP members.

The antagonism between broadcasters and newspaper publishers had its roots in the mid-1930s. Radio stations began to provide immediate news reports especially on international developments, thus challenging the monopoly previously enjoyed by Canadian Press. Denton Massey, a Conservative member of the 1936 House of Commons Broadcasting Committee, described the feud between the two forms of media: "There have been in this country and in the United States, more or less Wars of the Roses between the radio stations and the newspapers, in which incidentally, the objects of exchange have not

Josiah Blackburn immigrated with his brother to Canada West in 1850. In 1852 he purchased a fledgling weekly newspaper in London, Ontario called *The Canadian Free Press*, and founded a media dynasty that has flourished under the same family ownership down to the present. BLACKBURN FAMILY

Josiah's first son, Walter Josiah (at desk), was president and publisher of *The London Free Press* from 1890-1920. Later, his second son, Arthur Stephen, filled the same offices from 1920-1935. The aged oak desk still serves Martha Blackburn today. LONDON FREE PRESS

Walter Blackburn's parents, Etta Irene Blackburn (née Henderson) of Wardsville, Ontario, and Arthur Stephen Blackburn. Arthur, more than Josiah or Walter Juxon, was an intensely shy, withdrawn man. BLACKBURN FAMILY

Walter's three aunts (from l. to r.) Eleanor, Margaret and Susan, had a considerable influence on his life. Austere, but well-educated, they worked for the newspaper and consciously groomed the young lad for his future role as heir of the family enterprise. This photo was taken in 1934 while Walter was taking the aunts on a driving tour of the Gaspé. WALTER D. LAFNER/BLACKBURN FAMILY

(Above) *London Free Press* delivery boys lined up outside the mailing room, January 1922. (Below) Delivery trucks in the early fleet of the *Free Press*.
LONDON FREE PRESS

(Above) Constance Margaret (Blackburn) Orr, Walter's elder sister, in a photo taken in Cairo. Constance was a shareholder until Walter consolidated his ownership in 1958. BLACKBURN FAMILY

(Left) Miriam Irene (Blackburn) Smith, the second sister, in a photo by Karsh. Y. KARSH/ BLACKBURN FAMILY

Members of the Young Progressive Conservatives at the University of Western Ontario, 1933 (from left): J.E. "Jim" McConnell, "Art" Harriman, Frank Sanders, and Walter Blackburn. The distinguished visitor in the front is Prime Minister R.B. Bennett, who had come as a guest speaker to the university. Jim McConnell later became president of McConnell-Eastman Advertising, a large London firm, now with head office in Toronto.
CAIRNCROSS/BLACKBURN FAMILY

(Above) A radiant couple, Walter Juxon Blackburn and Marjorie Ludwell Dampier on their wedding day, 9 November 1938, emerge from St. John the Evangelist Church, London, Ontario. BLACKBURN FAMILY

(Right) Majorie Ludwell Blackburn, in a photo taken in 1959. BLACKBURN FAMILY

Celebrating: Walter Jr. offers a tidbit to his father. Beside young Walter is Charlie Dark, Arthur Blackburn's chauffeur, who later managed Thames Ridge Farm for Walter Blackburn Sr. Charlie's son Arthur (far left) when older, worked in the press room at the *Free Press*. LONDON FREE PRESS

Some years later, Walter and Marjorie enjoy Arthur Ford's humorous reminiscences at one of the many *Free Press* dinner-dances they attended together. The annual event was a popular occasion, a time for both merriment and serious reflection, as when "W.J." articulated his well-known address in 1959 on the "corporate philosophy" guiding him as owner and employer. LONDON FREE PRESS

The CFPL Orchestra, June 1947. Photo was taken right in the radio studio from where music went "live" on air. LONDON FREE PRESS

A crane erects the first, 500-foot TV tower for CFPL-TV in the fall of 1953. A short while later, on 28 November 1953, Walter Blackburn and Robert McCubbin, liberal MP for Middlesex West, cut the ribbon "live" on TV, to inaugurate what was the second privately owned television station in Canada.
BLACKBURN FAMILY

The Blackburn family photo taken for the Christmas 1954 edition of the employee publication *The Fourth Estate*. From left: Martha, Marjorie, Walter, Susan, and sitting, Walter Jr. with the much-beloved family pet, a German short-haired pointer named "Rip". BLACKBURN FAMILY been roses. . . . The vast majority of newspapers felt that a great many advertiser dollars might be diverted to the air that might otherwise have been expended for the printed page."[7] Like his father before him, Walter Blackburn not only saw radio and newspapers as complementary media, but also recognized that *both* media would bring in increased advertising revenue in the years ahead.

Radio had enjoyed its golden age throughout the war years. Canadians listened to foreign correspondents report the principal wartime developments, many of which affected the thousands of Canadian soldiers abroad. The enmity between the print and broadcast industries had grown during the 1940s and 50s. Obviously Blackburn was mindful of the print-broadcast rivalry when he presented his first, provocative report of the radio relations committee to the CP executive committee in 1952.

Publishers initially refused to provide wire service reports to broadcasters. A change of heart occurred in 1941. When newspaper owners realized that stations could simply scalp their stories, they established Press News (PN), a subsidiary of CP, to provide news to both the Canadian Broadcasting Corporation and private stations. In 1952 PN served eighty-eight privately owned stations. Blackburn observed that the CP subsidiary was impeded "by the broadcasters' distrust of Canadian Press motives in making CP news available to them." Moreover, he noted that "there is an ever-present suspicion among radio men that CP withholds news from radio until after newspaper publication." His report also drew attention to the apparent willingness of radio station owners to make arrangements for satisfactory news coverage independent of CP altogether. He called for the establishment of a new company to serve private stations exclusively, operating along the lines of Press News. "Five of the nine directors . . . [would] be named by CP; four to be chosen by representatives of client private stations from among their number."[8] The method of selecting the private radio directors was to be determined by the client stations.

The latter part of the report reflected Blackburn's understanding of how eager broadcasters were to provide radio news, and his recognition of the publishers' concern that the electronic medium could not provide the in-depth quality of news coverage demanded by the print industry. Blackburn could empathize with both positions. In the early 1950s his own station, CFPL radio, was on the verge of developing a radio news operation that would eventually supplement the coverage by *The Free Press* in southwestern Ontario. "Private broadcasters are increasingly conscious of importance of quality in preparation and presentation of their news bulletins," his report maintained. "Radio stations, like newspapers, are subject to criticism if their news reports are inaccurate and to court action if libellous or unprivileged. Sponsors demand that their newscasts be prepared carefully." Blackburn also noted that "generally, news gathered by radio stations is factual and written with good judgment." He underlined the advantages the proposed arrangement with private broadcasters could have for Canadian Press: "The Committee's view that the CP-PN service would benefit by receipt of certain news gathered by private radio stations— particularly over week-ends and between the production-periods of newspapers—is expressed with the understanding that quality of this news would be watched carefully." In 1953 Broadcast News Limited, a subsidiary of CP, came into being and in January 1954 it took over responsibility for the wire and audio services provided to private broadcasters. Press News continued to serve stations belonging to the Canadian Broadcasting Corporation.[9]

Charles Peters, former president of the *Montreal Gazette*, recalled that Blackburn rightfully deserved the title "The Father of Broadcast News." Peters had a first-hand look at the effort he put forth in the creation of the news organization: "It was mostly his energy and his ideas that carried this through [and] he had the advantage of being in broadcast media much earlier than most people ... this was an experience I had with him which showed me his character and particularly his thoroughness."[10]

Blackburn took the position that there was no point in making enemies with the broadcasters. There was always the possibility that broadcasters might establish their own news service independently of Canadian Press. Such action would

have deprived the national agency of revenue gained from having the broadcasters as clients. In time, the revenues of Broadcast News rose faster than those of CP, a development brought
about by the considerable expansion of the broadcasting industry.[11]

I. Norman Smith, former editor and president of the *Ottawa
Journal*, remembered that "the conflict [between print and
broadcast] was greatly eased by Walter." Smith recalled that
Blackburn sometimes would argue the case of the broadcasters
while "knowing damn well that the CP members were going to
say 'oh nuts to that.'" On one occasion, Smith and Blackburn
toured the Atlantic Provinces talking to radio station representatives about the CP service when relations were strained
between both sides. Blackburn changed from the slow, ponder-
ous approach he generally adopted at CP meetings to a more
assertive style which caught Smith's attention: "The broadcasters were always ready for kill . . . and they were alert, quick, fast-
thinking guys. . . . Walter changed his demeanour but only a
little bit . . . he was still able with that crowd to get their attention."[12]

The broadcasting perspective that Blackburn brought to the
Canadian Press helped the national news agency enter a new era
where electronic journalism would play a leading role. Indeed
during the 1950s his own station, CFPL, moved quickly to
streamline its news operation under managers Cliff Wingrove
and Doug Trowell. The arrival of Hugh Bremner from Brant-
ford in 1954 set the station on a new course in news and public
affairs programming. Bremner along with Ward Cornell,
Andrew Stuparik and Bill Scott formed the station's first major
news team. News copy from *The Free Press* was rewritten in broadcast style. CFPL began to provide listeners with more actuality
material of voices in the community, lending a greater urgency
to news heard over the air. There was little indication then that
in later years the station would sever its news connection with
the newspaper entirely.

CFPL, along with Toronto station CFRB and CHML in Hamilton, was involved in a radio news innovation undertaken with
Charlie Edwards, the head of Broadcast News. The stations pro-

vided a radio-service to each other that allowed for an exchange of news reports. Hugh Bremner recalled that CFPL used the newspaper's photo lines as the carrier for the sound and that this was really new at the time. In effect, this exchange was the beginning of an electronic Canadian Press. Stations paid for the service and all agreed to contribute to it on a co-operative basis. Broadcast news executives in the United States came to Canada to examine the experiment. The more refined Broadcast News audio service eventually succeeded this original method of voice reports.

Blackburn also approved another innovation made by CFPL radio in the mid-1950s, the introduction of radio commentaries on a daily basis. Bremner, who held the post of news director, began daily opinion pieces in 1955. Most private stations in Canada shied away from commentaries. With the exception of Gordon Sinclair on CFRB in Toronto and commentaries heard on CBC stations, private radio tended to treat the whole area of editorials somewhat gingerly. The nature of the medium, which was heavily reliant on advertising dollars, dictated a cautious approach.

This reticence was a carryover from the war years in the United States. In the so-called Mayflower Decision of 1941 the Federal Communications Commission had ruled that a broadcaster could not be an advocate, and outlawed on-air editorials. The decision was in response to an application by the Mayflower Broadcasting Corporation for a renewal of the licence for its Boston station, WAAB, after the station had voiced editorials in the late 1930s.[13] In Canada, however, there was no such strict prohibition. When CFPL radio began presenting regular commentaries, the editorial page of *The London Free Press* could no longer be seen as the sole moulder of community attitudes. Radio was prepared to be more adventuresome in its approach to public issues. The medium now interpreted news developments and did not simply report them.

Radio had earned its place as the second jewel in The London Free Press Printing Company (Limited). But it was television that consumed most of Blackburn's energies in the early

1950s. To understand the challenge that this medium presented in its pioneer days, it is worth while examining the political environment when the medium was introduced to Canada, and Blackburn's financial position as a media owner. The federal Liberal government had declared an interim television policy in 1949, the year the Massey Commission was established. It was designed to ensure that the public system would develop before private broadcasters entered the field. The position of the government was that the CBC should control licensing, networks and program distribution. The corporation was encouraged to seize the initiative by establishing its own TV stations. When it reported in 1951 the Massey Commission endorsed these notions. The Commission turned down a request by the Canadian Association of Broadcasters to establish a separate regulatory agency for broadcasting in Canada. The CBC was to continue to regulate the private broadcasters who were to be denied TV licences until the CBC could provide national programs.[14]

In September 1952 two CBC stations, CBFT and CBLT, in Montreal and Toronto respectively, began operation. Shortly afterwards private operators were allowed entry into this new electronic field. Towards the end of 1952, the CBC board announced it was prepared to hear applications from private broadcasters whose stations were intended to help distribute the programs provided by the public system. As in radio, the development of television in Canada proceeded in a hybrid fashion, with privately owned stations expected to serve as outlets for the national publicly owned system. The first private television station, CKSO in Sudbury, opened in October 1953.

Blackburn's eagerness for a TV licence had been evident as early as 1947 when he had visited New York to get a first-hand look at telecasting, prior to its advent in Canada. Blackburn's attention to this medium paid off. CFPL TV, the second station opened under private ownership, began broadcasting on 28 November 1953.

At the time of Blackburn's entry into television the corporate structure of his enterprise included the following: The London Free Press Holdings Limited, the holding company;

London Free Press Printing Company Limited, the new operating subsidiary with its print and electronics divisions; London Advertiser Company Limited, a non-operating company whose charter was kept alive following the closing of *The Advertiser* in 1936 to retain ownership and control of the name *London Advertiser*; and the London Echo Limited. This latter company, which provided economical advertising for the small retailer and served as a householders' weekly news digest, continued to operate at a loss until it was closed in 1957.

The weekly *London Echo* was one facet of his operation with which Blackburn had struggled continuously since acquiring the paper in 1946. He had shown a canny strategy in buying the paper: he had been able to forestall competition and prevent any potential buyer from getting into the market. But by 1956 the weekly's net annual loss was $10,500 which was $2,000 greater than the previous year. The paper was inadequate to meet the competition from the daily *Free Press* and the electronic advertising media. Finally on 20 March 1957 publication of the newspaper was suspended.

As of November 1950 the current assets of the newly incorporated London Free Press Printing Company Limited totalled $469,498 compared to current liabilities of $377,810. Its fixed assets including the newspaper plant totalled $552,504, still a relatively small company.[15] CFPL-AM had really just begun to be a profitable advertising medium. But when Blackburn moved to television, he was no longer a small business owner by any Canadian definition. Both the finances and the potential influence of this new medium put him into a small elite group of media owners.

Blackburn was acutely aware of the high costs involved in television which he later observed had "a fantastic appetite for both money and manpower."[16] Television could not be expected to be a major revenue producer for some years until advertisers saw its worth. Given the still comparatively small size of the company, Blackburn recognized the extent of the risks involved in the establishment of television. Still he argued before the board of directors of The London Free Press Holdings Limited in April 1953 that the move to television was necessary. That board had included as directors Blackburn's sisters Constance Orr and Miriam Smith. Both his sisters had grave reservations about the venture into television; they considered the new medium to be a costly proposition and too high a risk. Their outlook ultimately prompted them to sell their shares in LFPH to Blackburn. Blackburn himself still felt that since the company was involved in communications generally, entry into TV was essential to maintain the company's position in the radio and newspaper advertising field. Blackburn informed the directors of the company that a deficit from operations would undoubtedly parallel his efforts to develop television as a new service. In his application to the CBC Blackburn explained he "was prepared to invest an estimated $775,000 (comprised of $635,000 capital cost plus a budgeted first year loss of $140,000) in the project. If this estimated total investment should be exceeded, and this is not beyond the realm of possibility, we are willing and able to meet the excess required to do the job."[17]

As owner of a private family business, Blackburn enjoyed the advantage of long-term perspective. Unlike a public company where short-term results are measured every calendar quarter, he was able to withstand the initial financial loss that television's introduction incurred. Bruce Pearson, deputy chairman of what is now The Blackburn Group Inc., has explained Blackburn's favourable position this way: "The private company [owner] can say, let's put in that kind of investment. . . . It is going to take awhile to get it back, but I don't have to worry about paying out that dividend next month."[18] Less concerned about the short run, Blackburn was able to look ahead a whole generation. He foresaw that television one day would be highly profitable.

The advent of television came during the aftermath of other management initiatives whose impact still was felt in the early 1950s. Blackburn had implemented a salary administration plan in January 1950 for all departments of the newspaper division. As a result newspaper expenses increased by $321,543 for the fiscal year ending 31 October 1950, in large measure attributable to an increase of $213,000 in salaries. The salary plan was adopted following a report by J.D. Woods and Gordon, management consultants, which recognized that rates of pay were out of line in some departments of the company. Clearly, Blackburn saw implementation of such an expensive salary plan as a way to prevent an even costlier intrusion by unions.

He informed shareholders: "As you are aware, The Free Press is a non-union shop. Although our Press Room and Stereotyping Room staffs belong to unions, we have no signed contracts with them. For many reasons, it is desirable that we should keep it this way." He saw the need for the company to be competitive in its payment of salaries: "It is necessary that we keep our wages and salaries level with or, preferably, slightly higher than comparative union rates adjusted to the prevailing cost of living and average wage levels in London. Tied in with this is the necessity of keeping all wages and salaries within the Company on an equitable basis."[19] Blackburn admitted that the possibility of the newspaper's editorial department becoming unionized had spurred him on. He feared the influence of the American Newspaper Guild in Canada.

Additional expenses were also incurred by the company's expansion of its facilities at 442 Richmond Street. By March 1951 it occupied new offices at the corner of Richmond Street and Queens Avenue. Further additions and renovations were made to the newspaper's composing room. Within the newspaper division as well, ventilating and air conditioning equipment was included in all areas except the press room. A new oil heating system was installed and additions were made to the dispatch and mailing rooms. New bureaus were opened in Stratford, Woodstock and St. Thomas.

Looking ahead to 1952, the year before television arrived, Blackburn expressed caution: "The year ahead may well be a difficult one. Business generally is not rolling ahead with the same gusto displayed since the war and prior to the implementation by the government of its tighter money, higher interest rate, policy and credit controls. It will probably be a year of adjustment and it is impossible to foresee at the moment just what the year may bring."[20] But Blackburn plunged ahead.

As in radio, private television operators were reliant on the whims of politicians and regulators before they could proceed with the introduction of the medium. As a rule Blackburn had little time for politicians. He considered them unnecessary meddlers in the private sector and too hasty in their desire to issue regulations. He had a near, pathological fear about government encroachment into the mass media that could limit freedom of expression.

At the same time he had a certain admiration for C.D. Howe, who had dominated the Liberal cabinet as "Minister of Everything" during wartime. Like other private broadcasters, Blackburn had remembered that in the 1930s Howe had given strong backing to the role of private radio in the Canadian broadcasting system. When television arrived, Howe, the federal minister of trade and commerce, argued that the medium should be open to private enterprise. Blackburn recognized that private broadcasters would eventually be given an opportunity to introduce television: "We knew what we were going to do and had our applications ready and waiting to go. . . . We knew by what the Honorable C.D. Howe was saying . . . [that] he wasn't prepared to give the CBC everything . . . and set up the CBC as a monopoly as the BBC was in England."[21]

Blackburn initially had assigned Murray Brown, manager of the company's electronics division, Glen Robitaille, the director of engineering, and Bob Reinhart, who later became assistant manager of CFPL TV, to explore television developments in the United States. The CBC required that a sound understanding of the medium had to be shown in presentations before it, and the trio put together a water-tight feasibility study. The company filed two briefs with the regulatory agency dealing with both the engineering and social aspects of the medium. Robitaille regarded "Blackburn's interest [in] and appreciation for engineering [as being] ahead of all broadcasters of the time." He also recalled that it could be difficult working with him. There was hardly ever any casual conversation: "I felt some sympathy for the man, [but] it kept me very conscious of what you were saying to him regardless of the circumstance."[22]

The developments which preceded the opening of the television station on 28 November 1953 were both hectic and uncertain. The first deadline was in March when submissions had to

91

be made to the CBC board of governors. Problems arose when the original site chosen for the station near Egerton Street in southeast London proved unsatisfactory. The air service branch of the Department of Transport objected because the proposed TV tower in this location was too close to London airport and could cause problems for approaching aircraft. Before the company's technical brief could be filed with CBC, a new site had to be found to show the proposed location of the station. Eventually an 83 acre site on Commissioners Road in London just west of Highway 2, where CFPL TV is located today, was chosen. Plans were made for a 117,000 watt station transmitting from a 500 foot tower.[23]

The CBC board of governors gave close scrutiny to the company's brief. The board recognized that a television licence would enhance Blackburn's monopoly position throughout the London region. Clearly he would become a multi-media owner. In 1953 there was no radio station to compete against CFPL in the London market. The closest regional radio station was in nearby St. Thomas where CHLO had been on the air since 1948. But this station was not a strong competitor either for audience or advertising. Initially the CBC had largely overlooked the cross-ownership issue when a number of newspaper publishers had been awarded radio licences. But licencing these individuals to provide still another form of electronic media service in individual markets would inevitably reinforce the growing problem of media concentration.

Davidson Dunton, chairman of the CBC, maintained that the corporation was always somewhat more suspicious of a station owned by a newspaper publisher: "We tended to watch those people a little more carefully to see that they were not trying to blanket any area with one set of opinions."[24] While the subject of cross-ownership in newspapers and radio was debated in the late 1940s and early 1950s, the CBC took no strong action against such undertakings. But television was a different matter.

Dunton remembered that the board took a hard look at Blackburn's application for a licence: "We thought about it very carefully. . . . It would have been rather nice if there was another application . . . but the question didn't arise, because there was no other application of any substance." The CBC chairman also acknowledged the regulatory dilemma of whether the board had a right to deny television service in the face of a strong, well researched application. He asked, "Do you deny television to the London area when Blackburn wants to do it and there is nobody else with a sound looking project . . . It was a good sound application." The management of CHLO radio had appeared in opposition to Blackburn's application but did not file a brief for a TV licence.[25]

The CBC board of governors gave its approval to the company's application in May 1953. The sod was turned in June as the sign for work to begin. From then until November, time was the company's enemy.

Beginning in June 1953 contractors and workmen proceeded with the TV building, and electronic equipment was ordered. Throughout the summer radio personnel, who would later appear on camera, began learning the announcing techniques demanded by the new medium. In September the 500-foot tower which held the station's antenna was put in place, attracting widespread public attention. The following month it took three weeks to install the TV transmitter, $350,000 worth of sophisticated technology, turning the new building into a vital, electronic centre.

Bob Elsden, president of CFPL Broadcasting, has recalled the race against the clock to meet the deadline: "[Walter] was out here with Marjorie when we were building the station. It was nothing to see him with a broom in his hand . . . he came out to help every night. . . . He was as interested and as talented in the electronics as many of our people. He understood what was going on." Elsden likened the activity and family atmosphere surrounding the introduction of television to that of "a Mennonite barn-raising. Everybody helped. I think we all probably worked sixty or seventy hours a week for weeks on end."[26]

It all came together at 6:30 p.m. on 28 November 1953. CFPL TV, Channel 10, went on the air. The novelty of the new electronic instrument attracted a large crowd to the Hotel London, many of whom got their first look at this new visual medium. Blackburn was seen that night cutting the ribbon to mark the start of the new era in communications. He had promised the CBC board of governors that his station would open by November. His determination to hold to his word had meant an almost break-neck schedule for most of 1953.

Viewers received an indication of television's immediacy and its capacity to communicate living experiences the first night the station was on the air. While the station aired a Douglas Fairbanks movie, it flashed a bulletin telling of a fire in a downtown London laundry and dry cleaning establishment. Just an hour and forty minutes later, viewers saw film footage of the fire and visual reports on the story, a style of news coverage that foreshadowed the station's later award-winning achievements in television news.[27] As well as being only the second privately owned television station on the air in Canada, CFPL was the first private station to be connected by microwave to the CBC television network.

The viewing public was wildly enthusiastic following the introduction of television. After just twelve months of operation, Blackburn underlined the impact of the medium: "Acceptance of CFPL-TV by the public of Western Ontario has been phenomenal. CFPL-TV has been taken into the homes and hearts of the people. Hundreds of unsolicited letters, telegrams, phone calls, word of mouth comment, surveys, support this. Television-equipped homes in our coverage area has increased in one year from 20,000 to approximately 60,000."[28] The advent of television had created a new electronic media environment.

The days of radio as a national network service were numbered. TV became the medium of national attention. Radio's future role would be to service local audiences with news, information and vibrant programming formats. Still Blackburn, whose radio and TV stations were CBC affiliates, wanted to maintain a close working relationship with the corporation: "CFPL-Radio's friendly relationship with the CBC has been maintained and we have more than discharged our duties as a network affiliate by contributing originations to the Dominion and Trans-Canada Networks and the International Service." These programs included performances by the Earle Terry Singers and the Don Wright Chorus. Blackburn explained in 1954 that "revenue from Network commercial programs is now almost non-existent and the future of the Dominion Network is very uncertain. Network revenue has not been a vital part of CFPL's total income but the collapse of the network would seriously affect CFPL-Radio's programming policy."

By the mid-1950s the company's overall radio operation was recording reasonable profits. As Blackburn had expected, television's financial growth was slow. In 1955 the operating profit for CFPL radio was $127,000 while the corresponding figure for the television station was $23,000. At this time Blackburn had already undertaken plans to convert the TV transmitter in preparation for colour television which did not arrive for another decade. The expenses associated with television remained a concern to him.

Not surprisingly, he was somewhat distraught at the failure of advertising agencies to recognize the potential of this visual medium: "I was amazed at the conservatism of . . . advertising agencies. Everybody thinks they are go-go boys, ready to move . . . [with] any new idea that comes along, but they are far from it. We really had to get out and establish our audience and sell the product."[29] Blackburn realized also that the electronic media market in London would no longer be his private fiefdom. The CBC board of governors had licenced a new radio station with the call letters CKSL inthe fall of 1955. Blackburn was aware that this station would offer stiff competition, but he chose not to oppose the application because of the company's ownership of three media in London. He anticipated losing some clients to the competitor but felt that CFPL would be able to remain the top station in the market.

Despite the new challenges, the Blackburn empire showed strength. The consolidated financial statements for 1956, which reflected the combined financial position of the London Free Press Holdings Limited and the subsidiary companies, showed a net profit of $369,564 compared with $289,734 for the preceding year, a profit improvement of $79,830 or 27.5 per cent. But Blackburn did not treat his new radio competitor lightly. His own station was forced to adust its programming format when CKSL began broadcasting on 24 June 1956.

The ownership of the new radio station involved another long-established London family. Joseph Jeffery, a prominent lawyer and businessman whose grandfather had founded the London Life Insurance Company, teamed up with F. Vincent Regan, a young Toronto lawyer to form London Broadcasters Limited. "We're fed up with Blackburn's communications monopoly," Jeffery remarked, though he later admitted that Blackburn had never abused the influence his media ownership gave him.[30] At the same time, he was at a loss to know how to crack Blackburn's hold on the London market.

Jeffery was a close friend of newspaper magnate Roy Thomson, who in 1964 became Lord Thomson of Fleet, and John Bassett, whose family has dominated Canadian media for three generations. He contemplated an attempt to challenge Blackburn's newspaper. "My brothers and I had thought seriously of trying to start up a daily newspaper," said Jeffery. "But Lord Thomson and . . . John Bassett . . . said to start up a newspaper you can make up your mind for some years you will lose a million dollars a year. . . . I [wasn't] . . . prepared to do that." On the basis of what he had learned, Jeffery knew that any effort to compete against *The London Free Press* would be difficult: "Lord Thomson told me that it was a very well run newspaper . . . and he was very complementary about it. He said there wasn't very much that he could think of to improve it." [31] Instead Jeffery turned to radio, a medium that still had the aura of novelty.

CKSL initially did provide a level of competition which Blackburn could not fail to ignore. He reported to shareholders that in the fall of 1956 the new competitor had made serious inroads into the London radio market. The new station had prompted a change in CFPL radio's programming. Blackburn's company scoured markets in Canada and the United States to seek out a new style of radio that would give it greater advantage. It was decided to completely change the philosophy of programming and adopt a pattern very similar to that employed successfully by the Westinghouse radio stations in the United States. This new programming concept necessitated a sweeping change in the radio organization and also made possible substantial economies in CFPL's operation.

The company's shift to the new radio format was in keeping with its practice to be alert to new developments in the three media. Despite his fiscal conservatism, Blackburn was not prepared to cling to the past, especially when he was forced to confront his first major competition in the London market. Moreover, the introduction of television forced adjustments upon radio.

Radio in Canada generally was influenced profoundly by United States models. As Blackburn had noted, the music-news-service format that CFPL radio introduced in January 1957 was an American import. The days of the bloc programming in radio, which included lengthy entertainment productions such as the musical program "Make Believe Ballroom," women's shows and interviews, were no more. In the face of television, radio began to play to its strengths.

The development of transistors gave the medium a new portability. Radio was less cumbersome than TV, and, through remote broadcasts, could be with the people almost instantly. Radio developed a new itimacy with listeners. While television took over the evening hours, radio concentrated on information from the moment morning alarm clocks went off. Radio's staples were the morning and rolling home shows. These programs allowed the medium to capture the audiences from six a.m. to nine a.m. and again between three-thirty p.m. and six p.m.[32]

It was the fabulous fifties when CFPL brought this new age of radio to London, the era of rock and roll. The personality disc jockey had arrived, with his characteristic chatter interspersed between music and news. Perhaps most important of all, radio became more intensely community oriented. Television might boast a wider audience and more "glamour," but radio could have a more intimate and flexible relationship with Londoners.

The changes paid off for CFPL which was to dominate the radio market for the next two decades. The November 1957 Elliott-Haynes survey showed that CFPL led in 33 of 36 measured quarter-hour periods. The Bureau of Broadcast Measurement (BBM), which surveys Canadian audiences, also found CFPL to be leading its competitor almost two to one. While CFPL radio was moving ahead, in 1957 CFPL television enjoyed its best year financially with an operating profit (before taxes) of $241,000, an increase of $121,000 over the preceding year. In contrast, Joseph Jeffery, looking back on the first years of his station, remarked that "we carried CKSL for 20 years and didn't make a nickel out of it."[33]

Blackburn did not always have free rein in southwestern Ontario. He would grow impatient when the long arm of the broadcast regulator reached out to try to improve Canadian programming. Because of his overt, dedicated sense of social responsibility combined with his publisher-capitalist philosophy, he was greatly annoyed at the presumptuousness of regulators who suggested that his media outlets were not exercising responsibility or providing an acceptable level of service. His comments to shareholders in 1957 reflected his frustration with the broadcast regulator: the CBC's more vigorous scrutiny of radio and television operations would undoubtedly mean an additional burden to the company's financial problems due to increased programming costs and more severe limitations on commercial placements.

Blackburn was equally perturbed with bureaucratic delays that held back the introduction of new technologies. He tried to get permission to provide colour television on an experimental basis almost a decade before it was commercially introduced to Canada. Again he was rebuffed. The CBC had agreed to recommend approval for such a venture on the condition that the Department of Transport endorse the idea first. But the Department declined. The transport department argued that there was no existing policy on colour television at the time.

Private broadcasters often have complained about being royal commissioned to death. Just six years after the Royal Commission on National Development in the Arts, Letters and Sciences, under the chairmanship of Vincent Massey, had examined the state of Canadian broadcasting and discussed ways of promoting cultural nationalism, a second study, the Royal Commission on Broadcasting headed by Robert Fowler, presented its report to the government.

Murray Brown appeared before the Fowler Commission on 12 September 1956. There were few aspects to the broadcasting business that Walter Blackburn took more seriously than the preparation of briefs for broadcast inquiries or regulators. Brown wrote the first draft of the company's brief to the Fowler Commission, but Blackburn as always insisted on reading every word of it. *The Free Press* publisher could be exceedingly tedious when it came to the final version. "It drove me crazy at times," said Brown. "The wording had to be so precise. . . . [Blackburn] was very precise in his own speech and in his own writing and he expected everyone else to be."[34] In their brief to the Fowler Commission, The London Free Press Holdings Limited along with CJCH in Halifax and CKVL in Verdun, Québec, again broke ranks with the Canadian Association of Broadcasters and endorsed the status quo that would allow the CBC to remain both a broadcasting operator and a regulator.

In his appearance Brown endorsed the existing system of "co-ordination of public and private facilities under one responsibility to Parliament. The creation of a separate regulatory body would seem to be impractical and would duplicate the present system of national control." A new regulator might be a more restrictive supervisor of the private broadcasters and interfere further in the marketplace. "When markets could adequately support 'second' stations," Brown argued, "these should be obliged to reserve certain periods for Canadian programs produced by the CBC or themselves; 'complementary' was a better word to describe the place of private stations vis-à-vis the CBC than was 'competitor.'"[35]

Like the Massey report, the Fowler Commission failed to recommend a separate regulatory agency for broadcasting. However, it did call for a reorganization of the existing CBC board. The CAB had wanted a two-board system, an independent regulatory board and a CBC board, with no connection between the two boards. Fowler rejected the two-board system but suggested that the revamped CBC board be renamed the Board of Broadcast Governors. However, the new government headed by John Diefenbaker in 1957 ultimately accepted the CAB's position. The following year a new broadcasting act called for the establishment of the two-board system. The new Board of Broadcast Governors took the name but not the form that the Fowler Commission had envisaged. Eventually, however, the BBG evolved into the separate regulatory agency many private broadcasters had wanted.

Blackburn had lost on this issue. In time his fear that such a body would apply excessive regulation to the broadcast industry was borne out. The BBG was the first broadcasting authority to implement Canadian content (Cancon) quotas for broadcasters. Private owners could find themselves in a sensitive position at licence renewal time if stations had not met the Cancon requirements.

While he concentrated heavily on advancing the company technologically during the 1950s, Blackburn never lost sight of the need to maintain favourable relations between the company and staff. He promoted staff efficiency and loyalty largely through the day-to-day efforts of Russell Waide, the company's personnel services manager. Blackburn continued his practice of attending regularly the General Committee meetings of The London Free Press Employees' Association to monitor any irritants or concerns that arose in discussion. His wife would give him an early dinner on Monday evenings. Waide would pick him up at home and drive to *The Free Press* for the 7:30 p.m. meeting. In this way staff grievances could often be defused before they became major sources of friction.

However, Blackburn faced a short-lived strike among a handful of pressroom employees in April 1955. They were members of local 173, of the International Printing Pressmen and Assistants Union. This minor labour disturbance was seen as a low point in the company's history since Blackburn had assumed control in the mid-1930s. His entire managerial outlook was predicated on the notion that both company and staff had similar goals and that conflict could be avoided. Ten of the sixteen pressmen at the newpaper walked off the job, seeking better staffing arrangements and wage parity with workers in Windsor and Hamilton. Blackburn's reaction was both surprise and dismay. "I don't believe in a fundamental conflict between management and labor," he said. "I believe in a man's right to work. . . . I see men on the picket line. It's a pretty pathetic sight.

But they have not been pushed around by us. It is their own decision."[36]

The walkout ended in ten days after the company used supervisory staff to assist the men who remained on the job. The result brought an end to the pressmen's union at the newspaper. After the strike ended Blackburn thanked the staff who had remained loyal: "My great regret, as I know it is yours, is that 10 young men felt it necessary to declare industrial war on us all with a strike. . . . Their action remains unexplicable to me and all others who dealt with them. Perhaps they listened too much to outside advice." He gave the labour disturbance a terse six lines in his 1955 annual report to shareholders, stressing the solidarity shown by the majority of workers: "Loyalty was illustrated when ten youths whose average age was about 22 years decided, at the instigation of their union, to call a strike in the pressroom on April 18, 1955. Volunteer help moved in from other departments; no editions were missed or even delayed; every employee except the picketing strikers reported for work as usual; circulation went up during the strike; the strike collapsed in ten days leaving the pressroom non-union."[37] This unsettling experience which tested Blackburn's managerial approach prompted him to enunciate the company's philosophy referred to earlier at the 1959 company dinner dance — the notions of harmonious relations between company and workers, employer benevolence and employee self-help — that had always, implicitly, guided him.

As the 1950s progressed, his company grew and staff relations became normalized. Blackburn could look back on a successful decade. He now had control over four media outlets, the newspaper, AM and FM radio stations and a television station. This concentration of ownership would bring an increasingly watchful eye from regulators in the years ahead. It had been a busy time for the publisher who in 1958 had reached his forty-fourth year.

But regardless of how distracted he was by business affairs, he had always insisted that family matters must receive a high priority. With his three children now in their mid to late teenage years, he decided to provide the family with a new recreational outlet. Blackburn purchased an island at Pointe-au-Baril, Ontario, in the Georgian Bay area for $35,000. There was a main house, which Blackburn dubbed "Good News", and four cabins on the island. The cabin on the southwest side of the island, which became "Little News", was expanded by adding a small kitchen, bathroom with shower, living room and a small, unscreened deck. Beginning in 1959, the family would leave their home at 326 Victoria Street in London, where they had moved in 1952, for extended periods each summer at Pointe-au-Baril. There Blackburn had some of his most pleasurable moments enjoying the boating and fishing in the region. A man who enjoyed just about every form of electronics from digital clocks to the most up-to-date telephone and radio devices, he spent hours of delight in tinkering with his power boat and fixing things.

Blackburn owned two different boats at Georgian Bay, one with two outboard motors; the other was an inboard-outboard. The boats were chosen specifically for Georgian Bay use, powerful, and with room for family and friends who often enjoyed picnics together. He was fastidious in the way his and other boats were tied up at the docks and maintained. Blackburn was a skilled mariner. He had successfully completed the Canadian Power Squadron course and examination in navigation, and flew the squadron's flag on his boat. On picnics he was no chef, although he was good at barbecuing. "We had picnics galore", his wife recalled. "But [Walter] never, if he could avoid it, did any of the cooking." Instead he often helped gather wood for the fire. Whether at Georgian Bay or back home in London, Blackburn's favorite middle-of-the-night snack was a tin can of Campbell's tomato soup into which he added milk. He would break crackers into the soup and eat it that way until the can was finished.

His daughter Martha, too, recalled her father's interest in anything to do with boating: "Everything I know about tying knots I owe to him, but I never had the patience to learn to splice rope, an accomplishment at which he spent hours."[38] Blackburn's time spent at Georgian Bay was precious. "I've got to get my batteries recharged", he would say before departing from London.

The fabulous fifties would soon be replaced by the turbulent 1960s. He had modernized the newspaper, developed the electronic media and was looking ahead to even further communications advances. But the new decade would bring both professional and personal setbacks for Blackburn that would leave a lasting impact on the man.

CHAPTER FIVE

◇————————◇

A Publisher's Hopes Dashed
1958 — 1970

WALTER BLACKBURN FACED the most unsettling and uneven period of his life during the 12 years that began with John Diefenbaker's electoral sweep in 1958 and ended with the publication of the report of the Special Senate Committee on Mass Media in 1970. The year 1958 was the most profitable in the history of CFPL radio and television. But the performance of *The London Free Press* was less satisfactory — general business and competitive conditions restrained advertising revenue.

Blackburn was disenchanted with Diefenbaker essentially for two reasons; the Conservative leader's vascillation on defence policy and what *The Free Press* publisher perceived as Diefenbaker's preoccupation with his own self-importance. Blackburn was impatient with the prime minister's reluctance to arm Canada's anti-aircraft missiles with nuclear weapons. Blackburn also thought that Diefenbaker had lost control of the Conservative Party and the cabinet by letting his own ego too often get in the way of his decision making. As a result he chose to back Lester Pearson and the Liberals in the 1963 federal election.

There were two other developments during these eventful years that gave rise to first celebration, then deep sorrow. The company reached another milestone when its newspaper and radio operations moved into new headquarters at 369 York Street in 1965. The new home of *The Free Press* and CFPL AM and FM radio was estimated to cost $6,500,000 and contained the most advanced newspaper and radio technology. The company's handsome surroundings reflected Blackburn's belief that the development of both communities and nations was inextricably linked to the efficiency of their communications systems. In sharp contrast to this memorable occasion was the death of Blackburn's son, Walter Juxon, Jr., three years later.

These two events seemed to reflect the turbulent and often unpredictable nature of the 1960s, a decade characterized by both technological advance and personal upheaval for the company and its president. Blackburn also failed to be re-elected to the board of directors of Canadian Press, a development that ruined his ambition to become president of the national news agency. Nonetheless, the Special Senate Committee on Mass Media, chaired by Senator Keith Davey, gave a strong endorsement to his media empire in 1970, a verdict that drew national attention.

Like all owners of substantial private businesses, Blackburn was deeply concerned about the question of ownership-transfer to the next generation and the impact of estate taxes. In 1958-59 he arranged for the transfer of the business ownership to his children to keep the enterprise in the family. Bruce Pearson, a director of The Blackburn Group Inc., has explained: "He certainly set the thing up to succeed in the turnover from one generation to the other."[1]

Blackburn showed foresight in such family-related business matters and was highly conscious of his own anticipated life span. He once remarked to his secretary, Helen Daly, that he did not expect to live to a ripe old age. In the drawer of his oak desk, first used by his uncle, Walter Josiah, Blackburn kept a record of the family's medical history. His grandfather, Josiah, had died at age sixty-seven; his father and uncle at ages sixty-seven and fifty-seven respectively. The timing of their deaths suggested that longevity was not on Blackburn's side.

The London Free Press Printing Company Limited, the operating company which generated the earnings and carried on the business for the total enterprise, had authorized capital

106

in late 1958 that totalled $60,000. This amount consisted of 600 common shares of $100 par value each. Only three of the shares had been subscribed and issued. Each of the three directors of the company, Blackburn, Arthur Ford and London lawyer Huron Davidson held one share. The London Free Press Holdings Limited (LFPH) was the beneficial owner of all of the issued shares.[2]

LFPH had authorized capital totalling $1,000,000; 18,800 five percent redeemable preference shares of $50 par value each for a total of $940,000. Twelve hundred common shares of $50 each made up the remaining $60,000. The Blackburn family held 889 of the common shares that involved fractional breakdowns. Walter Blackburn held 351.970 shares while his sister Miriam Smith had 268.515 shares. Their sister Constance had died in 1953. Her estate also held 268.515 shares. The Southam Company Limited had 300 common shares while Elsie Lester of North Madison, Ohio, whose relatives had been connected with the company from its early days, held the remaining 11 shares. Under the terms of certain family wills and agreements, Walter Blackburn had voting control over the shares owned by his sisters. Therefore, including his own shares, Blackburn had voting control of 889 of the company's 1,200 issued common shares.

When Blackburn froze his estate for succession-duty purposes in the late 1950s, he created three trusts, one for each of his children, Susan, Walter and Martha. Concurrently, a new holding company was incorporated with the name Blackburn Holdings Limited. This company purchased the 889 shares of LFPH held by the Blackburn family. Blackburn Holdings borrowed from the Bank of Montreal and paid cash to buy the shares held by Blackburn's sister, Miriam, and the estate of Constance, his other sister. When he sold his own shares to Blackburn Holdings, Blackburn was not paid in cash. He took back debentures. Thus the holding company owed him money, an amount that was paid to him over an extended period. These 889 shares representing ownership of Blackburn Holdings were then issued to the children's three trusts. Walter Jr.'s trust held one-half of the 889 shares; Susan's and Martha's trusts each held one-quarter. As of 23 January 1959 Blackburn's three children were the owners of Blackburn Holdings Limited. At this point Walter Blackburn had no ownership interest in The London Free Press Holdings Limited, having transferred it to his children through Blackburn Holdings.[3]

This estate freeze prevented the profits from subsequent growth in Blackburn's media empire from coming into his hands. Rather it fell to the children through the trusts that had been created. Thus the estate tax that would have been paid later at his death was avoided. During the next 25 years, his media operations went from a business valued at not much more than a few million dollars, to a multi-million dollar enterprise. However, from the practical standpoint, Blackburn's personal estate did not grow during that period. The reorganized corporate structural hierarchy of his enterprise now consisted of Blackburn Holdings at the top, The London Free Press Holdings Limited in the middle, and London Free Press Printing Company Limited at the bottom.

The reorganization plan also allowed Blackburn to retain voting control of the enterprise initially through London Free Press Printing Company Limited, the operating company. He was able to outvote the trusts even though he had no ownership interest. This objective was achieved by having the operating company issue 120,000 voting preference shares proportionately to the holders of common shares. Each shareholder received 100 preferred shares for every common share. For example, the Southam Company and shareholder Elsie Lester were issued 30,000 and 1,100 preferred shares respectively. At the same time Blackburn personally received his proportionate number of 88,900 voting preference shares. While his children owned 889 common shares of The London Free Press Holdings Limited through Blackburn Holdings, Blackburn still retained direct voting control of the operating company, London Free Press Printing Company Limited, through his preference shares. In effect this gave him control of the enterprise from the bottom up.

More than a decade later following further tax changes which removed the disadvantages related to an individual's control of a holding company, Blackburn was able to operate the business, from the top down, through Blackburn Holdings Limited. On 4 January 1972 the 120,000 voting preference shares of London Free Press Printing Company Limited were redeemed, and in return Blackburn Holdings issued to Blackburn personally 50,000 voting preference shares at a dollar apiece. This action allowed him to re-establish his control of the enterprise from the top through Blackburn Holdings, rather than from the bottom of the corporate structure through the printing company.

Following the corporate reorganization and an increase in the authorized capital of the operating company, London Free Press Printing Company Limited paid $1,140,000 in stock and cash dividends. These were received by The London Free Press Holdings Limited, owner of all of the outstanding shares of the operating company. The receipt of these dividends enabled the holding company to pay a special dividend to its shareholders on 26 January 1959 of $120,000 in specie (120,000 printing company Class "B" voting preference shares) and $1,020,000 in cash ($850 per share). Blackburn advised shareholders that these dividends were special in nature and could not be expected to be repeated: "It is hoped by your directors, however, that in the near future conditions will warrant placing the company on a regular dividend basis. The amount of such dividends has not yet been determined but is unlikely to be greater than the rate which prevailed prior to the discontinuation of regular dividends in 1951."[4]

Ken Lemon, his financial adviser, underlined the conservative dividend policy of Blackburn's operation: "When you concentrate the ownership in the hands of the operator who is drawing a salary and who doesn't necessarily care about dividends, the money, instead of being diverted into dividend payout, can be ploughed back into the enterprise. . . . The company was highly conservative in its dividend policy and in fact modest dividends were paid back when the sisters were still shareholders. . . . Walter himself took virtually no dividends out of the place ever."[5] Similarly, back in the early days of the company, his aunts seldom received dividends. Most of the money was needed to build the business. This policy continued, and for the next twenty-five years his enterprise experienced sustained growth, without massive amounts of money being diverted in dividends paid to non-operating owners.

In July 1959 Blackburn accepted what turned out to be a somewhat controversial honour: his appointment as honorary lieutenant-colonel, 9th Signal Regiment, Royal Canadian Corps of Signals (Militia). Since he had not served in the country's war effort, military enthusiasts in London, historically a garrison city, wondered at the rationale behind the appointment and at Blackburn's acceptance of it.

Blackburn succeeded Lt. Col. Basil Grover who had died in November 1956. The tenure of his appointment was from 22 May 1959 to 21 May 1964. Although he agreed to accept the appointment Blackburn did not appear to have been at ease with his decision. "I didn't feel he was particularly comfortable," his wife Marjorie recalled. "He [just] felt he should do it."[6]

All applications for such honorary military appointments are processed through national defence headquarters in Ottawa and have to receive ministerial approval. Under the Canadian Forces Administrative Orders, the position of honorary lieutenant-colonel was restricted to retired officers of the Canadian forces and to distinguished Canadian citizens. In their recommendation of Blackburn for the appointment, senior military officials in Ottawa noted that in 1954 he had been the first Canadian to be elected secretary of the American Newspaper Publishers Association and was widely known in the broadcasting field. As Major-General J.D.B. Smith explained, "Mr. Blackburn has been responsible to a large extent for the very favourable publicity given the services through the press, radio and television in the London area."[7]

George Pearkes, the defence minister in the Diefenbaker government, approved Blackburn's appointment on 22 May 1959. In July Brigadier F.A. Clift, commander for the western Ontario area wrote a congratulatory letter to *The Free Press* publisher. He underlined the support that Blackburn had given to the military: "You have always been a staunch friend of the military in this area. 9 Signal Regiment and the Canadian Militia in general are fortunate indeed to have you associated with them in an official capacity and will appreciate your advice and interest as Honorary Lieutenant-Colonel of 9 Signal Regiment."[8]

Lieutenant-Colonel D.F. Hansford, commanding officer of 9 Signal Regiment, expressed satisfaction that Blackburn had accepted the appointment. He asserted that the regiment's prime purpose, as a milita unit, was to provide training in all phases of communications required by the army: "I am sure Mr. Blackburn's association with our regiment will be an inspiration to us all, because of . . . [his] outstanding contribution to the field of electronics communications."[9] Clearly officialdom in Ottawa considered Blackburn's contribution to the field of communications sufficiently outstanding to warrant this honour that had frequently gone to retired officers.

Tom Lawson, Blackburn's long-time friend who had served in the war, remembered that "there were a few eyebrows raised" about the appointment: "People had gone and served and . . . they thought the job should have gone to somebody else who had been overseas in the war. . . . Some people felt strongly about it."[10] Blackburn's enthusiasm for titles and the recognition they brought could have clouded his judgement. That his media had given favourable support to the military was undeniable; however, Blackburn chose to ignore the public perception of his acceptance of this military honour.

A year before Blackburn's tenure as honorary lieutenant-colonel expired, he had a major disagreement with Arthur Ford, *The Free Press* editor-in-chief, and a life-long Tory who had been influential in party circles. Their differences revolved around the newspaper's editorial position in the 1963 federal election. Ultimately Ford resigned.

The Conservative cabinet was badly split in 1963 over whether Canada's weapons systems, in particular two squadrons of anti-aircraft missiles, the Bomarc-B and five squadrons of CF–101B Voodoo interceptors should be equipped with nuclear warheads. This ambivalence had drawn criticism from the United States, a partner with Canada in the North American Air

Defence Command (NORAD). The American State Department was quick to note that the Voodoos simply were not effective without nuclear warheads. Lester Pearson, the Liberal
leader, reversed an earlier position and decided to accept
nuclear warheads for "those defensive tactical weapons, which
cannot effectively be used without them but which we have
agreed to use."[11] The Conservative government was torn between
the anti-nuclear views of External Affairs Minister Howard
Green and the pro-nuclear position of Douglas Harkness, the
defence minister. Early in February 1963 the minority Diefenbaker government fell in the commons. The Liberals were
returned on 8 April, albeit in another minority position.

At election time, the newspaper never made an endorsement without Blackburn's tacit approval. When it came to the
support of a particular political party, he was extremely sensitive to his newspaper's monopoly position. Blackburn had an
intense belief in a free press that could operate independently
without community pressure or government interference. Just
as he maintained that a broadcasting licence carried with it a
concomitant responsibility to the public, so too did he feel a
newspaper must be free to play a leadership roll especially at
election time. He therefore kept a watchful eye on the content of
the editorial page. However, by no means did he make a daily
practice of dictating editorial positions. As Norm Ibsen, the
newspaper's editorial page editor, remarked, "He did not like us
to presume too much in editorials and he sort of liked the calm,
measured approach rather than what smacked of hyperbole. I
don't think he liked to be too extreme in any direction."[12]

The Ford incident represented something of an historical
paradox as the newspaper broke sharply with its past. *The London Free Press* had been perceived as a newspaper aligned with
the Conservative Party ever since the publisher's grandfather,
Josiah Blackburn, had broken with George Brown, the Reform
leader, back in the mid-nineteenth century. After Ford became
editor-in-chief in 1920 this view was reinforced with his staunch
support of Conservative leaders such as Arthur Meighen and
R.B. Bennett. Ford's connections to the Conservative Party were
well known beyond journalistic circles. But just as Blackburn's

grandfather had shifted the London newspaper's orientation, so too did the third-generation publisher show an independence of mind during the Pearson-Diefenbaker era. "I really loved Mr. Ford," Blackburn admitted, "I had great respect for him. I admired him as a man. . . . [and] as a journalist. I admired him as our editor. But I had to stand my ground, or I couldn't have admired myself." In the 1963 federal campaign *The Free Press* endorsed Lester Pearson and the Liberals. Blackburn observed: "We did support the right man, in my judgment, at that time. Mr. Diefenbaker was a disaster."[13]

Blackburn was distressed over the incident because of his admiration for Ford. For about a quarter of a century the two men had had a smooth working relationship. Given their age difference, Blackburn had for years perceived Ford as a father figure. Ford had arrived at the newspaper some 15 years before Blackburn had taken over as publisher. He had assisted the young president through his difficult early period. With Ford's considerable experience, Blackburn was able to concentrate on building the business, especially from the technological standpoint, in both print and broadcast.

By the time this editorial difference arose, Ford was eighty-two, having served as editor for forty odd years. But his departure was not a major upheaval, for his successors were capable of taking over. His age had caused him to become somewhat absent-minded of late. John Elliott, who worked under Ford as the chief editorial writer, frequently scrutinized Ford's writing during his final years with the paper. On one occasion Ford's wife put in an urgent call to his secretary at work asking her to double check her husband's clothing. His wife had become curious when she noticed that a suit Ford had received from the cleaners was minus the jacket with the pants still in the closet. She wanted to know if he were wearing trousers.[14]

Reflecting on the 1963 election campaign, Ford said he had "never seen an election in which the voters were so confused, so puzzled and so deeply anxious over what course to take . . . to bring about stable government."[15] Blackburn remembered the final editorial meeting with Ford: "I asked him what we were going to do. I said I couldn't change my mind [from favouring

Pearson] and live with myself, and I suppose he couldn't change his mind and live with himself. So he decided to retire."[16]

Ford stepped down effective 29 March 1963 and became editor emeritus. He continued to write a front-page editorial each Saturday for *The Free Press*. As a veteran political observer he remained dubious about the future of Canadian politics: "The danger is that the public is becoming cynical in regard to parliament and losing faith in both the . . . old parties which is a bad thing for the country."[17]

Ford's successor was John K. Elliott, who had graduated from the University of Western Ontario in 1926 with gold medals in political economy and economics. His uncle, John Campbell Elliott, a former Liberal member of Parliament for the riding of West Middlesex, had become postmaster general following Mackenzie King's return to power in the 1935 federal election.

Elliott was a thoughtful, sensitive and conscientious man whose road to promotion as editor had been impeded by Blackburn's reluctance to ask for Ford's resignation at an appropriate time. The circumstances surrounding Ford's resignation served to underline what could be perceived as a weakness in Blackburn's managerial approach. William Heine, who succeeded Elliott and held the editor-in-chief's post for some fifteen years, explained: "The list of people whom he allowed to . . . let rise up to the point where the Peter principle applied and then in a sense of desperation had to cut them off at the shoulders was rather long."[18]

Blackburn's loyalty to certain staff members, while admirable, seemed at times to supersede his sense of proportion. Although Elliott suffered from health problems and did not appear to enjoy administrative duties, Ford's lengthy stay with the newspaper prevented him from receiving the appointment as editor much earlier. Yet throughout these circumstances which saw Elliott work under Ford for some twenty years, the two men maintained a close and friendly working relationship. Elliott too was made editor emeritus in 1970, three years after William Heine succeeded him.

Ford's retirement had marked the end of another era at *The Free Press*. Technological improvements had reached a new refinement by the mid-1960s when the company moved its news-paper and radio stations into its present headquarters at 369 York Street in London. The age of computers had arrived and Blackburn could hardly wait to get started. "The whole printing business is in a process of change," Ford explained to his friend Victor Odlum. "We are building a new plant and have spent a million and a half on new presses and machinery which in a decade may be scrapped. But we could not wait."[19]

Blackburn had a true sense of family history that often revealed itself on memorable occasions involving his company. Nowhere did it show more than on 19 March 1964 when he turned the first sod at the York-Colborne streets site for what he termed the "dream building" of *The London Free Press*. With some hundred active and retired members of the newspaper's organi-zation looking on, he recalled the company's early history, not-ing in the process the contributions of his ancestors: "Through Josiah Blackburn, publisher and editor, and Arthur Blackburn, publisher and broadcaster, I guess I have acquired honestly my own love of newspaper work and broadcasting. It is a very far cry from the small, hand-operated press that turned out the first copies of *The London Free Press* one hundred and sixteen years ago to the huge electronically controlled equipment which will take shape on this site."[20]

Blackburn equated the growth of his organization with that of the city of London, noting the symbiotic relationship between the newspaper and community. His remarks reflected the notion of localism, a characteristic Ontario attitude: "Yet, as we stand on the threshold of the biggest single undertaking in this company's history, we remember that it is on the founda-tions of hand-operated presses, box-like studios and pioneer villages that we build. It is our past performance and growth coupled ... with the performance of London and Western Ontario that makes it possible for us to invest $6,500,000 as our contribution to the future growth and prosperity of this com-munity." Blackburn told the crowd that "because our roots are in

London and Western Ontario it makes me extremely pleased that such a large number of the major contracts for this project have been won in fair bidding by London firms."

The *Canadian Printer & Publisher* magazine described how *The Free Press* built its new facilities, "one of the most advanced newspaper plants in the world," around a plan for easy production of a newspaper: "The operating areas of the newspaper were planned first for the most efficient production of a newspaper, and then the building was created around the smooth-flowing production departments." Architect Frederick E. Fletcher, a partner of Gordon S. Adamson & Associates, said that "from the beginning the publisher, Walter J. Blackburn, stressed that the men and women working in his organization are of prime importance and the plant was to be a human and desirable environment in which to work."[21]

The construction of the new premises was a total staff effort involving both print and broadcast operations. It involved numerous conferences of department heads under the chairmanship of W.G. Trestain, general manager and executive editor of the newspaper, and a smaller group, the building subcommittee, chaired by Mel Parkinson, which held some one hundred formal meetings in addition to daily informal conferences during the two-year planning stage. Before construction got underway employees could make any number of suggestions on the layout of the new building. They were able to examine a miniature of every office and department, which had been built on a grid with tiny pieces of plastic equipment to indicate various measurements and distances.[22]

The company published a handsome souvenir edition entitled *Communications in the Community* to mark the move to its seventh location in London. The newspaper staff began operating from the new premises on 3 July 1965, while both the AM and FM radio operations moved to their new quarters on 1 December of that year. The new 160,000 square foot building was designed clearly to help the various departments cope more efficiently with the time constraints involved in the publishing of the daily newspaper. As the company explained, "Time, again measured in minutes, has been gained in the modern conveyor systems which carry the river of folded, trimmed and counted copies of *The Free Press* from the press to the mailing room, through automatic bundle-wrapping and tying machines and down spiraling chutes into waiting trucks."[23] A ten unit Goss Headliner Press, worth $1,500,000 was installed to produce larger and more colourful editions at speeds of up to 1,000 copies a minute. In addition, new equipment in the plant's photography and engraving departments improved the reproduction of pictures and illustrations. The building contained a 500 ton air conditioning unit and a heating system designed to make the workplace conducive to improved productivity. When he moved into his new office, Blackburn retained the old oak desk used by his uncle Walter Josiah, the company's second president, and by his father, Arthur Stephen Blackburn, whom he had succeeded. "It is a reminder," said the third-generation publisher, "that we owe a debt to those who toiled before us. We are building for the future on the knowledge and experience of the past."

The York Street headquarters of *The Free Press* had been estimated to actually cost $6,975,000 in the final tally. To help finance the project, the company made arrangements with the Bank of Montreal for a term loan and a demand loan of $1,500,00 and $2,000,000 respectively. With these expenditures, Blackburn was grateful for unexpected revenue gains in 1964 and 1965. A corporation tax deferral, principally due to accelerated depreciation permitted on normal equipment acquired between 14 June 1962 and 31 December 1966, also assisted the company.

During this building expansion Blackburn kept a watchful eye on Canadian broadcasting developments. He recognized that the workings of the government-appointed Advisory Committee on broadcasting, under the chairmanship of Robert Fowler (the same chairman who had headed the earlier royal commission into Canadian broadcasting in 1957) could have important implications for his electronic media holdings.

In June 1965 Blackburn wrote to Fowler on the question of cross-ownership and whether newspaper owners should be allowed to have broadcasting licences. "I know of no case in Canada," he said, "where a newspaper has entered broadcasting just to sell the station later at a profit, although such cases have certainly occurred among non-newspaper owners." Blackburn was forthright: "The BBG [Board of Broadcasters Governors] has the authority and the responsibility to require any licensee to meet his obligations to the public and under the legislation during the term of his license; and in addition is in a powerful position at license renewal time to review past performance and require specific promises of future performance."[24]

Still Blackburn was concerned, as were a number of private broadcasters, when the Fowler Committee delivered its report in the first week of September 1965. Murray Brown, general manager of the broadcasting division, wondered if the recommendation for a new broadcasting authority would not leave the chairman of such an agency with such powers that he would be virtually a czar of Canadian broadcasting.

Another cause for concern was the report's general criticism of the performance of private broadcasters. The report called for private broadcasters to play a more active role in meeting the national objectives of the broadcasting system in addition to servicing their own local audiences. A controversial recommendation was Fowler's call for program performance standards to be established for individual private stations that would be enforced as a condition of licence.[25] Blackburn was uneasy with this latter recommendation; he also was concerned about the extent of control that a new independent board or authority might have over Canadian broadcasting.

In the mid-1960s Blackburn again had to face competition, not on the newspaper side this time, but from another London radio station, CJOE, which began broadcasting in 1967. The owner of this station was Joseph McManus, a self-made millionaire, who had accumulated his wealth through the selling of fuel oil and automobiles. With London's population growing and the city's business community expanding, McManus felt the London market was ready for another radio station; he was prepared to challenge Blackburn and Joseph Jeffery, part-owner of CKSL radio. CFPL did not oppose McManus's application for an AM station before the Board of Broadcast Governors in 1965; still some revenue loss was anticipated given McManus's wide range of business interests. However, under McManus, CJOE had several unsettling years from the time it began broadcasting in 1967; the station struggled to gain a foothold in the London market and frequently changed programming formats. Eventually CJOE was sold to Middlesex Broadcasters, when it assumed the called letters CJBK, the designation the station holds today. On 1 May 1987 Twigg Communications Limited, a privately held Canadian company, purchased CJBK and BX 93, a sister FM station in London, along with CHOK-AM in Sarnia.

Technological developments in television during the mid-1960s presented another challenge and dictated increased costs. On 1 September 1966 CFPL television began colour broadcasting through video tape, film and slides, an innovation requiring an expenditure of some $400,000 not including studio cameras. In this same year a decision was made to enter the cable television business in order to counteract the impact of cable which threatened to fracture the audiences of conventional TV stations.

Cable had its beginnings in London in 1952. Edwin Jarmain, a local handyman who owned a London laundry and drycleaning establishment, solved the viewing problems of his neighbours who were unable to get proper TV reception of American programming. Jarmain simply erected a large antenna and then enlisted his neighbours as subscribers by providing them with "hook-up."[26] In 1964 Blackburn had decided to hold discussions with Jarmain and representatives of Famous Players Canadian Corporation with a view to the establishment of community antenna television systems in Sarnia and Chatham. Blackburn saw cable as a profitable enterprise. He also recognized that the audience of CFPL TV, through cable distribution, could be increased in these two communities, a development which would bring greater advertising revenue. He also wanted to gain a fuller understanding of the cable business, a new communication service provided to homes by means of co-axial cable, a significant technological development.

The broadcasting regulatory agency, the Board of Broadcast Governors, approved the Chatham cable system in September

1966. The London Free Press Holdings Limited (LFPH) became a 50 per cent owner in Chatham Cable TV Limited. Jarmain Teleservices Limited and Famous Players Canadian Corporation each held a 25 per cent interest in the newly formed company. The total financial involvement of LFPH in Chatham TV cable, which commenced operations during the first week of September 1967, was approximately $200,000.

At about the same time Blackburn also set out to improve managerial efficiency. In 1966 Woods, Gordon & Company, a consulting firm, carried out an extensive survey of the print and broadcasting operations. The firm's recommendations had considerable impact on both print and broadcast sections of the company. The newspaper division was reorganized. All departments that dealt with the business side of the newspaper, such as display and classified advertising, circulation and promotion, were designated as the Marketing Group, under manager Charles G. Fenn.

The first major initiative of the Marketing Group was a study to determine whether *The Free Press* should continue to carry the Saturday supplement *Weekend* or switch to *Canadian*, a new competitor. Blackburn decided he would make an arrangement with *Canadian*. *Canadian* magazine founded in 1965 was published by Southstar Publishers Limited, a consortium of the *Toronto Star* and Southam Press. The magazine's content was devoted mainly to stories of general interest. *Weekend* magazine had been founded in 1951 and was published by the Montreal Standard Publishing Company. This weekend supplement also featured topical articles. Peter G. White, who became marketing services manager of *The Free Press*, recalled that the publisher drove a hard bargain when he opted for *Canadian* magazine: "He argued that *Canadian* . . . and the national advertisers in it were using his distribution system and therefore they should pay for it."[27]

Blackburn cancelled his contract with the Montreal Standard Publishing Company on 31 December 1967. Southstar Publishers Limited had urged him to pick up *Canadian* to help raise the supplement's circulation. Ross Munro, then publisher of *Canadian*, recalled his difficult efforts in the mid-1960s to get

Blackburn to carry the magazine: "[Beland] Honderich and [St. Clair] Balfour and myself went down to try to persuade Walter to take *Canadian*. . . . He was already taking *Weekend* and we had a really long, long discussion. . . . That was the toughest discussion I had with him [and] we needed *The London Free Press*." Munro admitted that he had "a hell of a time" to get *Canadian* off the ground.[28]

Blackburn negotiated a healthy financial arrangement with Southstar Publishers Limited effective 1 January 1968 to carry *Canadian*. In 1968 Blackburn received quarterly payments ranging between $56,959 and $58,144.97 from Southstar, totalling for the year $230,208. Thereafter he was paid the sum of $28,273 in quarterly installments in each of the years 1969 to 1977 inclusive. The contract also called for him to receive a share of Southstar's profits each year between 1968 and 1977.[29] Shortly afterward, both of the financially troubled magazines, *Canadian* and *Weekend*, folded. A new supplement *Canadian Weekend* was formed. In 1979 its name was changed to *Today*. It went out of business in 1982, amidst an economic recession.

Canada's centennial year in 1967 saw *The Free Press* organization in a sound financial position. London Free Press Printing Company Limited (both print and broadcast) had an operating profit of $2,181,000 for its fiscal year ending in October. Blackburn explained to shareholders: "The current financial position of the Company is reasonably good. Excluding the liability of the Company to the The London Free Press Holdings Limited from current liabilities, working capital at 31 October 1967 was almost $1,000,000."[30]

At the same time the company was well into the computer age. The vice-president of finance, B.E. "Bev" Lanning, who had joined the newspaper on 21 August 1967, noted the progress that had been made. "Conversion to electronic data processing techniques was initiated during the year. The first application was computerized typesetting, which conversion was made with a minimum of disturbance and is presently operating as anticipated in the Woods, Gordon feasibility study." Lanning explained that "the computer feasibility study was also updated by our own staff and a definite plan [was established] for conversion of various accounting and other applications to electronic data processing through 1970."

A new operating company, CFPL Broadcasting Limited, came into existence on 1 September 1968. It acquired the radio and television assets of London Free Press Printing Company Limited and became the licensee of CFPL–AM, CFPL–FM and CFPL–TV. The reason for the formation of CFPL Broadcasting Limited was to protect the operating company, London Free Press Printing Company Limited, from the need to provide confidential, financial information dealing with the newspaper to the Canadian Radio Television Commission, the broadcast regulator. It was also felt there was some merit "politically" in the new name: CFPL Broadcasting Limited was not so readily identifiable with *The Free Press*.

A significant personnel change in 1968 involved the replacement of W.G. Trestain, who had relinquished the senior management position of vice-president of the newspaper operation in June 1967. Trestain, who had joined *The Free Press* in December 1936, and Blackburn went back a long way together. At the start of World War II Trestain had become the newspaper's "roving reporter" providing colourful local features on events and personalities.[31] Later he had moved to the management side and was heavily involved in the planning and organization for the company's move to its new York Street headquarters. However, differences had arisen between Blackburn and Trestain in a number of areas, some pertaining to day-to-day administration of the company. Blackburn felt Trestain treated some of his directions aimed at improving the newspaper in a cavalier fashion; Trestain responded that Blackburn seemed more preoccupied with "non-essentials" rather than with the major, overall objectives of the newspaper operation.

Blackburn appointed William J. Carradine, an executive with the Procter and Gamble Company in Geneva, Switzerland, to fill Trestain's position. During Carradine's first day on the job, Blackburn introduced him to the technical aspects of the new, modern newspaper building. "I would have thought the thing to do was to go around and meet some of the managers," said

Carradine. Instead "Walter immediately took me to the bowels of the building, showed me the boilers . . . the ink system, took me up into the huge air conditioning part of the building [and] spent a happy hour up there just sort of twiddling dials."[32]

Carradine recalled an early meeting when he called the publisher "Walter" in front of senior executives: "There was a great hush," said Carradine. "It was as if the world had come to an end."[33] After this incident Blackburn called Murray Brown, vice-president of broadcasting, and Bev Lanning, vice-president of finance, into his office. He explained somewhat haltingly to them that, in public or socially, he would prefer if they referred to him as "Walter" and not as "Mr. Blackburn." Brown saw that he was uncomfortable: "That was what was embarrassing him. The fact that Bill Carradine was 'Waltering' him all over the place and to everybody else he was 'Mr. Blackburn.' He only went to two people, myself and Bev Lanning. . . . He felt that if one vice-president [was] calling [him] Walter they should all be."[34]

By the year 1968 the newspaper and radio operations had become attuned to their new facilities. CFPL–TV was now a mature fifteen years old. That same year the country was on an emotional high when Trudeaumania swept across the nation. But for Walter Blackburn 1968 was a time of tribulation that involved both professional and personal setbacks. In April he was distraught over his defeat when he stood for re-election to the board of directors of the Canadian Press (CP). In June his son's suicide shattered him.

Blackburn's defeat in the CP election occurred at the organization's annual meeting on 30 April 1968. He was a second vice-president and in training to become president of the news agency. In 1968 he had to stand for re-election to the board but failed to be elected as a director from Ontario.[35]

Ten candidates had been nominated. The CP membership had to elect three Ontario representatives. The winning candidates were Norman Smith representing the *Ottawa Journal*, Tom Nichols from the *Hamilton Spectator* and J.D. MacFarlane of the *Toronto Telegram*. In effect the vote had knocked Blackburn off the board of directors. Since he was not re-elected, he was not eligible to be a vice-president. In the end the second and first vice-presidents were Norman Smith and Beland Honderich, respectively, of the *Toronto Star*.

Throughout his career Blackburn had been a strong supporter of Canadian Press. His uncle, Walter Josiah, had been actively involved in the founding of CP. However, Blackburn saw his chance to become president disappear with the outcome of the 1968 vote. He was sorely disappointed and felt rejected; he believed strongly in CP and felt he deserved the presidency. "I can see [Blackburn] now, sitting in his favorite corner of a Royal York meeting room," Stuart Keate, former publisher of the *Vancouver Sun*, recalled. "At the morning sessions, he would puff quietly away on a briar to which was attached one of those 'windcheater' lids. After lunch or dinner, he would switch to Tueros, one of his favorite cigars." In Keate's view Blackburn's defeat, at that crucial rung on the ladder towards the CP presidency, "was one of those things that rocked the convention. Walter's demeanour was certainly downcast. . . . He had earned the right to be president of CP and a lot of us who had observed him up close . . . were outraged."[36]

No definitive reason can be given for Blackburn's defeat. The voting at CP annual meetings is by secret ballot. But Blackburn argued that he had been the victim of a bloc vote by the Thomson group; Thomson executives refuted this notion and steadfastly denied they had anything to do with a vote aimed at Blackburn's defeat. On this subject, Blackburn admitted to a certain ambivalence. Carman Cumming, Mario Cardinal and Peter Johansen have explained the incident in their study of group influence within CP: "Blackburn blamed a bloc Thomson vote for his own defeat . . . although he added that it appeared to be an accident, and that even the Thomson people were upset over the incident. . . . Blackburn lost, but said he did not think the defeat was caused by [an intentional] 'voting arrangement.'"[37] In the 1968 election none of the three Thomson newspaper representatives, James B. Lamb from the *Orillia Packet and Times*, G.B. Macgillivray of the *Fort William Times-Journal* and John B. McKay of the *Sarnia Observer* was elected to the board.

Some Thomson representatives had voted a number of proxies for publishers not present at CP annual meetings. But spokesmen for the newspaper group flatly denied that their organization had voted in a bloc deliberately to keep Blackburn off the board. In the 1968 election for Ontario directors, when Blackburn was defeated, the CP membership cast 73 votes including 18 by proxy. The Thomson organization cast 15 votes in person or by proxy.

St. Clair McCabe, a Thomson executive who at the time represented the *Moose Jaw Times-Herald*, maintained that his newspaper group never tried to stop Blackburn from the CP presidency: "I voted any proxies . . . in the interest of the Canadian Press and at no time did we ever try to block Walter Blackburn under any circumstances." McCabe was unable to recall a vote in which he did not endorse a member, such as Blackburn, who was already a vice-president: "We have got them in the line [for the presidency] . . . I thought of voting for people, not against people."[38]

Kenneth Roy Thomson, head of the Thomson newspaper empire, recalled that Blackburn spoke bitterly about the vote in 1968. He implied that the newspaper organization had knocked him off the board intentionally. "We did not do that," said Thomson, who maintained that Blackburn's defeat "was inadvertent. . . . There wasn't a bloc vote against him. It was just the way the vote went. But nobody got together I am damn sure in our group . . . and said 'don't vote for Walter.'"[39]

Beland Honderich, publisher of the *Toronto Star*, knew that the vote distressed Blackburn: "It was really quite an insult to Walter. As a matter of fact, I talked to him after the meeting and said 'Look I am prepared to resign Walter if this will help the situation' but it obviously wouldn't." Reflecting on the outcome of the vote, Honderich recalled that "Walter was not the most popular person around the Canadian Press. I think that people respected his opinion, but he was such a nit-picker that he drove people to frustration."[40] St. Clair Balfour, head of the Southam newspaper chain and president of CP when the election was held, remembered that Blackburn was "bitter, bitter, bitter."[41]

As owner of an independent newspaper, Blackburn was concerned about group bloc voting within CP. The minutes of the

1964 CP annual meeting showed that he had registered his disapproval about proxy voting arrangements: "Mr. Blackburn said the elections problem was not necessarily in the lack of candidates; it could be in the voting. He had seen one group representative vote a fistful of proxies last year. The membership should be informed about who holds what proxies." Blackburn suggested that "longer board terms might be an advantage. It took at least a two-year term to become informed on CP operation yet sometimes a director starting on the board did not get re-elected."[42]

In 1968 Blackburn also had to compete with three impressive candidates from large Ontario cities. Norman Smith, Tom Nichols and Doug MacFarlane could have simply proved, in this instance, more attractive to the CP members throughout the country who voted for and elected the directors. However, Blackburn's unexpected setback underlined for CP's executive committee the importance of protecting the progress of any officer who had been placed in the order of succession.

Blackburn was indignant at his failure to be returned to the CP board. But the death of his son Walter Juxon, Junior, whom he had seen as a potential heir to his family's media empire, was a stunning reversal of far greater proportion. Blackburn had experienced considerable family hardship before in his life. As a young man he had watched his diabetic father endure some difficult days before dying in 1935 in a diabetic coma. One of Blackburn's nieces, Stephanie, had suffered permanent injury from burns to her left arm, hand and leg when a nurse accidentally placed a leaking hot water bottle in her basinette shortly after birth. Blackburn was also distressed over his daughter Susan's divorce from Antonio Toledo, an executive with the Benson and Hedges tobacco company. As patriarch of a large group that was both business and family, he took each mishap very personally.

Walter Junior was a personable, friendly young man. Robert Turnbull, production manager at *The Free Press*, remembered his outgoing personality when he worked as a laboratory technician in the photographic department. His father wanted him to learn all phases of the newspaper business. As the boss's son, Walter took in stride the friendly taunting from fellow employ- ees who may have envied his position. "He never expected spe- cial treatment," said Turnbull.[43] Still his life was not easy. He had a history of medical problems and remained undecided about his career options.

At age fifteen when he attended Trinity College School, a private boys' school in Port Hope, Ontario, Walter was rushed to a Toronto hospital for an emergency bowel operation. He had become ill during a Victoria Day Holiday picnic. Although his father was not a regular church-goer, he often attended services in Toronto during the family crisis: "[Walter Jr.] came through that," said Blackburn. "But we realized that, as he improved, certainly his mental attitude towards life had changed very sub- stantially. . . . things went from bad to worse in the mental health area. [Still] he . . . had a very happy marriage."[44]

Walter Junior's wife was Judith Millsap, a Londoner, whom he married on 21 August 1965. The couple had known each other almost from childhood. The sister of Jill Millsap, wife of W.J. Carradine who had joined *The Free Press* in 1968, Judith had attended Central Collegiate high school in London with Walter, after he had returned from Trinity College School in Port Hope. Judith had attended Bishop Strachan School, a private girls' school in Toronto.

Walter, after spending time in both the newspaper and elec- tronic wings of his father's business, remained undecided about his future in either publishing or broadcasting. In March 1967 the couple, who had no children, moved to Montreal where Walter worked for RCA Victor in the field of educational televi- sion. In 1968 the couple moved to Toronto. Judith recalled her husband's excellent attitude towards children: "He went to the Crippled Children's Centre on Bayview [Avenue] . . . and he worked with them helping them to swim."[45] Walter Junior also had shown keen interest in flying and had obtained a pilot's licence. Jack Schenck, a licensed pilot since 1962, remarked: "I thought he would have been [an] excellent . . . commercial pilot."[46] He also loved farming and the outdoors.

Walter Junior did not show any particular eagerness to succeed his father. Blackburn eventually came to realize this fact: "I have often wondered whether I put him under more pressure than a young man should be subjected to at his age in indicating to him what my hopes and aspirations for him were." Blackburn felt his son's "bowel problem seemed to lead to . . . [a] mental problem." He reluctantly came to realize that Walter Junior would not be his successor, the Blackburn male heir who would take the communications empire into the fourth generation. "I had never questioned what I would do," said Blackburn. "To me it was just natural for him to do the same. It took me quite a while to realize that [the family business] was not going to be for him. Then I backed off but, by that time, he had been under a lot of pressure."[47]

Walter's wife, Judith, recalled one discussion with the elder Blackburn in the family's London home on Victoria Street. He asked her what he could do: "Wally wasn't very well. It was typical of him that he cared so much. If he was putting pressure on Wally, it was a very subtle pressure and one which he may have not realized himself he was doing. How much was self-imposed on Walt? You can't disassociate it." Judith described Walter Junior as "a wonderful person but [he] never could get his act together in terms of post secondary education, deciding what it was he wanted to do vis-à-vis what his father wanted him to do."[48]

This latter view was also shared by Blackburn's daughter, Martha, perhaps the family member closest to her brother: "Walt felt very strongly even as a young child . . . the responsibilities of ownership. I think Dad used to introduce him as 'my son and heir'. . . . Walt should have been a farmer. He loved the land, but he grew up with inbred expectations of what he thought he had to do."

Walter Junior's suicide occurred on 22 June 1968 at the age of 27. Blackburn's wife, Marjorie, who had assumed more than her share of this particular family burden, observed: "This was the ultimate tragedy in Walter's life."[49] Blackburn responded to the family crisis in a characteristic manner. He continued to immerse himself in his business and community projects, especially the construction of London's University Hospital.

The year after his son's death, the Special Senate Committee on Mass Media, under the chairmanship of Senator Keith Davey, began hearings that dealt with the politically sensitive issue of ownership concentration. As a cross-owner of newspaper, radio and television operations, Blackburn knew he would come in for close scrutiny. He was determined to leave nothing to chance in preparation for the committee's hearings. The Blackburn name and the future of his business, was once again on the line.

The senate hearings into the media began on 9 December 1969. Prior to the start of the committee's proceedings, Blackburn decided that he would attend all the sessions to obtain a sense of the questioning and direction of the committee. William Carradine, then vice-president and general manager of the London Free Press Printing Company Limited, remembered how determined the publisher was to put the company's best foot forward: "We prepared a three-ring binder that must have been three inches thick answering in exquisite detail every one of the questions that might possibly come out at the committee hearing. . . . That [was] the kind of person [Walter] was. He had an almost bulldog approach about him when he had a particular project or job that was terribly important to him. He would just become immersed in it."[50]

Blackburn took the offensive with the senate committee. He showed no reluctance to expose in full the workings of his media operations during the senate inquiry. He appeared before the committee on 21 January 1970 to give evidence and answer questions that related to the overall operations of the print and broadcasting divisions. On this same day Carradine and senior members of the newspaper staff appeared to deal with any queries relating to *The Free Press* and newspaper operations generally.

Murray Brown, who at the time was president and general manager of CFPL Broadcasting Limited, appeared before the committee along with his senior broadcasting executives on 25 March 1970. Brown, who co-ordinated the broadcasting brief, cleared just about every sentence of the document with Blackburn. The publisher wanted all his representatives to be the ultimate in precision on this important occasion. "Gosh

[Blackburn] was there a lot," said Senator Keith Davey. "It obviously gave him a feel of how we were going to operate and what our approach was, and I'm sure it gave him a good idea what to expect from us."[51]

When Blackburn appeared before the committee in Ottawa on 21 January, senators had before them an exhaustive brief that covered virtually every facet of the company's history, structure and methods of operation. In its set of guideline questions for owners of cross-media operations, the committee had asked the following question: "What advantages does the publisher of a newspaper gain from ownership of a radio and television station or vice versa?" In his brief Blackburn responded that all his media reaped some economies and benefited from sharing combined general administration and staff services such as finance, data processing and personnel.

He explained further to the senate committee: "In my opinion, there are two [additional] advantages. . . . These are: a direct knowledge of and exposure to the method of operation and current trends in radio and television, or in newspaper, as the case may be. Greater financial stability of total operation over the longer term, permitting better quality of present product, and in addition the development of knowledge of electronics." Blackburn observed: "In this changing, increasingly electronic world it is difficult to foresee by what means the public will wish to receive its news and information services, and one naturally wishes to remain a part of the communications industry regardless of changes in public decisions as to what 'hardware' system they prefer."[52]

Blackburn had a notable brief exchange with the committee chairman. Senator Davey argued that *The Free Press* publisher was in a decidedly monopoly situation in London. While he agreed that his media were dominant in the area, Blackburn frowned on the chairman's use of the term "overwhelmingly dominant." He also disagreed with the senator on the extent of the competition that faced CFPL radio. He informed the committee that there were two other London stations and other outside broadcasters who reached the London audience.[53]

A Liberal senator from New Brunswick on the committee,

Charles McElman, told Blackburn that as a respected publisher his views on the "raw, naked, unadulterated power" of media owners would carry great weight. In reply Blackburn said he could hardly agree that publishers were in positions to exercise such power. Moreover, he did not think the public would stand for it, if that were the case. The hearing, at which Blackburn appeared, began in the morning and was continued at a special night sitting. Senator Davey drew attention to the great interest of the committee in Blackburn's media operations and in his ownership philosophy.[54]

When the senate committee released its report on 10 December 1970, Blackburn was euphoric. The committee recognized that his style of operation, with the three media acting independently, achieved the desired results, namely independent editorial judgement and quality programming. While it maintained that "London, Ontario ... is a classic monopoly situation," the report praised Blackburn's three media outlets:

> The Blackburn family owns the *London Free Press*, CFPL Radio and CFPL-TV. On the face of it, this would constitute one of the tightest information monopolies in the country. And yet the *Free Press* is a very good community newspaper; and CFPL and CFPL-TV are among the best local programmers in the country. It is significant that in five cities near London — Sarnia, Chatham, St. Thomas, Woodstock, and Stratford — the *Free Press* has achieved an average combined circulation that totals 41 per cent of the circulation of the local dailies. This is a tribute to the editorial performance of the *Free Press*. . . . Both the radio and TV outlets are serious about local news and entertainment programming — to the point where local programs frequently draw larger audiences than do the CBC network offerings.[55]

Significantly, the committee cited *The Free Press* as an "exception to the apparent rule that monopoly promotes mediocrity, competition promotes quality." The senators found Walter Blackburn's analysis of the media markets in London and western Ontario to be both thorough and persuasive: "In his appearance before the Committee, Walter Blackburn forcefully argued that his properties do *not* enjoy an information monopoly. In

131

the seven-county area served by the *Free Press*, CFPL and CFPL-TV, his presentation outlined that there were forty-two newspapers (including six dailies), thirteen radio stations, two tv stations and fourteen cable-tv systems." Thus the report concluded: "The Blackburn media are providing good service to their community, we suggest because their owner *wants* them to provide good service, and is willing to spend to get it."

Blackburn enjoyed especially one aspect of the report; the committee's conclusion that media owners should not be placed in a straight-jacket of regulations by the establishment of fixed guidelines or immutable cross-ownership policies. This passage doubtless appealed to his belief that media owners should be able to operate freely with minimal government interference: "Again, the moral is that there is no moral. There are not, nor can there be, any sweeping criteria that will determine now and for all time which ownership-concentration situations militate against the public interest, and which ones are operating in its favor. In every case the arguments for and against are quite finely balanced. Each case must be judged in the light of individual circumstances."

CFPL radio interrupted regular programming to announce the favourable findings of the committee. *The London Free Press* gave the report front-page coverage. The committee's positive review was a pleasant way for the 56-year-old publisher to begin a new decade and provided solace for him following his earlier setbacks. In addition the year 1970 brought more positive economic news. The operating profit from the newspaper, radio and television totalled $3,023,000 for the fiscal year ending 31 August 1970. Working capital increased during the fiscal year by over $300,000 to a level of almost $3,200,000.

Blackburn had defended and consolidated his media holdings in London. He could build towards the future and still find time to concentrate on those community projects, such as the London Health Association, that were close to his heart. He was also about to take his first bold step outside of London to expand his media operations. A somewhat turbulent decade was behind him. Tomorrow seemed to hold greater promise.

CHAPTER SIX

The House that Walter Built
1970 — 1974

As A MEDIA OWNER Walter Blackburn preferred to operate on a regional rather than a national basis. He prided himself on the service his media provided to London and southwestern Ontario. He had no aspirations to become a national media baron who owned a chain of newspapers or a group of broadcasting stations. When the electronic media began to grow and to provide investment opportunities in the country, Blackburn seldom showed a desire to acquire additional media properties: "For many years I was really running the newspaper rather than sitting on top as a [financier] looking for new ways to make more money. . . . I was concerned about keeping up with the demands that were being made on the company by increasing circulation . . . [the] size of the city . . . increases in broadcasting revenue and spending more money on programming."[1]

Blackburn had been publisher of *The London Free Press* for some 35 years when the Special Senate Committee on Mass Media brought down its report in 1970. Members of the print and broadcast industries in Canada had regarded him largely as an owner who enjoyed an enviable monopoly position in London. Blackburn was always sensitive to charges that his position potentially gave him an inordinate amount of influence in southwestern Ontario. Stuart Keate, a former publisher of the *Vancouver Sun*, recalled that Blackburn confronted his critics head on: "What it all boiled down to was: 'C'mon in the water's fine'. . . . A strong challenger would doubtless make *The Free Press* and the electronic operations better performers. All this was stated in congenial tones which undoubtedly infuriated his opponents."[2]

Blackburn had broken with established practice when he purchased a half ownership of Chatham cable television with the Jarmain family in the mid–1960s. Then in the early 1970s he made his first media acquisition outside his home territory when he purchased CKNX radio and television in Wingham, a small community of a few thousand people north of London. The irony of the transaction was in the timing. Blackburn completed negotiations for the purchase of the Wingham media operation in December 1970, the month the senate committee released its report that underlined the dangers of media ownership concentration both regionally and nationally.

W.T. "Doc" Cruickshank, owner of the Wingham stations, had been a long-time friend of Blackburn. In a sense the Wingham purchase was as much a rescue operation as it was a media business venture. "It was almost like helping a friend," concluded Douglas Trowell, a former CFPL radio manager.[3]

"Doc," as he was affectionately known from the time he worked as a chauffeur for a local physican, was an early radio pioneer. In 1926 he built his own transmitter assigning it the call letters JOKE. When he received a broadcasting licence, the station designation became 10BP and was changed in 1935 to CKNX. His Wingham radio station concentrated heavily on agricultural programming to serve rural western Ontario.[4] After Blackburn had encouraged him to take the move, Cruickshank established a television station in 1955 to serve the rural residents of Bruce County and portions of the counties of Huron, Grey, Perth and Wellington.

On 8 March 1962 a major fire swept through the studios of CKNX radio and television housed in an old schoolhouse. The studios were virtually ruined but the stations' transmitters remained intact. The aftermath of the tragedy solidified the friendship between the London and Wingham media families, for when Blackburn heard about the fire, he promptly called Cruickshank to see what assistance could be provided. "[Doc] outlined what he needed and we sent . . . cameras, engineering assistance, microphones for radio and TV, all the gear that we felt he would require to get him back on the air. We got him back on air within a day or two in temporary quarters."[5]

Blackburn and Cruickshank reached an agreement on the sale of the Wingham stations on 10 December 1970. Blackburn acquired for $1,300,000 cash all of the shares of Wingham Investments Limited whose wholly owned subsidiary, Radio Station CKNX Limited, operated the AM radio and television stations in the tiny community. Clearly Blackburn was the natural purchaser of the Wingham electronic media because of his long establishment in southwestern Ontario. "Doc asked us if we would buy the [stations]," Blackburn recalled. "He told me that I was his first choice and really the only person he would want to run the [stations] . . . he knew we would run . . . [them] in the same manner that he had."[6]

At the time of the purchase the Wingham television station, a CBC affiliate, found itself under financial threat. The private network, CTV, had decided to establish a rebroadcasting transmitter in the Owen Sound area. Viewer access to CTV in the area covered by the Wingham TV station had severe financial implications for Cruickshank. Officials of his company had informed the CRTC in October 1970 that the Wingham station would die if the CTV application were approved. They argued that national advertisers would not buy time on CKNX television, a local station serving a small market. Murray Brown, president and general manager of CFPL Broadcasting Limited, explained prior to the purchase: "It appears evident that the Commission [CRTC] feels our purchase of CKNX (at least CKNX-Television) is the logical means by which present television service to the Wingham area may be maintained and the Cruickshanks saved from possible financial disaster."[7]

The CRTC was comfortable with the notion of Blackburn buying the Wingham radio and television stations, despite any concerns it had over the question of concentration of ownership. At the time the CRTC, under its vigorous new chairman Pierre Juneau, had received no clear directive from the government on the subject of media concentration. Like its forerunner, the Board of Broadcast Governors, the commission treated each case individually on its own merits, an approach that in the Wingham purchase worked to Blackburn's advantage. Appearing before the CRTC on 16 February 1971, Murray Brown forecast an increasing clamour from the public for the fullest range of services that technology made possible. "Desirable as it may be from the public's point of view to have a wide choice of television viewing, this development will have a devastating effect on many smaller Canadian television stations. "The very survival of these smaller stations," he warned, "may depend on acquisition by a metropolitan-based station similar to that which they were proposing for CKNX. In this way," Brown concluded, "the larger stations could make a further contribution to the future health of Canada's broadcasting system."[8]

The commission endorsed the application by The London Free Press Holdings Limited to buy the Wingham stations on 11 March 1971. "Doc" Cruickshank did not live to see the commission's approval. He had died the preceding month of cancer at the age of 73. But his wish prior to death had been fulfilled. The Wingham stations would continue, the CKNX staff maintaining responsibility for their own operations.

The Wingham television station had struggled unsuccessfully to attract national advertisers. But after Blackburn bought the TV station, CFPL and CKNX combined their advertising rate cards. This move allowed advertising to be sold in a package arrangement. To buy commercial time on the London station, a national advertiser had to do likewise on CKNX. This brought in the big advertising revenue which allowed locally focused programming to continue.

At roughly the same time that he purchased the Wingham stations, Blackburn decided to withdraw from Broadcast News, the Canadian Press subsidiary that he had helped to found in the early 1950s. His move coincided with a decision by CFPL radio's management to relinquish the BN voice service the station had taken since its inception and carry the Canadian Contemporary News Service (CCNS). Unlike BN, CCNS served its client stations on an exclusive basis, only one station in each radio market. CFPL's competitor in the London market, station

CKSL, had subscribed to the BN voice service on 1 February 1971, a move that was of some concern to CFPL station manager C.N. "Bud" Knight and Gordon Whitehead, the station's news director. Both stations would be carrying similar reports removing the earlier competitive advantage CFPL had enjoyed.

Blackburn had begun to see himself with a conflict of interest in his role as a director of Broadcast News. He explained his reluctance about continuing as a director in a March 1971 letter to John Dauphinee, the general manager of Canadian Press: "Since some CP members began to fuss several years ago about . . . [CP's] cash return from BN and it was suggested by one that CP's BN directors who have broadcasting interests might be biased in favour of broadcasting and against CP's best interests, I have questioned whether I should remain as one of CP's BN directors."[9] The manner in which Blackburn handled his resignation from BN was illustrative of his general practice to keep an arm's length relationship from senior management decision making on policy issues in which he might have an immediate, personal interest.

When CFPL was on the verge of dropping the voice service, Blackburn urged Murray Brown, the president and general manager of CFPL Broadcasting Limited, to make a courtesy call on his long-time colleague Charlie Edwards, the BN general manager. His memo to Brown on 30 March 1971 underlined some of the difficulties that Broadcast News had faced over the years: "BN voice was Doug Trowell's idea when he was CFPL Manager. CFPL talked BN into starting it. The service has never received enough support from broadcasters to yield the money required to do a top job. It has been forced to limp along, and is now losing money." Blackburn also told Brown that he had informed John Dauphinee that CFPL was soon to drop its contract with BN: "The above facts provide no reasons why we should not drop BN voice in our own competitive interest and to improve our Voice service if we can at a price you are prepared to pay; nor does the fact that I am a BN director. The late Bill Burgoyne [*St. Catharines Standard*] set a precedent by dropping BN voice when he was on the Board." But Blackburn felt that since he was a BN director, the situation demanded courtesy: "I strongly suggest that you give Charlie Edwards ... a chance to talk with you, Bud and Gord Whitehead before you decide whether or not to approve Gord Whitehead's recommendation [to drop BN], recognizing that we are dealing BN voice, which is already losing [money], a substantial blow by removing $8,300 a year in revenue, and the support of a good news station."[10]

In the end Blackburn endorsed the decision of his news director Gord Whitehead, who had been critical of BN's coverage. Whitehead favoured the adoption of CCNS. Blackburn informed John Dauphinee: "If there is any merit in the opinions of our News Director, and I believe there is, BN Voice, however, will have to do a better job to stay in business over the long haul against developing competition." With reference to the decision to leave BN and opt for another voice service, Blackburn was apologetic but pragmatic in support of his broadcasting executives: "I am sorry about all of this, but this is the way it is with CFPL. Happy to say, however, there is at present general satisfaction here with BN wire service."[11]

Both Broadcast News and CP executives made a valiant effort to keep Blackburn from resigning his BN directorship. Charlie Edwards noted the historical role that *The Free Press* publisher had played: "The great difficulties and obstacles faced by CP in the 1940s and early 1950s in efforts to serve broadcasters were resolved largely through the wise recommendations of the CP committee that studied the situation under your patient and informed chairmanship. Your counsel as director during BN's early years contributed much to bringing newspapermen and broadcasters together effectively to form a news organization that I know has benefitted both industries tremendously and in fact has been the most effective and unique organization of its kind anywhere."[12]

I. Norman Smith, CP president at the time, hoped Blackburn would remain on the BN board: he felt that the cross-fertilization of ideas between broadcasting and newspapers was an asset. In making his plea to Blackburn, Smith recalled their long years of friendship: "We are too old a set of friends, Walter, for me to give you malarkey. I will feel BN will make wiser decisions — and CP will so benefit — if you remain at least one more year on the Board."[13]

However, Blackburn held to his earlier position and resigned from the board in the fall of 1971. A resolution passed by the Board of Directors of Broadcast News Limited at a meeting in Victoria, British Columbia, on 21 September 1971 noted that "the members of The Canadian Press have particularly benefitted over the years from Walter Blackburn's forceful presentation to them at CP meetings of the broadcasters' side of the story."[14] A pioneer of Broadcast News and a board member for 18 years, *The Free Press* publisher had served longer than any other director.

There were other challenges to take up. Blackburn was an enthusiastic supporter of the Ontario Press Council established in 1972, and *The Free Press* was an early member of this body which served as a watchdog on the print media and heard readers' complaints.

But there were personnel changes once more within the newspaper wing of his media operation that occupied his attention. William Carradine left *The Free Press* in 1972 to join the Southam organization. Peter G. White, who had married Blackburn's daughter, Martha, in 1967, joined *The Free Press* in 1970, and assumed the position of planning and development manager for the newspaper in 1972. White had been born in London, England. He spent four years at the Aluminum Company of Canada before pursuing his Master of Business Administration degree at the University of Western Ontario. Martha Blackburn meanwhile, now in line for succession to the Blackburn empire, became a member of the board of directors of London Free Press Holdings Limited, London Free Press Printing Company Limited and CFPL Broadcasting Limited in 1975. With the departure of Carradine who had earlier envisaged the possibility of becoming publisher of *The London Free Press*, Walter Blackburn took on the duties of general manager. This notion had been discussed with Blackburn who had not ruled it out entirely, though he never had made a firm commitment to Carradine. The interest of his son-in-law and daughter in the newspaper, and Blackburn's own strong dynastic feeling about the family business, however, produced a set of circumstances that prompted Carradine to accept a senior position with the Southam company in Toronto.

About the time he left in 1972, Carradine had a mild disagreement with Blackburn on a matter also involving electronics, the purchase of a new computer. Blackburn was leaning towards the purchase of a large, costly Digital Equipment Corporation (DEC) computer system. "Walter would want to know every nut and bolt of the computer," Carradine remembered. "I think he felt ... [the large computer] would probably last him almost on into the future as long as he could see. . . . I had a sense that the large monolithic system was really not going to serve our purposes as well as a system of small computers."[15] However, in April 1972 negotiations were authorized for the acquisition of the Digital Equipment Corporation computer equipment. The cost of the DEC 10 system was estimated at $953,000 in the first year accumulating to an ultimate cost of $1,024,000 including duty and federal and provincial sales taxes.

With the Wingham purchase completed and plans for the next family generation to succeed him now underway, Blackburn was able to enjoy the acclaim he received for his role in undertaking numerous civic endeavours. During the early 1970s he was able to watch a number of projects in which he had been personally involved come to fruition. Perhaps the most notable of these was the opening of University Hospital in September 1972. Blackburn, who was essentially a private individual, preferred to be an influential backstage presence in his community activity. This discreet posture was decidedly an "old London" custom. It was in keeping with the approach to civic endeavours taken by the publisher's ancestors, in particular Josiah Blackburn, his grandfather. Still, Blackburn devoted both time and money to support London educational and medical institutions as well as the artistic community. His contribution had considerable impact on the city's quality of life. His wife, Marjorie, explained that "he was ... bent on service to the community. That was ... [how] he could forget about all the [personal] unhappiness and he got enormous satisfaction from it."[16]

When Blackburn received an honorary Doctor of Laws degree from the University of Western Ontario, he was described as "a physicist manqué" who had become "his own newspaper's resident guru in the arcane field of computer technology and electronic editing systems." Western's president, Dr. D. Carlton Williams, read the citation which outlined the extent of Blackburn's community support for social agencies, the arts and in the educational and medical fields: "Journalist Blackburn's corporate policy has, as one of its principal commitments, service to the people of London and its environs. Citizen Blackburn has pursued the same ideal in his personal service to such varied community institutions as the London Symphony, Theatre London, the YM-YWCA, the Salvation Army, and the Board of Governors of this University." Williams noted that Blackburn provided strong support for the establishment of a Department of Journalism in the mid-1940s, "a support without which our present Graduate School of Journalism could not survive." The publisher was commended as well for his work with the London Health Association (LHA) over the years and the significant role he played in "the development of our splendid University Hospital." Blackburn undoubtedly was pleased with the reference made to his grandfather: "Josiah Blackburn, founder of the *Free Press,* did battle with the old *Globe* in 1877 over the Toronto paper's contention that the Western University of London should not be allowed to open in competition with the University of Toronto. To what extent Josiah's eloquence decided the issue, I do not know, but then, as now, a Blackburn stood as a staunch ally of this university."[17]

From 1963 to 1975 when Blackburn served on the university's board of governors, he emerged as something of an establishment radical. During the 1960s restlessness pervaded campuses throughout North America as students and faculty sought to obtain a greater role in the day-to-day administration of universities. The University of Western Ontario did not have to contend with the level of disturbances that occurred at some other Canadian universities. Still students were critical of the board of governors and voiced their resentment at lack of representation on university administrative bodies. As a governor

Blackburn did not escape criticism from students and faculty who saw the board being dominated by business-oriented individuals. Their criticism was based on the belief that a university was fundamentally different from a business and could not operate along similar lines.

However, Blackburn insisted that the views he espoused at the time brought his position much closer to that of the faculty and students than either group realized. His attitude towards their demands on the university administration was largely similar to the views he had espoused while dealing with employees in his own media business. In fact, Blackburn was so insistent on university reform that he eventually clashed with Dr. G.E. Hall, the then university president.

Blackburn resented the students' attack on him because it was untrue. "My interest [on the board] was as a graduate and as a Londoner and as a responsible citizen I thought," he recalled, "[the students] were attacking me without knowing. They had never interviewed me [and] they had never sought my opinions about these matters." He argued that protesting students would have been surprised if they had realized fully his stance on the question of whether their activity should be heightened in the operation of the university. "They would have been astounded if I had shown them a letter I wrote to the President, urging him to bring the faculty and students into the management of the university," he said. "I couldn't convince them and they thought I was for the birds . . . I could never get the board to agree but I did my damndest to do it." In the 1970s both groups would have far greater representation in the university system, as Blackburn had envisaged: "I was saying three cheers. I knew it could be made to work and that the university would be better for it."[18]

Blackburn was pleased when he saw faculty become more involved in day-to-day matters, such as the parking and roads system at the university: "They knew what was needed. The board would have stumbled and bumbled and had consultants and all sorts of stuff, probably [ending] up with a shmozzle."

On the question of greater involvement by students and faculty in the university administration, Blackburn was consistent with what he had practised in his own business. The Free

Press Employees' Association was the mechanism he had established as a substitute for union organization. "Many businessmen ... talked with me about our employees' association here and the first thing I [told] them is ... you have to ... give up your sovereignty.... You no longer have the privilege of making decisions in matters that fall under joint jurisdiction, naturally, on your own."

Blackburn's role in the development of University Hospital, the province's first on-campus teaching hospital, gave him a sense of great accomplishment. The hospital, built and fully equipped at a cost of just under $39,000,000 became closely identified with Blackburn's efforts as a civic builder after its opening on 21 September 1972. He was later presented with a sketch of the medical institution by artist Sylvia Clarke bearing the inscription, "This is the House that Walter built." At the time Blackburn remarked, "I was the leader, yes, but there were so many more involved and the credit is due them more than me."[19]

He admitted his great admiration for prominent, community-minded individuals such as E.V. Buchanan and Colonel Ibbotson Leonard who were actively involved in the London Health Association at that time. In Blackburn's eyes, they were role models for the community, men to be commended for their contribution. Still Blackburn had immersed himself for more than a decade in this project which could be regarded as the high point of his community involvement. He served for seven years as chairman of the hospital's planning and building committee and was president of the London Health Association, the owner and operator of the hospital, during the four years that culminated in its completion and opening. University Hospital now ranks as one of the world's leading health-care institutions.

The building of a hospital or any new structure of similar magnitude was bound to have appeal for Blackburn. He had gone through such an experience in the mid-1960s, with the establishment of new headquarters for *The Free Press* and CFPL radio. His inclination towards engineering came to the forefront as he busied himself with the details of planning and construction. His friend, J. Allyn Taylor, a former president of

Canada Trust and board member of the London Health Association, explained: "Walter was essentially an engineer and architect in his own right. He loved the bricks and mortar and the
planning of [the hospital]. . . . He unquestionably made a tremendous contribution to it."[20]

Blackburn worked closely in the development of the hospital with the late Jack Stevens, a former chairman of Emco Limited, and Dr. Harold Warwick, who served as vice-president of
Western's health sciences in the late 1960s. When Premier John
Robarts announced a $30,000,000 government allocation for
construction of the hospital in January 1967, the way was then
cleared for detailed planning to begin. "This is great news for
us," Dr. John Neilson, the hospital's executive director, remarked
at the time. "We know now what monies we have."[21] Although he
had been involved earlier, Blackburn's contribution became
most significant in the five-year period prior to the hospital's
opening in 1972. "I look upon Mr. Jack Stevens as really the
driving force in getting that hospital going," Harold Warwick
recalled. "But Walter Blackburn . . . really carried it through
with most of the detailed planning of the hospital. . . . It was
Walter who did the leg work . . . with those of us in the university,
the medical staff, the nurses and the physicists . . . and the architect Wilf Lamb."[22]

Blackburn travelled extensively in Canada and the United
States, often at his own expense, to view similar hospital con-
cepts in preparing for the establishment of the proposed London hospital. These journeys included forays to the University
of British Columbia and to medical centres at the Universities of
Missouri, Kentucky and North Carolina. On these fact-finding
excursions, Blackburn adopted a no-nonsense approach.

In a downtown Vancouver hotel room he became perturbed
with Harold Warwick during a conversation that involved officials from the University of British Columbia (UBC). A teaching
hospital was also being planned at UBC. "I had a great interest
in salmon fishing," Warwick remembered. "I would see them
bringing in fish from the boats and I was sitting at the window
sill watching while this other chap was telling Walter details of
the planning of the hospital." Warwick recalled that Blackburn

became upset: "He ticked me off. He told me that we were out there on business and please pay attention to what they were doing. It was all nicely said and so I lost my interest in salmon fishing right at that moment."[23]

Blackburn preoccupied himself with just about every aspect of the London hospital from heating systems to the size and makeup of the bedrooms. In a 1967 report he went into considerable detail on the location of sewers to serve the hospital, access roads to the property, and steam requirements that involved the university's heating plant. He seemed to revel in this kind of engineering detail. He went to great lengths to ensure that the hospital's bedrooms would be suitable and meet all requirements.

Jack Stevens, the president of the London Health Association in the mid-1960s, drew the board of directors' attention to Blackburn's interest and enthusiasm for the project: "With Hospital planning reaching the point where actual room layouts are most important, this Association is most grateful to Mr. Blackburn for making available 3,000 square feet of space in the *Free Press* building for this purpose."[24] Blackburn insisted on seeing how the bedrooms would be laid out with the furnishings and supplies in them. As a result full-scale models of the various types of bedrooms were constructed in the basement of the newspaper building on York Street. When the mockups of the rooms were completed, suppliers moved in the furniture that would be in the patients' rooms. All of this took up a great deal of space in the newspaper building normally reserved for newsprint.

During the planning stages, the matter of hospital beds became something of a sore point for Canadian manufacturers. It was decided that the beds would be purchased in the United States. "There was a tremendous amount of lobbying," said Diane Stewart, director of nursing. The manufacturers "particularly wanted that contract. We were able to prove to Mr. Blackburn ... that those beds [in the United States] ... were most [suitable]. ... He supported us to the end of the world on that."[25]

Blackburn also spent a period in the United States when he examined closely the companies involved in the production of hospital equipment. Patrick Blewett, executive director of the hospital, found Blackburn to be a man who left nothing to chance: "We were looking to purchase a new CT scanner and he came along with us to visit General Electric and also went to the large American radiological meeting to look at all the equip- ment that was there. [He] brought back not only brochures on equipment but also looked at the financial stability of the com- panies with whom we were planning to do business. That was kind of indicative of the person."[26]

Blackburn's capacity for thoroughness and his eye for detail often made him a demanding Health Association president. When the hospital was about to open its doors, a directive from the Ontario Ministry of Health stipulated that 60 of the hospi- tal's 451 patient beds should not be in operation. The govern- ment's objective was to reduce health-care costs. Blackburn, who often lamented the notion of voluntary hospitals in the prov- ince being brought under ever increasing government surveil- lance, disagreed with the health ministry's decree. He saw the government's action as another example of needless meddling. He explained: "We feel that it is uneconomic to hold out of service available brand new beds which are so well supported by the most modern diagnostic and treatment services. Operating costs reductions available in this hospital through this reduc- tion in patient beds are minimal."[27]

Later Patrick Blewett, the hospital's executive director, was able to get 30 of the 60 beds opened following negotiations in Toronto. Blewett was boastful before the hospital association's board of directors of his accomplishment. When he broke the news, Blackburn listened and then asked ponderously, "Patrick, how come only 30, what happened to the others?" When the meeting broke up, Blewett wryly remarked to Blackburn that he was off to see about the remaining 30 beds. To this Blackburn responded, "Patrick, you have no remorse at all, have you?" Blackburn was later to remark to Bill Brady, a CFPL radio execu- tive who served the hospital in a public relations capacity: "You know, Bill, you have to kick Patrick in the ass once in a while."[28]

The official opening of University Hospital occurred on 21 September 1972. The late arrival of Ontario's premier, William

Davis, distressed Blackburn on this formal occasion. The proceedings that included several speeches by prominent dignitaries were well underway when a noisy helicopter carrying the premier passed overhead. At the time the hospital had no helipad. The helicopter landed on a grassy knoll next to a nearby parking lot after causing an excruciating racket that drowned out the speaker at the moment. Davis then was driven the short distance to the opening ceremonies. Some of the guests were amused at the premier's grand entrance. Not Blackburn. "I don't think W.J. ever forgave him," Bill Brady recalled. "He thought it was gauche. His comment to me later was, 'that was not necessary for Bill to do that.'"[29]

Gold keys that fit the hospital's front door were presented to Dr. Wilder Penfield, director emeritus of the Montreal Neurological Institute, and to Blackburn as president of the Health Association. "I don't know what I'll do with it," said Blackburn. "I might have it framed and keep it in my home. We certainly don't need two keys."[30] At the opening Blackburn acknowledged the contributions from the public and government in support of the hospital. The federal and provincial governments contributed some $33 million in about equal shares. The Richard Ivey Foundation in London put up $2.4 million, the major private donation. The Health Association's contribution was $3 million.

Reflecting on the success of University Hospital, which added a new prestige to London as a city, Harold Warwick remarked: "I don't for a moment believe that [London] would have achieved the eminence it has as Canada's main transplant centre ... unless University Hospital had developed. Walter could see all points of view. He was scrupulously fair too I felt to all people concerned. . . . Fitting in teaching with the service aspect is not an easy thing."[31]

In his final annual report to the association's board of directors in May 1973, which Blackburn described as his "swan song," he said it was time for him to assume a less active role and pay more attention to family matters: "I appreciate immensely the opportunity to serve in the several capacities entrusted to me; it has been the busiest and most satisfying period of my life."[32]

More than a decade later the hospital would build a separate multi-organ transplant unit that carried Blackburn's name, a testimony to his contribution.

Besides the support he gave to London's educational and medical institutions throughout his career, Blackburn also nurtured the growth of London's artistic community. He preferred to offer his support privately. In the early 1970s he must have had a sense of satisfaction as he watched the growth of the London Civic Symphony, which he helped to rescue financially in its early years. The symphony evolved from a group of part-time community musicians to a fully professional orchestra, later called Orchestra London. Following the Second World War, the London Civic Symphony experienced financial difficulties and its conductor Bruce Sharpe resigned. Blackburn helped to keep the organization in existence.

In a phone call to Millard "Mac" McBain, who was chairman of the London Kiwanis Club music committee, Blackburn suggested he attempt to build community support for the symphony. *The Free Press* publisher hardly knew McBain, having met him on only a couple of occasions at the local Chamber of Commerce. McBain was heavily involved at the time with a mass choir oratorial project that included 550 singers from 62 choirs and symphony musicians. When McBain asked Blackburn why he had contacted him, Blackburn replied: "You have the only committee that . . . is properly organized to be able to cope with the crisis at the moment."[33] Blackburn offered to donate $500 immediately for the symphony and an additional $1500 later to assist the committee, if it fell somewhat short in its attempt to gain community-wide financial support. All of this he insisted should be kept confidential.

"We did call some of the symphony members together with the members of our committee," said McBain. "[We] told them if they would select a conductor who would have the confidence of the community that we would try to sell . . . the idea of an association with a board of directors representing the varying organizations and groups throughout the community. This was done. Martin Boundy was the man they selected as the conductor." Reflecting upon the incident, McBain wondered how often

Blackburn might have adopted this kind of practice: "Anything [Blackburn] felt he wanted to support, he undoubtedly did it through someone else who he thought probably could do it more effectively . . . than if he tried to do it . . . [with] the limitations that went with being a media [owner] and so on."

Another Londoner prominent in artistic circles, Libby Murray, recalled that Blackburn tended to avoid the acceptance of a seat on boards of arts organizations: "I think in that way it kept him a little more remote. Also I don't think he wanted that kind of visibility. He wasn't a man who joined boards for the sake of having his name on a list." At his *Free Press* office Blackburn frequently entertained delegations representing artistic groups involved in fund-raising. These representatives were inclined occasionally to question the comments or remarks of newspaper critics and reviewers. Blackburn supported the arts in a corporate sense, but tried to refrain from interfering in matters related to editorial decision making. "He made it very clear he was the publisher," said Murray. "He was not the person who set that kind of policy. He would direct you to a features editor or someone like that."[34]

Perhaps next to the Investors Club, the theatre crowd gave Blackburn his most pleasurable moments away from the pressures of business. Murray remembered him "entering the spirit" of numerous events with enormous enthusiasm: "I have seen him at costume parties where he was just super. . . . Maybe in his public posture he tended to be very dignified and rather remote and proper. . . . [But] he was not a stuffy person at all. He was very warm, very affectionate towards friends."

Blackburn especially enjoyed the ballet and attended the Stratford Festival regularly. His wife, Marjorie, an English major at Western, often took the text of a Shakespeare play to the theatre: "If the first scene or two is familiar, you are going to get off to an easy start, especially with Shakespeare. Your ear tunes into the rhythm and the music of the language." Privately with the publisher, his wife could be hard on *Free Press* reviewers and critics of local theatre: "Sometimes [I] got upset because I felt the criticism was unjust at that point . . . in the development of the theatre." On the literary side, Blackburn enjoyed *The New*

Yorker magazine. His wife explained: "I often read to him in the car when we were going along. . . . We would start with the 'Talk of the Town' where all the high standards of journalism [are], not only in the point of view but in the quality of the writing itself. . . . That is how he would catch up on things."[35]

Although Blackburn was reluctant to bow to community pressure from artists and other self-interest groups, he did encourage editorials that commended individual achievement he considered important. "The publisher . . . had individuals whom he felt deserved a lot of credit in the community," said Norm Ibsen, editorial page editor. "[These were] people whom he thought we should react favourably to when they spoke out. . . . Allyn Taylor was one and E.V. Buchanan was another. He thought the community owed people like that a lot. They deserved an occasional editorial pat on the back."[36] These were generally prominent figures whose roots, like Blackburn's, were deep in the community.

Blackburn's generous financial support to cultural organizations within the community represented only a small segment of the range of regional and national activities he and his company assisted financially. Helen Daly, the corporate secretary, kept two, three-ringed binders for Blackburn, one marked "personal" and the other "company," to record the various amounts of money given to the different organizations over the years. The corporate donations policy stipulated that 60 per cent of the company's contribution to any project should come from the print operation with the remaining 40 percent charged to the broadcasting wing of the company. This 60/40 split was seemingly related to revenues and profits at that time; in 1988 corporate donations were split on an even 50/50 basis between print and broadcast.

During a two-year period, in the early 1970s, for example, the company gave $71,000 to three groups, the London Health Association, which received $39,000, Theatre London and the London Symphony Orchestra. In 1972 the sum of $10,000 was given to St. Paul's Cathedral in London. Over the years other religious bodies including the Talbot Street Baptist and Holy Trinity Ukrainian Greek Orthodox churches also had received smaller donations. Among the hundreds of organizations that received financial support were the University of Western Ontario, Western's business school, the University of Toronto, the Banff Centre School of Fine Arts, the Canadian Mental Health Association, the Canadian Diabetic Association and the World Wildlife Fund, to name only a handful.

By the mid-1970s after the purchase of the Wingham electronic media and the opening of University Hospital, Blackburn was obviously thinking seriously about the future and the next generation of family members who would be in charge of the newspaper and broadcasting operations. He also turned again to something that had festered in the back of his mind for years: *total* control of his communications empire.

It will be recalled that Mrs. Elsie Lester, at one time a resident of North Madison, Ohio, had received ten shares in 1939 from the estate of her mother, Philippa Mathewson, and an additional share from Philippa's husband, George, after his death in March of that same year. At the time of her death, Mrs. Lester had lived at High Point, North Carolina, where Blackburn travelled to discuss valuation of the shares with Thomas, her husband.

The fact that George Mathewson's father, Henry, had been an early shareholder in the London newspaper, dating back to the days of Josiah Blackburn, had a considerable bearing on the negotiations. Blackburn showed a loyalty towards individuals such as Mathewson, whose connection with the newspaper dated from its early beginnings. He did not adopt a strictly business-like posture with Lester. Blackburn appeared to be preoccupied with what he felt the Lester estate should be paid rather than a desire to obtain simply the most favourable market price for the shares. In the end on 8 March 1974, he purchased the eleven shares of The London Free Press Holdings Limited, held by the estate of Elsie Lester, from her husband Thomas H. Lester, for $225,000 in United States funds.[37] Blackburn now had 900 of the 1200 common shares of LFPH. Only the 300 shares held by the Southam company were still outstanding.

Regardless of how consumed he was by business or his com-

munity involvements, Blackburn maintained close social contact with the Investors Club, that coterie of London individuals
from the business community where he could lighten up. Now
in their riper years, the Investors enjoyed recalling the club's
beginnings at the start of the Second World War and some of the
activities they undertook. They could often turn a meeting at
the usually sedate London Hunt Club into a vibrant social gathering. On one occasion the Investors put on an exotic meal of
Chinese food. A group went to Chinatown in Toronto and
ordered some twenty-five pounds of rice, enough to feed about
500 people. The cooks at Wong's cafe in London prepared the
meal. As owner of a radio station, Blackburn naturally had
access to an extensive record collection and he provided the
Chinese music. Although perhaps not one of their more imagi-
native events, it was still a memorable occasion for the Investors
with the waiters at the Hunt Club in Chinese regalia serving the
oriental dishes.

In the mid-1970s, he also found time for trips to England
and Europe. Blackburn preferred to visit historical sites and
enjoyed superb restaurants. On one of these journeys abroad
Blackburn and his wife, Marjorie, accompanied by their friends
Mel Pryce, Fred Jenkins and their respective spouses, Ruth and
Sally, dined at an Italian restaurant in London's Soho district.
"We were escorted into the basement," Fred Jenkins remembered. "Walter's nose was about this high. He liked better restaurants than this." Moreover, the three wives were in a giddy mood
which did not alleviate Blackburn's discomfort. "We all ordered
Italian food," said Jenkins, "and Walter ordered partridge I
think, and the women were laughing. That wasn't one of Walter's
nights."[38]

CHAPTER SEVEN

A Life-Time Ambition Fulfilled
1974 – 1976

*T*HE GROWTH OF concentration in the Canadian mass media was a subject of extensive debate during the 1970s. The focus was on the phenomenon of cross-media holdings, the common ownership of newspaper-broadcasting entities, group-owned broadcasting stations and the expansion of large newspaper chains. Walter Blackburn emerged as a leading voice for independent newspapers at a time when most dailies had fallen under chain ownership. London, Ontario, remained one of the few Canadian cities where a family, whose ancestors dated back to the mid-nineteenth century, continued to own and operate the community's daily newspaper.

Blackburn argued that an independent, locally owned newspaper had a corresponding responsibility to be responsive to the region it served. Decisions that pertained to the newspaper's level of service could be made with a full understanding of the regional environment, not in some remote head office. The more independent the newspaper, the greater its freedom from political and community pressure.

Blackburn was skeptical of widely owned media companies that might have to consider shareholders' profits ahead of media service. He was also uneasy about the potential influence the Southam and Thomson organizations could wield within newspaper organizations such as Canadian Press. A prominent lawyer and former CP solicitor, J.J. Robinette, remembered

Blackburn's "fiercely independent" attitude: "He did speak [especially] in the later days for the independent newspaper."[1]

For the most part, generational continuity in family newspaper operations had given way to economies of scale. A newspaper chain, through both its talent and resources, had a decided advantage over a single owner in the distribution of its operating costs. Tax legislation also spurred media concentration. Succession duties had often forced the sale of a family-owned newspaper, almost invariably to a group or chain, to help pay the substantial taxes that followed upon the death of the owner.

Blackburn had been especially concerned about this aspect of media ownership. He had tried unsuccessfully to get Senator Keith Davey, chairman of the Special Senate Committee on Mass Media, to take appropriate action: "I and others drew to Davey's attention the basic problem which is the estate taxes which force private owners to sell."[2] To avoid the succession duties, Blackburn had frozen his estate in 1959. This action gave him voting control over the enterprise but removed him from the ownership aspect of the business.

Along with the economic aspects of media ownership, Blackburn remained sensitive to the deleterious effects of editorial concentration, always perceived as a potential danger in the kind of enterprise he operated. "As the newspaper publisher I am responsible for the editorial policy ... and accept that responsibility," he said. "I also have to be aware ... that, if I were to throw Blackburn's views around in all the family-owned media, I [would] get into difficulty ... I encourage ... [the three media] as a matter of policy to compete and place no restrictions whatsoever on true competition."[3]

In his day-to-day management of the media operation, Blackburn seldom was seen in the radio premises of the York Street building that housed both the newspaper, AM and FM radio stations. However, the notable exception to this behaviour was his appearance in the radio studios during the night of virtually every civic, provincial and federal election. Just as he was extraordinarily cautious about the newspaper's endorsement of political parties, so too did he expect CFPL radio to provide thorough campaign and election-night coverage of voting returns.

The Free Press station CJGC, forerunner of CFPL, had been a pioneer in election coverage on radio ever since the federal campaign of 29 October 1925. The station provided up-to-the-minute reports of area riding results and national returns as well. Its successor, CFPL, continued this approach. In the 1970s the station adopted a more adventuresome practice. The station endorsed parties and candidates at election time. This kind of electronic endorsement was rare among private broadcasters in Canada. Such decisions were taken after the radio station's editorial board under the then news director, Gord Whitehead, had considered the parties' stands on the central issues in the campaign. The 1974 federal election, which saw Pierre Trudeau win his third consecutive campaign, was illustrative of the contrasting editorial stances *The Free Press* and CFPL radio adopted.

With the exception of the 1963 federal election, *The Free Press* tended to support the Conservative Party at election time. When Pierre Trudeau arrived on the national political scene, in Gordon Donaldson's memorable phrase, "like a stone through a stained-glass window," Blackburn was cautiously optimistic about the level of political leadership he would provide.[4] As Trudeaumania subsided and the idol began to develop feet of clay, *The Free Press* publisher had misgivings about both the prime minister's style and his approach to government. Clearly Blackburn did not agree with many aspects of Trudeau's philosophy of government.

Norm Ibsen, the newspaper's editorial page editor, recalled: "He was disappointed in Trudeau very quickly. The style of . . . [Trudeau] of course was a little alien to everything 'W.J.' represented. He always had a sort of underlying suspicion of Quebec. He felt Quebec had a disproportionate influence on national affairs [and held] the notion that politicians were always out to appease Quebec."[5]

Still Blackburn seemed to recognize the importance of providing thorough coverage of Quebec politics through both his own newspaper and the Canadian Press. At the time of the Quebec referendum on 20 May 1980, he encouraged CP to streamline its service to provide a fuller account of the principal developments taking place in that province. Blackburn wanted three additional reporters to provide Quebec coverage. Their reports would be filed to CP members as an extra service. However, a number of the smaller newspapers in CP considered his suggestion an unnecessary expense.[6]

In the 1974 federal election *The Free Press* did not give its outright backing to any political party. Instead it adopted a neutral approach three days before the 8 July election. The paper argued that "Canada needs a balanced majority government." At the same time it noted that such an outcome was "unlikely to happen." The editorial clearly reflected Blackburn's concerns about the lack of regional balance in the federal system and the heavy reliance of the Liberal Party on the province of Quebec. "The Liberals gained their razor-thin edge in 1972 with overwhelming Quebec support and with only token representation out west. In fact, in terms of seats, they won only Quebec."[7]

In contrast to *The Free Press*, the CFPL radio editorial heard on 5 July gave unequivocal support to the Liberal Party: "CFPL radio favours a Liberal majority government on July 8th. A majority government is essential so that the party in power can provide vigorous leadership. The Liberal Party has the talent and leader best able to deal with the present day economic ills and maintain a healthy degree of national unity." The radio editorial raised strong doubts with the following question: Was "the prices and incomes program proposed by [Conservative leader] Robert Stanfield ... an adequate replacement for the selective measures and supply stimulus advanced by Pierre Trudeau?"[8] At the time the editorial heard on radio was a major irritant for the numerous Tory supporters in London. Its contents naturally did not coincide with Blackburn's confrères at the London Hunt Club and other local Tory bastions. Still the 1974 election gave credence to Blackburn's repeated assertions before regulatory bodies that uniformity in editorial positions need not necessarily result from commonly owned media. Blackburn deliberately had structured his organization to nurture editorial independence.

Yet by the mid-1970s the trend towards concentration became even clearer. There were even instances of some newspaper chains taking over other chains. Looking back in 1980 on what it described as a "fateful decade," the Royal Commission on Newspapers, under the chairmanship of Thomas Kent, under-lined the persistent problem: "In the old sense of head-to-head competition between similar dailies in the same morning or afternoon market, competition no longer exists at all."[9]

Blackburn's career served as an exceptional counterpoint to the general economic trend that had occurred in Canadian media. While leading newspaper chains swallowed up indepen-dent dailies, and major broadcasting groups acquired local radio stations, *The Free Press* publisher chose to march to the beat of a different drummer. In fact, going directly against the flow, Blackburn actually purchased shares away *from* the Southam chain — that 25 percent interest in his family newspaper that went back to the days just after Confederation. This initiative in 1975 allowed him to fulfill a life-long ambition, "an instinctive desire to get the ownership back in the family."[10]

The history of the Blackburn-Southam connection is worth a brief review. William Southam, the founder of the Southam newspaper dynasty, had formed a partnership with Josiah Black-burn, John Kingsley Clare and Henry Mathewson under the title "The London Free Press Printing and Publishing Company" in 1871. Southam had subsequently sold his interest in 1877 when he went to Hamilton and acquired a 50 per cent interest in the *Spectator* newspaper. The London Free Press Printing Company was incorporated in October 1878. In 1907 Southam had bought back a 25 per cent interest in *The London Free Press*.

In the early 1930s there had been attempts on the part of both the Blackburn and Southam families to gain total control of the London media enterprise. But no agreement was reached. Arthur Blackburn, Walter's father, refused flatly to sell. Neither did the Southam company wish to relinquish its healthy 25 per cent interest. After Walter Blackburn succeeded his father, though he often thought about it, apparently there were no serious discussions relating to the purchase of stock until the mid-1970s. The negotiations in the spring of 1975 were seem-ingly prompted by Blackburn's guess that the Southam com-pany, which had planned to proceed with a new plant for the

Hamilton Spectator, might be open to an offer. Blackburn had learned that the company's expansion plans could require 20 to 25 million dollars in financing. He reasoned that Southam might be in a receptive mood and willing to sell if an agreement could be struck.[11]

The two central figures in the 1975 negotiations, Blackburn and St. Clair Balfour Sr., chairman of Southam Press Limited, were not only long-time business associates but also close friends. Balfour had begun to attend *Free Press* annual meetings as the Southam representative in the early 1950s. He had become a member of the board of directors upon the resignation of Arthur Ford some ten years later. Blackburn and Balfour were similar in many ways; aristocratic, intensely proud of their families' newspaper tradition and both decidedly reserved and formal in demeanour. "I had a long and happy, close relationship with Walter," said Balfour. "He paid extraordinary attention to detail personally. He dotted every *I* and crossed every *T*."[12]

Similarly Blackburn had "every regard for the Southams and the manner in which they [managed] their affairs."[13] When both men mentioned their grandfathers in conversation, a sense of family history and fascination with the past was readily apparent. Josiah Blackburn and William Southam had been partners in the early 1870s. Now more than one hundred years later their grandsons were about to sever an historic relationship unique in the newspaper industry. Fred S. Auger, a former publisher of the *Vancouver Province* and president of the Canadian Daily Newspaper Publishers Association, assessed the long-standing connection between Southam and *The London Free Press*: "Never did anything arise between Walter and Clair Balfour that was not sincere on both sides and ever led to any kind of personal animosity. There was lots of room for it . . . when you think of the inter-locking arrangement between Southam and the London organization and you think how far back the history of that went. Where it began is really a legend in Canadian publishing."[14]

At the same time Blackburn and Balfour were not always in agreement as to their methods of operation. Their outlooks were dictated largely by the different companies they headed. Blackburn perhaps enjoyed greater independence and autonomy in the operation of his private company. He could both decide the level of service and determine the extent of the profits he hoped to realize. Balfour, as president of Southam, a public company, naturally wanted to maximize profits for shareholders. This contrast in business approach led to frequent debates between the pair at board of directors' meetings in London.

William Carradine remembered a few frosty exchanges that were always followed by a friendly lunch afterwards: "Walter's feelings obviously were that the market was more important . . . that he didn't need the money and he was not prepared to meet Clair's demands for more profit." At times it was simply a case of views clashing: "So in the board meetings, it would tend to be a little of the two schools and the managers . . . Murray Brown and [myself] . . . we felt we were a bit like the ham in the sandwich at times . . . While we sympathized with Clair's beliefs that we could make a lot more money, we also obviously supported Walter's feelings . . . [namely], why squeeze the advertisers and the readers for money if it isn't absolutely necessary to do so?"[15]

Balfour was of the opinion that *The Free Press* should have returned a greater profit: "I used to make available to . . . [Walter] the comparable staffs of our newspapers of similar size. . . . I felt the . . . [*Free Press*] was over manned at that time. It didn't . . . earn the return on the investment that some of our comparable papers [earned]." Moreover, Balfour had some misgivings about Blackburn's penchant for electronics, including new presses with considerable colour capacity, and large computers. "When they brought out the computers initially, I thought that they over-computered at the time," he said. "[They] over invested in hardware based on our experience of what one needed to do the job that I thought he was proposing to do."[16]

While Blackburn seemed to understand Balfour's position, *The Free Press* owner could be unusually single-minded when he came to determine the nature and scope of the family business. Though occasionally in disagreement, he still listened carefully to Balfour. The Southam president brought to *The Free Press* a backdrop of newspaper developments in a dozen or so cities throughout Canada. Through Balfour, Blackburn had a window on the industry which he appeared to welcome and from which he learned. In his assessment of the Southam company, Blackburn remarked: "They are a public company and naturally one of their main interests was to do the right thing by their own shareholders ... maybe at times they thought our standards were higher than they needed to be."[17] Still a close, personal friendship between the two men flowed from their business association, and manifested itself in numerous holiday trips the two publishers and their wives took throughout the world.

Before examining the manner in which the negotiations were conducted and how the price of $11.25 million dollars was arrived at for the Southam shares, the financial state of the three wholly owned subsidiaries of The London Free Press Holdings Limited (LFPH) should be considered. In 1974 the after-tax earnings (profit) of the three companies were as follows: London Free Press Printing Company Limited, $1,229,242; CFPL Broadcasting Limted, $876,214; and CKNX Broadcasting Limited, $183,194. Blackburn's financial advisers had placed a fair market value of $600,000 on the company's 50 per cent investment in Chatham Cable TV Limited.

After assessing the relevant factors, such as the maintainable future earnings, to determine the fair market value of all of the shares of LFPH, the figure was set at approximately $23,500,000 in May 1975. This amount was based on a calculation of the current assets of LFPH that totalled $1,269,678 minus current liabilities of $394,024, leaving a figure of $875,654. The $23,500,000 figure also included an estimate of the market value of the holding company's investments in each of its three subsidiaries: London Free Press Printing Company Limited, $13,750,000; CFPL Broadcasting Limited, $6,800,000; and CKNX Broadcasting Limited, $1,400,000. The figure of $600,000, the value of the investment in Chatham Cable TV, was also taken into account in the figure showing the total value of the company.[18] This financial backdrop was used as a general basis to arrive at the value of the 25 per cent interest in the London Free Press Holdings Limited held by the Southam company.

Several discussions had been held among *Free Press* officials, culminating in a meeting on 6 May 1975 attended by Walter Blackburn, his daughter Martha, and son-in-law, Peter White, the vice-president of finance, Bev Lanning, and Ken Lemon, a senior partner in Clarkson Gordon and the Blackburn family's financial adviser. The participants at the meeting agreed that the Southam interest was worth approximately 6½ to 7½ million dollars. They reasoned that as much as 8 million could be paid for the 300 shares of common stock without involving a premium. At this time arrangements had been made with the Bank of Montreal for The London Free Press Holdings Limited to obtain term financing of 4 million dollars and an additional line of credit of 1 million dollars.

The following day Blackburn, Lemon and Lanning met with St. Clair Balfour and his company's representatives at Southam's office in downtown Toronto. Lemon recalled that the chemistry between Blackburn and Balfour in the board room during the negotiations was exceedingly formal: "They were the greatest of friends . . . [but] the friendship didn't really show in the transaction. It could have been two total strangers negotiating."[19] Blackburn offered 7½ million dollars for the Southam shares. (His advisers had placed the fair market value of LFPH at $23,500,000). Balfour responded promptly that the Southam asking price was 15 million dollars, double what Blackburn had proposed. "He was shocked when I told him what we wanted."[20] Southam had placed the total value of the newspaper and broadcasting operations at 60 million dollars. Their figure of 15 million was one-quarter of the amount.

At Ken Lemon's suggestion, this meeting on 7 May in Toronto also explored the possibility that The London Free Press Holdings Limited, rather than Blackburn Holdings Limited, might acquire the shares. The latter company had acquired the shares of Blackburn and his two sisters on 23 January 1959 and the 11 shares held by the Elsie Lester estate on 8 March 1974. Lemon had advanced the notion of Free Press Holdings making the acquisition as perhaps one way that Southam's asking price might be reduced.

Bev Lanning later explained to Blackburn the implications

if Free Press Holdings as opposed to Blackburn Holdings acquired the shares for redemption: "The presumption in the former case is that the bulk of the transaction would be a deemed dividend and therefore not subject to tax, while the residue, which would be a capital item, would not be large enough to incur any significant amount of capital gains tax to Southam." He also informed Blackburn that "Lemon [had] made a rough calculation that this [arrangement] might be worth as much as 1.5 million to Southam and Balfour's response was they would consider a reduction in their asking price to the extent that capital gains tax could be avoided."[21]

At the 7 May meeting in Toronto, Balfour had explained there was no particular urgency for his company to obtain the 20 to 25 million dollar financing that had prompted Blackburn to offer to purchase the shares. Both sides had also explored whether a first refusal element might reduce the newspaper chain's asking price, that is, Southam would have opportunity to match any comparable offer that Blackburn might receive, if he chose to sell his media enterprise. At the conclusion of the meeting, it was generally agreed that even with the capital gains tax avoidance possibility and a dollar value attached to a first refusal clause, the offering and the asking prices were probably still too far apart. However, Balfour, as chairman of Southam Press Limited, agreed to present Blackburn's offer of 7½ million dollars to the executive committee of the Southam board of directors.

Balfour telephoned Blackburn on 13 May, six days later, to tell him that the Executive Committee concluded unanimously that his offer was too low. Southam's tax advisers had agreed that capital gains tax could be nearly eliminated using the method of Free Press Holdings' purchase for redemption suggested by Lemon. Balfour now informed Blackburn that Southam was prepared to accept a price of 12.5 million with no first refusal clause. Near the end of the telephone conversation, Blackburn asked for three weeks to consider this new figure to which Balfour agreed.

On 20 May Blackburn, Lemon and Lanning held a meeting to discuss the changed circumstances and the price that Balfour had conveyed. After this session Blackburn, who frequently made notes as reminders to himself, wrote: "Ken [Lemon] suggests going back (if at all) at 10.5 and settle at 11.5, assuming we want to buy and are prepared to pay a premium price."[22] Lemon obviously considered the Southam price too high.

The next meeting between *Free Press* and Southam representatives took place on 2 June 1975. Blackburn, Lemon and Lanning this time met with Southam executives Gordon N. Fisher and Brian Shelley. Fisher, president of Southam, was a great-grandson of William Southam and son of Philip Fisher who had served previously as president of the company. With reference to Balfour's 13 May phone call, Blackburn explained to the meeting that he felt the 12.5 million dollar price was more than *The Free Press* should pay. Blackburn then offered 10 million dollars for the quarter interest in LFPH. The notion of Southam having first refusal rights was again discussed. Blackburn held to his earlier position that he would prefer no such clause in any agreement. Subsequent to the Blackburn-Balfour discussions, Fisher had discussed this matter with Balfour. Both Balfour and Fisher had agreed that there was no need for their company to request any right of first refusal.

After Blackburn made his offer of 10 million dollars, the matter of valuation of *The Free Press* print and broadcast operations received extensive discussion at the 2 June meeting. Fisher maintained that the 12.5 million dollar figure was fair. Southam had "if anything bent over backwards" to reach a reasonable price.[23] He held to his company's earlier stand that *The Free Press* operations were worth at least 60 million dollars. The proposed price of 12.5 million was as low as Southam could go.

It was obvious that the two sides were in major disagreement over the earning capacity of *The London Free Press*. Southam continued to take the view that the newspaper should earn at least 2 million dollars after tax as opposed to its actual current earnings of just over 1.2 million in the year ended 31 August 1974. Southam did not accept Blackburn's argument that the earning capacity of a newspaper, such as *The Free Press*, with morning and evening editions and the accompanying costs, was not as great as a single edition paper of the same revenue size.

In the end Fisher suggested that the difference between the 10 million and the 12.5 million prices might be split. Blackburn, Lemon and Lanning then met separately. Blackburn agreed to split the difference; a purchase price of $11,250,000 was suggested. Fisher recommended the acceptance of this price to his executive committee and board of directors. A Southam offer to finance the transaction was discussed but formed no part of the final agreement.

By 4 June 1975 a deal was in the making. Fisher informed Blackburn in a telephone conversation that he had contacted all but one member of Southam's executive committee. They were prepared to accept the offer subject to execution of a satisfactory agreement including provision for approval by the Canadian Radio Television Commission.

Clearly representatives of Southam Press Limited were aware of Blackburn's eagerness to regain the 300 shares that would give his family total control of the London enterprise, something that had been his life-long ambition. With the purchase, Blackburn Holdings had done just that, and achieved a certain, intangible peace of mind. Free Press Holdings paid $11,250,000 to the Southam company for its quarter interest. LFPH subsequently cancelled the shares.

The agreement reached with Southam brought to an end an historic family relationship in the newspaper industry. On 3 June 1975 Gordon Fisher wrote to Blackburn an expression of his appreciation "for the friendliness that you have continued to show towards us, specifically during our recent negotiations." Fisher explained that he was reluctant to sever the 100-odd year relationship between the two families: "For reasons which I think you already understand, neither Clair nor I will feel at all happy about separating the historical partnership between our two families. I am glad that, having established our willingness to deal, we were able to complete the transaction on what I am satisfied is a completely reasonable basis for both parties."[24]

The various *Free Press* operating companies, London Free Press Printing Company Limited, CFPL Broadcasting Limited and CKNX Broadcasting Limited, had liquid funds available totalling $4,750,000. The balance of the price of the shares acquired from Southam, $6,500,000, was borrowed from the Bank of Montreal on a seven-year term basis that required quarterly repayments of approximately $232,000.[25] For tax purposes, the operating companies rather than the holding company borrowed the money to pay Southam. The interest then could be deducted from their earnings, whereas Free Press Holdings had no taxable income from which to deduct interest expenses incurred through borrowing.[26] The borrowing was arranged through the operating companies that would lend or pay the proceeds, in the form of dividends, to Free Press Holdings. LFPH then paid Southam Press Limited the required amount.

After he had made the payment to Southam, Blackburn phoned his longtime friend John Ralph and, in his characteristic mild manner, remarked: "I have just signed a cheque for eleven million [*sic*] dollars." In Ralph's view, "Walter was never [really] prominent as a civic figure until he bought out the Southams in 1975."[27] Blackburn, as an owner of a private media enterprise, was always discreet about his public spending and the financial extent of his holdings. "He wore his money well," said C.N. "Bud" Knight, who headed the radio division at the time of the Southam deal.[28] The Southam transaction touched off considerable speculation in London and the rest of the country as to the financial worth of his communications empire. Obviously, the figure depended on one's perspective, as the negotiations indicated, anywhere between 23½ and 60 million. A neutral evaluation, all things considered, would have put it at around 35 million.

With the cancellation of the 300 Southam shares, Blackburn Holdings held the full 900 common shares of Free Press Holdings that it had acquired earlier. Once again, it was all in the family.

The acquisition of the 300 shares despite the steep price was some solace for Blackburn's fiercely independent spirit. His proud mood was apparent in his 1975 annual report to shareholders: "Perhaps the most important event of the year was the repurchase for cancellation of the shares owned by Southam Press Limited in The London Free Press Holdings Limited. This 25% minority interest had existed for about 100 years, but on

August 14, 1975 the ownership of your companies is once again 100% in the Blackburn family. The cost of this move . . . was financed by both internal resources and bank borrowings."[29]

The regaining of the Southam shares left an indelible imprint on Blackburn's family business, and was his last major corporate undertaking as publisher. In the next few years he would again become heavily involved in Canadian Press, while at the same time beginning to play a more detached role in the daily management of the family business.

Blackburn was about to enter the quiescent years of his life. The business had always come first. Now there would be additional time for family and his six grandchildren. In the meantime, the newspaper continued to grow and keep pace with the new technology of the computer age. On 5 December 1975 the last hot metal page was cast when the newspaper moved to electronic editing and photo typesetting. An application was filed with the Canadian Radio Television Commission in October 1975 to establish an FM radio station in Wingham, estimated to cost $225,000. CRTC approval would come two years later.

Blackburn seemed to sense it was time to revitalize the business internally, and so in 1975 he instituted significant personnel changes to the board of directors of The London Free Press Holdings Limited as the business prepared to move into the fourth generation of the Blackburn family. Blackburn's daughter, Martha, the fourth-generation publisher, joined the boards of Free Press Holdings Limited, London Free Press Printing Company Limited and CFPL Broadcasting Limited. "Dad tended to keep Free Press matters separate [from family]," she recalled. "In fact he didn't really ask me, he just sort of put me on [the boards] in 1975. . . . Once he felt comfortable with my interest in the business, then he began to make the motions . . . to see that financially the business would remain with [my] generation."[30]

In June 1976 Blackburn relinquished the presidency of the newspaper, a position which he had held for 40 years, to Peter White who assumed responsibility for day-to-day administration of *The Free Press*. White now became president and general manager. Blackburn continued to hold the titles of chairman and publisher.

In April 1974 Blackburn and his wife, Marjorie, saw construction begin on a new house the couple had planned together. They left their previous dwelling at 326 Victoria Street and entered 11 Kingspark Crescent, an elegant home with a backyard view of the 16th fairway of the Hunt Club golf course, on 15 May 1975. There would be more time for travel and golf in the days ahead, the game he enjoyed winning against his friends and business associates. They played for big stakes — ten cents a hole!

Blackburn's involvement with the Commonwealth Press Union (CPU), an organization he had served as vice-chairman of the Canadian section, afforded him and his wife opportunity for extensive travel. In the autumn of 1974, the couple took a worldwide trip that included stops in New Delhi, Bangkok, Singapore and in Hong Kong where the CPU meeting of press representatives was held that year.

But the most memorable trip that Blackburn and his wife enjoyed during his final years was in 1981 when they holidayed with St. Clair and Helen Balfour in Australia. Marjorie Blackburn recalled: "Australia is a revelation to anyone. You are introduced to a whole new world, basically an English one. Here is a country with wonderful public buildings and beautiful gardens. When you are older, your capacity for enjoying it is much increased." The repurchase of the Southam shares had fulfilled a long held wish; Blackburn now prepared himself to take a little more time to smell the roses.

CHAPTER EIGHT

◇————————————◇

The Final Years
1976 – 1984

W ALTER BLACKBURN liked to describe himself as a "liberal Conservative" or a "critical Conservative."[1] He believed in social welfare measures that aided the sick and the elderly. He felt that governments should see that proper medical care was provided. But Blackburn could never understand why wealthy Canadians including himself should be entitled to the old age pension. At the same time he was a fiscal conservative who believed governments should behave responsibly and strive for balanced budgets. Unfavourable economic indicators, especially the Trudeau government's introduction of wage and price controls in 1975, had induced extreme caution in the man.

An avowed defender of the restraint policies advanced by Louis Rasminsky, the former Bank of Canada governor, Blackburn repeatedly issued warnings to his staff that the country was living beyond its means. Blackburn urged editorials and stories that brought home to the public the notions espoused by the governor of the bank: inflation had to be brought under control and restraint must be practised. Ultimately governments would be called to account for reckless spending.

Norm Ibsen, *The Free Press* editorial page editor, said that "[Blackburn] was a great admirer of Louis Rasminsky, so much so that on occasion he had us run the governor's annual reports a couple of times ... in full. ... [The publisher] thought [Rasminsky] was a great prod of the national conscience ...

169

[but] some of us were not too keen on running these long governor's reports which were couched in language that really the average reader didn't respond to very well."[2]

Blackburn had voiced concern about the Canadian economy since the 1950s. His misgivings lasted into his later years. In September 1979, the year he turned sixty-five, he told the General Committee of The Free Press Employees Association that the problems Rasminsky had talked about were still with the country: "We're mortgaging our future and the future of our children and have been doing so for many years."[3]

The acquisition of the Southam shares had occurred when economic conditions were tight. Blackburn never liked to incur debt in the operation of his enterprise, so his decision to expose himself to the bank was a commentary on his keen interest in regaining the 300 shares held by the Southam company. While economic conditions did not seem favourable, Blackburn's sense of timing had its benefits. When the bank loan of several million dollars was repaid, inflation worked to his advantage. If he had taken a similar course when the recession struck in the early 1980s, the move could have created greater hardship. Peter White, then president of *The Free Press*, underlined the Southam deal as an example of Blackburn's sense of the marketplace: "In our favour, frankly, was inflation because we were paying . . . [the debt] off with inflated dollars. . . . His gut feel told him it was right to do it and he did it."[4]

Nevertheless, Blackburn was anxious to get rid of the debt his companies faced following the Southam transaction. In order to help raise the required cash and clean up the debt as quickly as possible, several steps were taken to sell those financial interests no longer considered necessary to Blackburn's enterprise.

In 1977 The London Free Press Holdings Limited sold to Canadian Cablesystems Limited its 50 per cent interest in Chatham Cable TV Limited. Although the Southam deal eventually prompted this sale, the move had been contemplated as early as August 1973. Blackburn had suggested to the board of directors that the company divest itself of ownership in cable. At that time the holding company wanted $600,000 for its common shares in the Chatham cable system. Murray Brown, president of CFPL Broadcasting Limited, had argued strongly for the company removing itself from the cable business. He thought that they were competing against themselves. With its ownership of television stations in Wingham and London, the company remained concerned about the extent of audience fragmentation that could result from the establishment of cable systems.

While Blackburn had filed no formal opposition to the licensing of cable in the Wingham area with the Canadian Radio Television Commission (CRTC), the company made the CRTC aware of cable's capacity to inhibit the local service of CKNX–TV. These views were expressed while Free Press Holdings continued to be a half-owner of the Chatham cable system. But Brown wanted to be free to speak his mind. "In addition to that, we . . . were anxious to get our bank loan paid off. We were seeking funds from every source we had."[5]

Other divestitures included the disposal of property at the corner of Queens Avenue and Richmond Street in downtown London, near a former site of *The Free Press* building, and the selling of twenty-six acres of land located at the television site in the city's southwest section.

The arrival of Blackburn's daughter, Martha, as a member of the board of directors in 1975, almost coincided with the departure of St. Clair Balfour following the Southam transaction. Blackburn was sorry to see Balfour, his friend, leave after their long association: "[However] there was no reason why he would want to remain and in fact we specified that he should not remain."[6] Blackburn frequently went into detailed explanations on the background of issues to familiarize his daughter with all facets of the media operation. The fourth-generation publisher was now in training for her future position. "I can remember Dad going into the longest [explanations]," she said. "This [was] quite tedious at times but . . . I never said 'you know I know all that or you don't have to tell me.' I had too high a regard for him . . . [and] this was important to him . . . slowly he realized that I understood the background."[7]

Following his relinquishing of the presidency of the newspaper to his son-in-law, Peter White, in 1976, Blackburn eased up

171

considerably in his day-to-day control of the paper. Instead, he turned his hand to other favourite projects. These included serving on the boards of the London Health Association, Canada Trust and the John P. Robarts Research Institute. This latter agency focused its research on stroke and aging, immunology, heart and circulation. Another distraction from daily *Free Press* matters was his chairmanship of Canadian Press's assessment committee between 1978 and 1982 in which role he led in the difficult task of establishing a new rate structure for member newspapers in CP.

He preferred more time for family, including his six grandchildren. The three children of his daughter, Susan Toledo, were all teenagers; 18-year-old Tony, Kate, age 16, and Kyra, 15. The children of Peter and Martha White were younger; 12-year-old Richard and daughters Sarah, age 10, and Annabelle, 7. At times, he would almost dote on his grandchildren and seemed to enjoy recalling for them the family's history dating back to the days of his grandfather. A special feature on the *Free Press* publisher in the employees' newspaper, *Fourth Estate*, showed Blackburn, in his later years, at Fanshawe's Pioneer Village in London. He demonstrated for his grandchildren the operation of the Washington printing press that *The Free Press* had used in its early years.

By the late 1970s Blackburn had lost three of his closest friends who had been prominent community figures. George W. Robinson, a former chairman of the London Board of Education and city transportation commission, passed away in 1971. Peter V.V. Betts, a lawyer and director of the London Health Association died suddenly in 1975. John Rathbun, a professor of pediatrics at the University of Western Ontario and chief of staff at the War Memorial Children's Hospital, died in 1972. All of these circumstances combined to draw him closer to his immediate family.

But even with his reduced role as publisher, Blackburn continued to oversee the general policy of the newspaper. Editorial quality still concerned him. Just a few years after the Southam buy out, *The Free Press* was caught up in an imbroglio from which its reputation suffered a major setback. The newspaper was accused of tampering with the electoral process.

There were few journalistic responsibilities Walter Blackburn took more seriously than the necessity of balanced election coverage and sound editorial judgement prior to voters casting their ballots. *The Free Press*'s endorsement of political parties and candidates was a matter of the highest priority to him. For this reason, the Harry Smith affair, which involved his newspaper in an ill-conceived arrangement for the husband of an employee to stand for election to the London Board of Education, made him furious.

The Free Press decided to run a hidden candidate for the board of education in the 1978 civic election. His name was Harry Smith, the husband of Emilie Smith, the newspaper's education reporter. In a confidential memo after the incident, *The Free Press* editor-in-chief, William Heine, explained the aim of the exercise to Jack Briglia, the managing editor: "[It] was intended to provide a dramatic example to the voting public of London of the relative ineffectiveness of a significant portion of the vote for members of the board of education and to bolster a case for the ward system for election to the board" rather than on a city-wide basis.[8]

Smith took the normal course of filing nomination papers and qualified as a candidate, with his name appearing on the ballot. But he did no campaigning. On 13 November, election day, he received 8,310 votes, finishing twentieth among the 23 contenders for 12 board seats. In its coverage of campaign meetings in the civic election, *The Free Press* consistently reported that Smith had not been in attendance.[9]

The idea to run the concealed candidate originated with Emilie Smith. Jim O'Neail, the city editor, endorsed the proposal. Briglia, the managing editor, was in Mexico on vacation at the time. Heine became aware of the incident only after nomination papers had been filed and the candidate had qualified. Heine's reaction "was deep concern, indeed a surge of fear."[10] He recognized that *The Free Press* would be accused of election tampering. Heine tried unsuccessfully to reach Blackburn but explained to Peter White what had happened. Clearly Smith was not a genuine candidate. *The Free Press* had been part of a hoax and had not levelled with its readers.

Once the die had been cast and Smith had qualified as a candidate, newspaper executives found themselves with virtually no options. Heine explained to Briglia the newspaper's dilemma: "We discussed blowing our cover, and running a story … but felt, rightly I think, that doing so would draw so much attention to Harry Smith that he might well be elected." Heine was of the opinion that *The Free Press* itself would have become an election issue, overshadowing the campaign: "We agreed that there was virtually no chance of his being elected but could think of no effective plan if he were elected. After considerable discussion, we could think of no way to stand down the candidacy without making matters worse."[11] The newspaper later broke the story, explained its position in an editorial, gave page one coverage to those critical of the dubious practice and carried several letters to the editor with both sides of the issue represented.

Blackburn had not realized what was happening until he showed up at the newspaper's editorial meeting the day following the municipal election. "The reference was made to the Harry Smith story which he hadn't even read at that point," Norm Ibsen recalled. "When he realized what we had been a party to, the colour started rising. … He was livid [because] he felt very strongly that a responsible newspaper does not interfere with the electoral process in any way."[12]

Blackburn's anger and disenchantment continued for some time. He was obviously distressed at the damage to his own reputation as publisher and to the family name. In January 1979 he issued a terse memo to Heine: "Never again is deception which involves the election process to be engaged in in the newspaper by any member of the *Free Press* staff. There shall be no exceptions and no approvals given. This particular deception has damaged the prime asset which a newspaper has, its credibility, an asset which is built up over years of development and can be lost overnight. The penalties for breach of the policy set forth above will be dismissal for cause; your staff is to be so advised."[13]

The Ontario Press Council came down hard on *The London Free Press* in an adjudication on 12 February 1979. The council's

174

ruling was perhaps the strongest since its inception in 1972. Blackburn had given solid backing to the formation of the press council, a forum for readers to appeal the judgements of publishers and editors. Now his paper was on the receiving-end of the watchdog's sharp criticism.

The council upheld three complainants in the Harry Smith affair. John Whaley, a London lawyer and unsuccessful board of education candidate in the election, Kenneth Bambrick, a journalism professor at the University of Western Ontario, and Peter Jedicke, a student and school board candidate in 1976, questioned the newspaper's approach. The council concluded: "*The London Free Press* committed a breach of journalistic ethics, meddled in the electoral process and may have altered the results by arranging to have the husband of an employee stand as a candidate in the London board of education elections.... the newspaper's action, aimed at demonstrating it would be better to elect candidates by wards than at large, was all the more mischievous since on that same election day electors were voting on a proposal to adopt the ward system."[14]

Blackburn no doubt was especially distraught when he read another section of the council's adjudication: "The action violated the trust of the community which should be able to expect that newspapers and other media will report news events accurately, fairly and fully." Blackburn was always keenly aware of his position as publisher of a newspaper in a monopoly position and its special role at election time, so the Harry Smith affair was the antithesis of his concept of proper journalistic standards and ethics. He admitted his shame as publisher of a newspaper that would do such a thing.

The press council's adjudication at the start of 1979 was a humbling experience for *The Free Press* publisher. But this same year was also to provide a special reward for Blackburn. He devised a new assessment formula for the newspapers belonging to the Canadian Press. This new rate structure determined the amounts members of the news co-operative paid for the news service. Blackburn immersed himself in the assessment committee's work. He saw his achievement as a form of compensation for his failure to become president of the news agency, a setback that haunted him until his death.

The politically sensitive issue of the charges levied on both small, medium and large newspapers in CP was almost as old as the news agency itself. The task faced by CP's assessment committee periodically was to restructure the rates charged to the various member newspapers in an equitable manner, as new circumstances developed within the newspaper industry. Blackburn, as chairman of this committee, formulated a new assessment structure that shifted assessments to a total weekly circulation concept, away from the basis of average daily circulation for CP members. The new arrangement had to take into account the size of the different papers, their costs and various publishing patterns which could range from five to seven days a week.

To understand the nature of Blackburn's accomplishment, the background to the assessment issue is worth a brief examination. When it began in 1917, CP divided its costs among daily newspaper members primarily on a population basis. City population was the original base.[15] Later circulation was introduced as an element in CP assessments. But the price that members paid to the news co-operative for the CP service remained a controversial issue. In the late 1970s, executives of the *Toronto Star*, the largest CP member, expressed sharp dissatisfaction with one assessment increase. They argued that it would be to their advantage to abandon CP and invest the money that was saved in their own service.[16] The Toronto papers frequently complained that they carried too much of the financial burden in the co-operative. The stronger members of CP were expected to help the weaker ones.

When Blackburn assumed the assessment committee chairmanship, the average daily circulation of member newspapers remained the basis for assessments. But Sunday editions of newspapers began to appear. The arrival of these papers gave rise to a further assessment problem. The Sunday circulation often tended to be much higher than the average daily circulation through the week.

After considerable thought and experimentation, Black-

burn along with Glen Witherspoon, then treasurer of CP, concluded that assessments should be based on total weekly
circulation. For example, if a newspaper publishing five days a
week had an average circulation of 20,000 a day, it would be
charged for a total of 100,000 papers. A paper publishing seven
days a week with a similar average circulation would be charged
for a total circulation of 140,000. This new formula attempted to
distribute assessments more equally. The new structure reduced
the costs slightly for smaller papers; it did not have a material
effect on the larger dailies but raised costs somewhat for the
medium-sized papers.

Blackburn's skills as a compromiser and negotiator were
apparent. He gained a consensus from the assessment committee on the new method of rates for members. He then sold the
total weekly concept to the various CP executive bodies. The
new formula was passed at the news agency's annual meeting in
May 1979. "I can recall Martin Goodman of the *Star* referring to
Walter as the man who had devised a formula that was acceptable to everyone," explained Glen Witherspoon. "[Walter] took
this very seriously. He felt that he didn't receive the recognition
[in CP] he should have. . . . It was his chance to do something for
an organization which he really treasured."[17]

Blackburn appeared to have been delighted with the
response to his initiatives. After the proposed formula received
unanimous support from the assessment committee on 19 January 1979, Paddy Sherman, publisher of the *Vancouver Province*,
wrote to Blackburn: "I didn't get a chance to say it after the . . .
meeting, but I really was highly impressed with the job you did
in the assessment formula. And to have got Clair [McCabe] to
make acceptance unanimous was as near a miracle as these old
eyes have seen for a long time."[18]

Blackburn responded to Sherman: "A pat on the back goes a
long way these days when agreement on financial affairs (and I
guess almost all other affairs of consequence) seems to be so
difficult to achieve. Budgets and attitudes are taut." At the same
time Blackburn questioned the position adopted by some newspaper chains: "Whereas I was delighted with the unanimous
vote, I feel now that we still face a problem with Thomson, and

probably with Sterling. They seem to want the *Toronto Star* to pay a larger share, with that piece of gold used to reduce further the smaller papers. Regardless of their ability to pay, they apparently place an extraordinarily low value on CP service."[19]

In early February 1979 Ross Munro, president of Canadian Press, commended Blackburn for his assessment work: "I've been going back and reviewing CP activities of recent months and I wish to express my belief to you that the most significant achievement was yours — developing the new assessment formula for the [forthcoming] Annual Meeting. It took a great deal of time, energy and thought on your part, Walter, and I speak for everyone in recognizing your contribution to our news service, which I am confident will remove the greatest single point of discontent among many of our members."[20] Blackburn replied modestly and paid tribute to CP president, Keith Kincaid, and Glen Witherspoon.

When the new assessment formula was passed at the CP annual meeting in May 1979, Blackburn was jubilant. He was unable to restrain his enthusiasm and could not remain in the meeting room at the Royal York Hotel in Toronto. Witherspoon recalled: "He went outside and told the secretarial staff, 'They have approved my formula.'" Characteristically, the following day he presented Witherspoon with a small computerized calculator as a recognition for the help he had provided. "Walter liked ... [almost] everything about CP," said Witherspoon, "except the way directors were elected."[21]

Ross Munro remembered the CP board meeting held in London, Ontario, in September 1979: Walter "held forth at some length" on the question of electing CP directors.[22] He was sensitive to the influence of newspaper chains within CP, and emerged as a spokesman for the independent newspapers. Blackburn felt that the Thomson vote had done him in back in 1968, but there appeared to be no proof of malintent toward him. Nevertheless, mindful of his bitter experience when he failed to be re-elected to the board and was not eligible to be a vice-president, Blackburn urged that a new method for the election of directors should be adopted that would relate to the assessments of member newspapers.

Walter Blackburn had the ability to choose men who were competent and dedicated, as he was, to work with him. St. Clair Balfour (top left) sat on *The London Free Press* board for many years; Huron R. Davidson (top right) had the same meticulous concern for detail as Walter and helped negotiate the buy-back of shares from Southam. Arthur R. Ford (bottom left) was mentor to Blackburn and editor-in-chief for forty-three years. Probably his closest, long-term working relationship and friendship was with Murray T. Brown (bottom right), former president of CFPL Broadcasting and still member of the operating board. LONDON FREE PRESS

A proud "W.J." stands beside the entrance to the new newspaper-broadcast building at 369 York Street, completed in 1965. The plant cost almost $7 million to build and equip, and was considered by industry analysts to be one of the most modern presses in Canada.
LONDON FREE PRESS

The composing room at *The London Free Press* building, April 1975.
LONDON FREE PRESS

The main house at Sandeman Island, which was originally purchased in 1958 and renamed "Good News". For years thereafter, and to this day, the Blackburn family used the island as a getaway to relax and enjoy nature. "W.J." loved to drive and tinker with the boats.
BLACKBURN FAMILY

Another "escape" was travel abroad; here "W.J." is at the Acropolis in Greece, April 1969, looking the well-dressed tourist, camera always in hand. JACK GOULD/BLACKBURN FAMILY

Nothing evoked greater concern and careful presentation from Blackburn
and his executives than the periodic governmental inquiries into media
ownership and regulation. Here he addresses the Kent Commission in
London, February 1981, while Peter G. White (left) and Kenneth W. Lemon
(right) listen. LONDON FREE PRESS

The General Committee of the Employees' Association, 1971. The logo has
since been modernized but the motto reads now as it did then: "Mutual
Understanding Brings Mutual Benefits." LONDON FREE PRESS

One of Blackburn's long-standing associations was with the Investors Club where he could relax with colleagues, friends, fellow businessmen and professionals from London. This photo was taken in December 1959.
BLACKBURN FAMILY

Walter and Marjorie Blackburn, with the employees, celebrate 125 years of continuous publication in London, at *The London Free Press* Employees' Association Dinner-Dance, December 1974. LONDON FREE PRESS

"W.J." with Mitchell Sharp, Minister for External Affairs in Trudeau's Liberal government, both looking pleased as punch after receiving honorary Doctor of Laws degrees from the University of Western Ontario in 1977.
BLACKBURN FAMILY

Moments later, Blackburn, ever the technological wizard, could not pass up the opportunity to explain the intricacies of a movie camera to young admirers. BLACKBURN FAMILY

Martha Grace Blackburn. After serving her apprenticeship on various boards of directors since 1975, Martha became the fourth-generation owner of the Blackburn group of companies upon the death of Walter Juxon Blackburn. The company has grown dramatically under her guidance.
BLACKBURN FAMILY

"W.J." wearing his favourite Irish sweater and playing with his second youngest grand-child, Sarah White. Guess who was left holding the pop bottle? BLACKBURN FAMILY

"Grandad" Blackburn enjoying the garden at 11 Kingspark Crescent with his youngest grandchild, Bella White, after his surgery for cancer in August 1982.
BLACKBURN FAMILY

The minutes of this CP meeting in London again under-lined Blackburn's belief that large newspaper organizations wielded undue influence through proxy voting within CP: "Mr. Blackburn said he favors a new way [for elections] that would be fairer. Thomson almost has control of the voting because of the number of its members, but would have less voting power if votes were based on assessments."[23]

Margaret Hamilton, a Thomson executive, then entered the debate: "She was disturbed at the suggestion that the Thomson block was the cause of an unsatisfactory board. If that was the case, there would have been cases where Thomson would have had more members elected to the board. Thomson usually has two directors which is not out of line considering assessment." In rebuttal, Blackburn said he wanted to make his position clear: "He was not suggesting Thomson and Southam used votes to the detriment of the board but it was necessary to face realities. The groups have exercised their power with discretion."

In the early 1980s CP did adopt a different approach for election of directors, though it still was not the method Black-burn favoured. This method was based on the practice adopted by the Canadian Daily Newspaper Publishers Association. In the past, a separate nominating committee called for nomina-tions; it then attempted to make sure a contest for directors was held in each of the geographical and language divisions of CP. This procedure was altered when the 1980 annual meeting approved bylaw amendments that empowered CP's Advisory Committee to recommend a slate of directors for approval by the annual meeting; this method replaced the earlier attempt to ensure a competition in each division. Michael Davies, pub-lisher of the independent Kingston *Whig-Standard*, said the change that allowed for a formal slate was prompted by a con-cern about bloc voting in CP elections.[24]

During the years that Blackburn headed the CP assessment committee, *The Free Press* embarked on another new venture: it entered the shopper publication business and within ten years was well on its way to the establishment of a national chain of weekly "pennysaver" advertising tabloids. Peter White along with R.A. "Sandy" Green, director of marketing for London

Free Press Printing Company Limited, had urged the entry into the shopper business. Green had joined *The Free Press* in 1976 from Alltrans Group Canada Limited, an Australian-owned international transportation company. Green undertook a market survey that found *The Free Press* could be vulnerable to competition from a well-run weekly newspaper.

Green discussed the nature of the business with Cal Tremblay, a shrewd businesswoman who headed the Harte Hanks pennysaver operations in California. She warned that the shopper business should be conducted separately from *The Free Press*. Moreover, Green would have to exercise patience. Tremblay estimated that it would take at least three years just to break even with a shopper in London, Ontario.

Based on Green's research, LFPH initiated a publication called *The Forest City Shopper* in London. Green explained that shopper publications have a controlled circulation: "By offering a shopper . . . we are able to zone it and say [to advertisers] 'you'll just get that sector of the market'. So they had very . . . targeted advertising, just their own market, and certainly the rates were more attractive."[25]

During the course of Green's contact with the major pennysaver operation in California, Tremblay had encouraged him to contact Harding Dawe, the owner of the *Pennysaver* in Ottawa. Green telephoned Dawe in August 1978 and learned that he was in need of financial help with his shopper. Green and White flew to Ottawa and reached an agreement to purchase the shopper from Dawe in November, along with the rights to the *Pennysaver* name. The negotiations were at times complicated. Green recalled: "After going through quite a long harangue with creditors and a lot of other problems . . . we looked after [the creditors]. *The Free Press* way of doing things was followed to a T. There was no creditor who wasn't paid 100 cents on the dollar."[26] The staff at the Ottawa Pennysaver were retained.

Four years after the establishment in 1978 of *The Forest City Shopper* in London, the Pennysaver Division was ready to stand on its own feet, and was launched as a separate, wholly owned subsidiary of The London Free Press Holdings Limited on 26 August 1982. It later assumed the title Netmar Inc., and formed two operating divisions, Netmar Publications and Netmar Systems, the latter a distribution service. The company publishes free distribution weekly shopping guides and distributes advertising flyers. During the course of the Ottawa acquisition, White and Green realized that there was potential for this type of publication not just in London but in other parts of Canada as well. By 1982 pennysaver weeklies that served small advertisers had been established in Victoria, British Columbia; Edmonton, Alberta; and at Windsor, Ottawa, London and St. Thomas in Ontario. Subsequently shoppers were established in the Ontario centres of Chatham, Guelph, Cambridge, Brampton, Mississauga, Kitchener-Waterloo and in Calgary, Alberta, Saint John, New Brunswick, Winnipeg, Manitoba and Vancouver, B.C. The shopper publication in St. John has since been closed; a distribution service operates in St. John and Moncton as licensees of Netmar Systems.

Blackburn remained cautious about the shopper experiment. He was uneasy about expansion plans that were new and took the company beyond London. The farthest he had previously gone beyond London for a major acquisition was Wingham. Several years earlier he had explained: "I must say that there were times when I wondered if we ought not to move into western Ontario and pick up some of the papers that I knew were becoming available in order to keep them away from Roy Thomson." However, Blackburn tended to exercise discretion: "It seemed to me not in our interests to do that. We had always been concerned about the accusation of monopoly which comes our way from time to time, more so earlier than now."[27]

However White and Green saw the potential to build a Canada-wide business. White sensed that Blackburn was cautious: "He was sensitive to the problems of distance and problems of unknown markets and he was concerned that we would be dissipating our energies and that Sandy or I would lose sight of what he called 'the mother lode', the home base. . . . But eventually he could start to see that this was a viable business and in his later years he became very supportive."[28]

Green was especially enthusiastic: "We then dedicated some resources . . . to look at the potential for weeklies and shoppers across Canada and a direct distribution system of the type that we were developing here in London. It became apparent to us that the potential was there, so we were off and running with the concept." When the shoppers were introduced, four *Free Press* employees became part of this new enterprise. The shoppers thus provided opportunity for some individuals to move eventually into managerial positions. Overall, though, the introduction of the pennysavers had minimal impact on the total Blackburn operation.

In the late 1970s there were a couple of years when the shoppers did not pay their way. The directors of The London Free Press Holdings Limited wore a collective frown. "The faces were somewhat long and there were a lot of very probing questions," said White. "The inference was clearly there, 'what are you guys doing?'" But, Blackburn's daughter Martha felt her father became highly supportive once he understood the nature of the pennysaver business, and threw himself wholeheartedly behind it. Ironically, as the shoppers expanded in various markets throughout Canada, Blackburn suddenly found himself in competition with several of his Canadian Press colleagues, including St. Clair Balfour. Southam Press Limited owned *The Citizen* in Ottawa where the first entry into shopper publications outside of London had been made.

By the time *The Free Press* entered the shopper business, the bank debt from the Southam purchase had been virtually paid off. During the recession of the early 1980s, the development of the pennysavers throughout Canada saw 600 jobs, including 300 full time, added to the economy.[29] In corporate structure, the relationship of *The London Pennysaver* to the total Blackburn enterprise remained similar to that of the other media divisions. The weekly functioned independently with separate staff, just as the print and broadcast sectors, a form of decentralization Blackburn insisted upon largely to stifle critics of media monopoly.

The issue of media concentration came under intense review yet again as the 1970s came to a close and a new decade began. In 1979 the CRTC examined its policy on this media question. Then, a Royal Commission under the chairmanship of Thomas Kent was established on 3 September 1980, shortly after the closing of two long-established daily newspapers in Ottawa and Winnipeg, an event which marked the culmination of a series of takeovers in the newspaper industry. An Appendix to the Kent Commission's report contains the text of the Order-in-Council by which the commission was established, and points to the core of the concern of then Prime Minister Pierre Trudeau that "there has been increased concentration of ownership and control of daily newspapers in Canada." Blackburn had professed to no interest in retirement even though he had entered his twilight years, and he gave both these inquiries high priority.

Indeed, the CRTC's examination of media concentration engaged him immediately following his return from a month's vacation in Egypt and Portugal in the spring of 1979. The CRTC enquiry conducted "a review of . . . cross-ownership within the context of the broader issue of concentration of ownership" and sought the views of broadcasters on the subject.[30] The London Free Press Holdings Limited commissioned a brief which outlined its corporate structure, its historical roles in London and southwestern Ontario and the level of competition in the region. The submission urged a retention of existing CRTC policy whereby cross-ownership cases in the media were treated on an individual basis: "By considering the merits of each ownership application separately rather than trying to impose fixed guidelines to meet a multitude of circumstances, the Commission can best deal with this issue on an equitable basis and, most important of all, in the public's interest."[31]

Blackburn preferred the status quo in the regulation of media concentration as opposed to a policy of fixed guidelines or a clear directive from the federal cabinet to the regulator. He felt the commission's existing practice yielded the flexibility required to examine particular market conditions, the nature and influence of present and anticipated competition and the economic and organizational resources of media owners. All of these notions were reflective of his passionate belief that media owners should be relatively free from government interference.

After its reception of briefs from broadcasters, the CRTC chose to hold to its existing policy. The CRTC had originally intended to hold a public hearing into the question of cross-ownership. However, after the majority of briefs from media owners urged the continuation of the commission's present approach, the public hearing was cancelled. Cross-ownership entities would be assessed on an individual, case by case basis.

Meanwhile, the electronic media market in London had changed noticeably during the 1970s. CFPL radio faced a much higher level of competition: for instance, no less than 17 FM stations were available to cable subscribers. CRTC demands for a more distinctive type of programming on FM radio had prompted CFPL to develop a new "Stereo 96" FM format in the mid-1970s. As well CFPL radio had severed its connection with the CBC in 1978. Since 1936 the London station had served as an affiliate of the corporation's Trans-Canada, Dominion and CBC Radio networks.

Blackburn was taken aback at the findings of the second inquiry. The Kent Commission in 1981 sought to correct what its report described as "the very worst cases of concentration that now exist."[32] He had appeared before the commission during its hearings in London on 3 February 1981, the last time he would present his views before a government media inquiry.

In an opening statement before the commissioners he outlined his concept of press freedom in a democratic society: "Freedom of the press simply is an extension of . . . [the] same human freedom which every citizen enjoys: the right to seek, receive and impart information and ideas through any media. . . . Freedom of Speech and of the Press, in my opinion, preclude government licensing, discriminatory taxation and prejudicial legislation."[33] Blackburn told the hearing: "A good newspaper becomes a vital part of the public record of events, and a key to interpretation of events, in a way which broadcasting can't duplicate. . . . No other medium provides the reader with the opportunity to browse at his own speed through the events of the day."

Blackburn accounted for the decline in newspaper competition that had given rise to single newspaper cities throughout the country: "In my view, daily newspaper competition in Canada was bound to decline over the years as operating costs and the capital investment required to modernize increased. This has been the trend over the 45 years I have been a publisher, and was the trend before that."

The Free Press publisher's skepticism towards unions was still apparent: "A daily newspaper in a competitive situation is extremely vulnerable to a strike. . . . A struck paper which ceases to publish is out of business without readers and circulation revenue and without advertisers and advertising revenue, but with ongoing costs." He argued that, in competitive newspaper markets, "publishers are forced to settle at higher wages and/or fringe benefits than their judgments dictate, or take a strike. In recent years . . . the *Vancouver Province* took a strike and upon resumption of publication found that it had fallen from first to second position." Blackburn further told the commission that "the concentration of ownership in newspapers . . . [was] being made necessary because of . . . economic and technological pressures . . . . Although current activities and possible future activity may be discussed and analyzed on the basis of control of information, it is economic pressures of various kinds and the final decision for simple survival that force concentration."

Ken Lemon, Blackburn's financial adviser, and Peter White also appeared with Blackburn. Lemon reminded the commission of "the old economic maxim that inflation results in confiscation of capital. I think we can modify that to say that the combination of inflation and capital gains tax based on inflationary gains results in a dramatic confiscation of capital." He explained further that this was the reason "why Mr. Blackburn and other people in his position are forced to conclude that ultimately their enterprises must be sold to larger business enterprises, so they will have the liquid funds to pay the tax which falls in on death."[34] White informed the commission that the newspaper continued to monitor developments in new technologies, such as Videotex and Teletex, and to assess their impact on medium-size, independent newspapers such as *The Free Press*.

Under questioning from commissioner Laurent Picard,

Blackburn opposed the notion of a Press Ownership Review Board. The Special Senate Committee on Mass Media in 1970 had recommended such a review mechanism. "My concern is that it smacks of licensing of newspapers," he said. "[This is] something that I am adamantly opposed to, because of the dangers of control of editorial content. . . . I would not want the ownership of newspapers to be determined by an agency of government on a political basis."

Blackburn told acting chairman Borden Spears that monopoly media situations need not necessarily mitigate against the public interest. He did not think *The Free Press* would be a better newspaper if it faced daily competition. Economic factors weighed heavily on his mind: "I've seen what's happened to our radio station, just to some extent, by having to . . . compete with new radio stations. . . . I don't like our radio operation as well as I used to, when we had less competition." He maintained that "if *The London Free Press* had competition here, we would be splitting the revenue available, and there is a limitation to that in a community of any size, and a lower limitation in London than in a larger city, or more affluent city."

The chief counsel for the Kent Commission, Donald Affleck, touched a sensitive area when he inquired if *Free Press* executives had seen any "concerted action" by a newspaper chain or group to dominate the Canadian Press news agency. Blackburn recalled his torment in 1968: "I was, in fact, defeated when I was Second Vice-President of Canadian Press and running as a director . . . with ultimate destiny of being President. . . . I was defeated in an election by a group vote. And it happened that I was aware of it because, by strange coincidence, the group vote was cast immediately ahead of me. I was next in line, and saw the fistful of proxies. The Canadian Press has been very concerned about this." His recollection before the Kent Commission marked the second occasion he claimed to have witnessed this form of proxy voting. At the CP annual meeting in 1964, he had described seeing one group representative vote a fistful of proxies the preceding year.

As an owner of both print and broadcast holdings and proud of the level of service he had provided, Blackburn felt betrayed when the Kent Commission released its findings on 18 August 1981. The commission recommended divestment of existing cross-media concentration: "While the economic reality of daily newspaper monopoly in most communities has to be accepted, there is no economic necessity for the same ownership of other media in the same community. Such a reduction in the diversity of sources of information is without justification."[35] There was no solace for *The Free Press* publisher in the report.

Blackburn promptly denounced the recommendations. He saw the Kent findings as an unprecedented intrusion by government that would kill "the kind of newspaper that we've spent a lifetime with." He expressed amazement at the cross-ownership recommendation that could have forced him to sell either *The Free Press* or his television and radio stations. "To me," he said, "this doesn't make any sense at all." He recalled the findings of the Davey Committee eleven years earlier to buttress the view that his media operation was sound. "We run our media responsibly," he said.[36] Blackburn saw the creation of a Press Rights Panel, which had been recommended to monitor implementation of the commission's proposals, as the replacement of community opinion with government bureaucracy that would determine how a newspaper operates.

Blackburn's attitude towards regulators and government inquiries into the media could be seen to have a slight undercurrent of paranoia. He felt he had extended himself to operate a respectable newspaper that was an asset to the community. In his eyes, the Kent recommendations represented an injustice. Norm Ibsen, *The Free Press* editorial page editor, described his reaction: "He felt a little betrayed that . . . [Kent] would think . . . even considering the fact that this monopoly existed, that it would be run in any way except . . . fair, community spirited and responsible."[37]

The Kent report was undoubtedly a setback for *The Free Press* publisher. No less wrenching for him was the decision to terminate the evening edition of the newspaper that he had presided over for forty-five years. Again family and tradition weighed heavily on him. Josiah Blackburn, who had started *The Free Press* as a daily in 1855, launched an evening edition in May 1875 to

counter *The London Evening Advertiser*. Since the evening paper
had served Londoners for 106 years, the third-generation publisher was highly reluctant to break with the past. The decision
to terminate the evening edition was taken essentially for economic reasons in the midst of the recession during the early
1980s. The action resulted from a document entitled the "Newspaper Planning Report" that *Free Press* executives Robert Turnbull, Bill Heine and Sandy Green had prepared.

By the early 1980s the circulation of the evening paper had
declined steadily. In the ten-year period between 1971 and 1981,
the morning city circulation had increased 117 per cent. The
evening paper had decreased 19 per cent. Turnbull, Heine and
Green concluded that the newspaper could not continue with
both editions and remain adequately profitable. Peter White
was aware of the problem the evening edition faced: "We consciously spent money in the early 70s in getting through the
technical revolution," he recalled. "But we all knew that . . . we
had to make a higher level of return on the investment. We . . .
[had a] morning and evening combination which was expensive."[38] In fact, the move had been considered for some years. In
1971 the newspaper had dropped its afternoon editions on
Saturday for the summer months. Five years later all subscribers
received Saturday morning newspapers the year round. Now the
end had come.

The notion of dropping the evening edition was an absolute
bombshell for Blackburn. He was uncomfortable with the proposal and for weeks refused to read the Newspaper Planning
Report. White recalled: "He would talk about his reluctance and
his unhappiness and . . . about tradition and so forth, all based
on the past. . . . He had great difficulty in coming to terms with
this." The board of directors made the decision to shut down the
evening paper on 24 June 1981.

Blackburn's daughter, Martha, adopted a position on this
subject reminiscent of her great aunts, Susan May and Margaret
Rose Blackburn, when they had urged her father to close *The
Advertiser* in 1936. She argued that if the evening edition were to
cease publication, no employee should lose his source of liveli-
hood. Largely for this reason an early retirement program was

instituted that made for a smooth transition from two editions to one. The result was minimal job dislocation.

Industry watchers observed these progressive management practices. *The Financial Post* cited this initiative as a reason for the inclusion of The Blackburn Group Inc. on the list of Canada's top 100 companies: "In 1981, the newspaper informed employees that it would eliminate its evening edition, making more than 40 jobs redundant. The staff cuts were made without nasty surprises for anyone through a generous early retirement offer and attrition. Fortunately, when the recession hit shortly afterward, the leaner staff needed no further trimming."[39]

The final edition of the evening paper rolled off the press on 2 October 1981. Cartoonist Merle Tingley showed his mascot, "Luke Worm," on the front page bidding good-bye to the 106-year-old evening edition. The caption underneath read: "So Long Ol' Buddy — see you in the morning!"

William Heine, editor-in-chief, explained the reasons for the evening paper's demise: "What confirmed the decision to convert the paper to morning distribution all week was the slow but steady erosion of afternoon-paper readers. The impact of television news had been increasing in the past decade, leading many newspaper readers to supper-hour and late-evening news broadcasts. As afternoon sales fell off, morning paper sales increased. In time, the decision to drop the afternoon edition more or less made itself."[40]

In his column, "Looking over Western Ontario," L.N. Bronson provided an historic look at the newspaper from its launching in 1875 when London lacked waterworks, postal delivery and any form of social legislation: "Victoria was queen of the empire on which 'the sun never sets.' In the U.S., Sitting Bull, the Sioux leader, was making news — Custer's last stand against 'the hostiles' was to come the following year. Closer to home, the stage coach war along the Lucan-London route raged. In 1880, the Biddulph troubles came to a head when the vigilantes massacred the Donnelly family."

The evening *Free Press* had a peak run of about 46,000 subscribers in September 1977. But when it published on its final day, the number of subscribers had dwindled to 15,000. Correspondents Del Bell and Gordon Sanderson recalled the newspaper's earlier days: "Who can count the characters who found their way up to the clutter of the second floor newsroom in that Victorian building on Richmond Street? Most have moved on and left behind only hazy legends. A few like CBS-TV's Morley Safer have gone on to become media superstars."

Walter Blackburn had tried to postpone the inevitable. For reasons of family and tradition, he had hesitated to stop publication of the evening paper. Ironically, now near the end of his career he had to face the same kind of decision relating to newspaper consolidation as he had at the very outset of his tenure when *The Advertiser* closed in 1936. The newspaper's staff sensed his disappointment: "The evening edition was launched — as was the morning paper — by Josiah Blackburn. The wrenching decision to discontinue evening publication fell to his grandson, publisher Walter J. Blackburn."

Perhaps the loss of the evening paper was partially redeemed by the bold launch of another newer medium of information dissemination. In 1981 London Free Press Printing Company Limited joined with Cableshare Inc. of London to enter the field of videotex technology. Videopress, an information and advertising medium based on the Telidon videotex technology, was launched on 1 December. Early in 1982 the federal Department of Communications contributed more than a million dollars in grant money to fund half of the terminal acquisition costs related to the Videopress operation. Videopress displays were located in two London shopping malls where advertisers could provide data stored in touch terminals from which mall patrons were able to access information on such items as gift ideas and winning lottery numbers. *The Free Press* entered the agreement with Cableshare, a data processing and high technology company, to gain experience in videotex technology and to learn of future developments that could relate to broadcasting and print. Another technological innovation introduced in early 1982 involved the conversion of the editorial and advertising divisions of the newspaper to a new Atex computer system. The move required extensive training for the technical staff and users of the new equipment.[41]

An economic recession took its toll on Canadian businesses in the early 1980s. After more than 45 years at the helm of *The Free Press*, Blackburn told employees in March 1982 that he had never witnessed a time "that ... [was] so troublesome from an economic view.... And I don't see a light on the horizon." Although seldom an admirer of Pierre Trudeau, Blackburn agreed with the prime minister that Canada could only be described as a high-cost economy: "We'll suffer ... if we don't watch our step. We're not competitive. We lose business and we lose jobs." As the newspaper and broadcasting media tried to cope with the unfavourable economic circumstances and aimed to seek greater revenue, Blackburn argued that *The Free Press* could never become the *Globe and Mail* of London: "We don't have the revenue base of a large city ... we have to relate our-selves to the economy of the community."[42] In the face of the recession, *The Free Press* had taken defensive action that included the cancellation of the afternoon edition, a hiring freeze and a cutback in the size of the daily paper.

A few months after Blackburn's ominous words in the spring of 1982, the sixty-eight-year-old publisher underwent a serious operation for bladder cancer. Following the operation on 11 August Blackburn spent several months recuperating. While he had lost considerable weight, the prognosis was for a complete recovery. During this period, one of the few public glimpses of Blackburn was a picture in the *Fourth Estate*, the Employees Association newspaper, that showed him and his wife, Marjorie, in the garden of their Kingspark Crescent home in London.[43] For the moment, Blackburn had a respite from the illness that would eventually claim his life. The state of his health no doubt prompted him to finalize transactions that related to the family business and complete arrangements for an orderly transition of his media enterprise to the fourth generation.

A high priority for him was to determine the family member who would have voting control of the business. After considera-ble family discussion, his daughter Martha, purchased the shares held by her sister, Susan Toledo, in December 1982. This action left one branch of the family in charge of the enterprise.

The historical precedent for this purchase was Blackburn's buy out in 1959 of the shares held by the estate of his sister, Constance Orr, and his other sister, Miriam Smith. While his three children owned Blackburn Holdings Limited, which acquired his sisters' shares in 1959, Blackburn had retained voting control over the total enterprise.

Prior to the purchase of her sister's shares, Martha Blackburn had received a startling introduction to the personal rivalries within family-owned businesses. She and her husband, Peter White, had attended a seminar for members of The Young Presidents Organization (YPO), an international network of young executives, in 1979 in New York. The YPO, founded in 1950 in New York City, has 5,600 members. The 1989 edition of the *Encyclopedia of Associations in the United States* noted the make-up of the YPO membership: presidents and chief executive officers of corporations with a gross annual revenue of at least $4,000,000, or average assets of $80,000,000, and a minimum of 50 employees. Each member must have been elected president of his corporation before his fortieth birthday, and must retire from YPO by 30 June the year after his fiftieth birthday. The YPO provides seminars for young executives and their spouses on business, the arts and world affairs.

Participants at this first seminar on family businesses had learned of some disquieting developments that had occurred in family-owned companies. "I must say that our eyes were opened to the most incredible situations that can happen with family-owned businesses," Martha recalled. "The aunts, the uncles, and the cousins sitting on the board, the in-fighting and the competition as to who drives what kind of car. . . . It just made my hair stand on end and I can remember coming home and sitting down and telling Dad about the dreadful things I had heard and saying . . . 'I can't imagine that happening with us.'"[44]

Blackburn was greatly concerned about the notion of succession. He discussed the subject thoroughly with family members and Ken Lemon, his financial adviser. Ultimately, he decided to give his younger daughter, Martha, voting control. His wife, Marjorie, raised some concern about their daughter, Susan, who would be excluded from the business. Initially,

Blackburn thought he would give voting control to his wife who turned down the idea because of the burden and responsibility that was involved. "It narrowed down to a choice of Susan and myself," said Martha. "I guess it wasn't such a difficult choice. Susan had not been involved in the businesses as I had. . . . I felt probably because of discussions I had had with YPO people that the businesses should be concentrated on one side of the family. Dad certainly had recognized that."

Susan was somewhat uneasy about the transaction, but in the end she knew her interests were beyond the family business. "I wasn't very happy with selling [my] shares, because I felt the business [always] would provide for the whole family," she said. Nonetheless, "Dad gave Martha control . . . [He] knew I wasn't interested in publishing. . . . I'm interested in horses, art [and] architecture."[45] Horses have remained a preoccupation with both of Blackburn's daughters, who own large farm properties northeast of London. Susan's property was named Beltempo Farm, Martha's Kilbyrne Farm.

When the transaction took place in December 1982, the ownership of Blackburn Holdings was divided equally between the trusts held by his two daughters. The shares previously contained in the trust for Walter Juxon, Jr., had been redistributed equally between his sisters. Martha White's purchase of her sister's shares, which was a long-term buy-out to be completed on 31 December 2002, essentially removed Susan's ownership interest in Blackburn Holdings. The transaction meant that Susan effectively was converted from a 50 per cent owner into a creditor of the holding company. Martha's trust was left as the sole owner of common shares. As a result of the arrangement, Susan's trust acquired a large number of redeemable preference shares. These shares were worth what the family had agreed was half the value of the business enterprise. The value of the companies was carefully assessed to provide the fairest treatment for Blackburn's older daughter. Upon redemption of all preferred shares over a period of time, Susan's trust would be left with cash. She would have no further financial interest in Blackburn Holdings.[46]

As Blackburn's once energetic life slowly wound down, he

received considerable satisfaction when yet another federal broadcast regulator endorsed his performance as a media owner. The Canadian Radio Television and Telecommunications Commission gave CFPL AM radio a highly positive review. The CRTC hearing in March 1983 was conducted in a new regulatory environment. In accord with the conclusions of the Kent Commission, the CRTC had received a federal government directive on 29 July 1982 not to grant or renew broadcasting licences to daily newspaper proprietors unless it concluded that such refusal "would be contrary to overriding public interest considerations, taking into consideration all relevant factors including consequences that would adversely affect service to the public or create exceptional or unreasonable hardship to the applicant, and the level of existing competition in the area served or to be served under the broadcasting licence." Blackburn, still recovering from his illness, was unable to attend the hearing. He was kept informed of the proceedings by telephone. By the time of the CRTC ruling in August 1983, Blackburn had stepped down as president of The London Free Press Holdings Limited, to be replaced by Peter White. Blackburn's daughter, Martha, remained a member of the board of directors of The London Free Press Holdings Limited, London Free Press Printing Company Limited and CFPL Broadcasting Limited.

White had led a 15-member delegation, of which Martha was a member, before the commission in March 1983. The London Free Press Holdings Limited (LFPH) intervened in the CFPL and CKNX AM (Wingham) licence renewal hearings to address the cross-media ownership issue. In its submission, LFPH stressed that the philosophy and operating realities of the company reflected three basic principles; autonomous and competitive management, editorial independence and program quality, and service to the community.[47] The company's brief recalled the past contribution made by the Blackburn family throughout several generations: "The Blackburn family began their enterprise in London, Ontario, over 130 years ago, and they together with management and employees can rightfully claim to have established and maintained a tradition of continuous ownership and excellence in both business and community service...

194

If dispossession is to be the reward for honest enterprise, particularly in the absence of cause, or of compelling social necessity, and in the face of recognized good performance, surely that is the imposition of excessive hardship on the applicant."

The CRTC, in its ruling on 17 August 1983, went to great lengths to pay tribute to Blackburn and the manner in which he had conducted his media operation: "The Commission considers CFPL London to be an essential and integral part of this large and diverse mix of media sources available in the London area. Through the efforts of the station's owners, its management and its employees, CFPL provides a useful, locally oriented service to residents in the London area and has developed a news and current affairs service of outstanding quality and responsibility. . . . the Commission is satisfied that failure to grant a licence renewal for CFPL London would be contrary to overriding public interest considerations."[48]

In other words, CFPL was recognized as an exception to the rulings that had so shocked Blackburn in 1981. He noted proudly in the Employees' Association newsletter: "It encourages us to do a good job in broadcasting. We take pride in acting in an effective and responsible manner." He wondered how comfortable the commission was with its new directive from the government: "They realized their decision would be subject to cabinet scrutiny and they wanted cabinet to know we were worthy of licence."

One of the last public appearances for Blackburn was at a Hunt Club retirement party on 23 August 1983 for C.N. "Bud" Knight, the vice-president and general manager of CFPL radio. Blackburn's final public outing was when he attended the 22 October 1983 annual dinner-dance of the Free Press Employees' Association, an occasion that marked the 40th anniversary of the organization that he had founded in 1943. He was determined to attend despite his illness. but three days later Blackburn was back in University Hospital when his cancer became more acute. Throughout his ordeal, he had spoken a great deal with his friend, Dr. Harold Warwick, with whom he had worked closely in the building of University Hospital. "He kept asking me what his chances were," said Warwick. "I felt I should be very honest with him. . . . One could be pretty sure what would happen with a hundred such [cancer] cases. A large percentage would be in trouble, but there would be the occasional patient who would do well. I advised him to accept the facts as they were and enjoy himself [as much as possible]."[49]

During the fall months of 1983 Blackburn's health continued to deteriorate. By mid-November his condition had taken its toll. Martha Blackburn remembered his insistence on manners and decorum while in hospital: "I said 'yeah' and he turned to me and said 'Martha, it is not yeah, it is yes'. . . . I can remember also never, never going in to see him in hospital dressed in riding clothes or wearing pants. I always wore a skirt because I knew it would please him."[50] He was still in hospital by early December when his doctor decided he should return home. His wife and family had urged him likewise. "He felt secure at University Hospital because of the role he played in the building of it," his wife, Marjorie, explained. "His own physician, Robin Shearer, really knew the value of a patient going home. . . . It was very hard to persuade Walter [but] he was finally persuaded that it would be really better."[51]

He returned to his Kingspark Crescent home, where the hospital had installed a bed for him, on Sunday 11 December. Three nurses specially trained in palliative care for the terminally ill were at his side. The calm and serenity of home replaced the steady din of the hospital corridors. No longer would Blackburn leave his bed, as he did at University Hospital, and push his intravenous pole to the office of Dr. Cal Stiller, chief of the hospital's multi-organ transplant service, to inquire how the research into diabetes was progressing. The end was near and it would come peacefully.

The Blackburn family was preparing for Christmas. Despite his illness Blackburn still felt the merriment of the festive occasion. W.J.'s grandchildren had erected the tree and it was time for the decorations. He felt the happiness, his wife remembered. "It is almost as if he said, well now is the time to go." Blackburn never gave instructions to her about the funeral. But he did remark, "You know it is going to be a big funeral."

Among his close friends who saw him during these final

days were J. Allyn Taylor and St. Clair and Helen Balfour. Taylor was impressed with the forthright manner Blackburn adopted during his illness, especially when he informed employees of the newspaper: "Walter just looked it squarely in the eye and said 'I have cancer and we are doing everything we can and there's the story.'" Taylor visited him three days before his death: "Right till the end ... I came away almost in disbelief at the courage the man was showing."[52]

The Balfours had wanted to come to London earlier to visit Blackburn at the hospital. His wife had suggested they wait until he arrived home. "Clair and Helen were really the last people we had any kind of social visit with," said his wife. "[They] came in and we had lunch. Walter stayed in bed. But after that, that was it. I think he had a bad round of pain and he simply just gave up. We called in our rector and had communion." Blackburn died at his home on 16 December 1983, just five days after he had arrived home from University Hospital. As William Heine explained, Blackburn simply saw his death as "the inevitability of the human condition ... again [displaying] the courage of the nineteenth-century English gentleman."[53]

The day after Blackburn's death *The London Free Press* described the tributes that poured in: "At the heart of all immediate reactions to the death ... of Walter J. Blackburn by those who knew him was one profound quality — unwavering respect." His chauffeur, Tom Wild, who had been born on the same day and in the same year as Blackburn, described him as a twin brother: "I was never an employee, I was always his friend. [He] always worried about where I was going to eat, whether I was all right." He remembered Blackburn would pick up nails off the floor he thought would get in somebody's way: "He worried more about his employees than they ever realized."[54]

David Peterson, who was then two years away from becoming Liberal premier of Ontario, paid tribute to *The Free Press* publisher: "You always hear about the Tory mafia, the Tory conspiracy in London. But never, ever, ever once in my career have I ever seen that power manipulated by Mr. Blackburn." William Davis, then still Premier of Ontario, described Blackburn's death "as a great loss for Ontario." Paul Martin, former high commissioner to Great Britain, had known Blackburn for 25 years: "We had many involvements together and I always found him a public spirited man, full of integrity who was interested not only in his own company but the affairs of Canada." Pierre Juneau, president of the Canadian Broadcasting Corporation and former chairman of the CRTC, had encountered Blackburn during the late 1960s: "He seemed to assemble people around him who reflected the same qualities of trustworthiness. He knew the real purpose of the business but served also other purposes than just making money. I had a great respect for him."[55]

The Free Press underlined Blackburn's considerable contribution to the community and his newspaper's support for a range of civic projects: the establishment of University Hospital, the development of the University of Western Ontario, the construction of the London Regional Art Gallery and Theatre London. Blackburn's newspaper had also endorsed less visible quality of life projects throughout the post-war years. These included the need to reduce pollution on the Thames River and to improve the city's water supply through greater reliance on Lake Huron water that would replace wells around the city.

Seven hundred and fifty people attended Blackburn's funeral at St. Paul's Cathedral in London on 20 December. Premier William Davis was among the dignitaries and community business-leaders at the service that was built around a theme of thanksgiving for Blackburn's full productive life. Reverend R.K. Farrell, rector of the Church of St. John the Evangelist that Blackburn attended, remembered his love, hope, patience and kindness: "These are the qualities of heart that turn people into people builders rather than people destroyers. Walter Blackburn was, first and foremost, a people builder."[56] Blackburn was buried in Woodland Cemetery in London. Fittingly, the pallbearers during the service were past and present chairmen of The London Free Press Employees' Association: Gerry Shaw, Ron Richardson, Dave Hill, Graham Boon, Bob Schroeder and Ted Kostecki.

Following Blackburn's death, a *Free Press* editorial entitled "A deep sense of loss" noted that Blackburn had left "a vastly

expanded and debt-free media corporation to the fourth generation of Blackburns to publish a newspaper in London and
Western Ontario."[57] *The London Free Press* thus began another
new era. For the first time in the history of the family company, a
female publisher was in charge.

CHAPTER NINE

The Fourth Generation
1984 – 1988

*M*ARTHA BLACKBURN WHITE'S accession to the top position as publisher of *The London Free Press* ushered in a
new era for the Blackburn family's media dynasty. A vibrant and
energetic woman, she became the only female publisher of a
privately owned daily newspaper in Canada. The thirty-nine-
year-old daughter of "W.J." had been groomed for the position
since 1975 when her father had placed her on the boards of the
various companies in the family-owned business. She had married Peter White in 1967, raised three children and had served
on various community boards. Her primary outside interest was
her farm. Now she found herself atop the corporate structure of
the family business. On 31 January 1984 she became chairman
of the London Free Press Holdings Limited, and publication of
The London Free Press, the same day her father had become publisher forty-eight years earlier. Two years later on 14 November
1986, Martha became chairman of the boards of the operating
companies, CFPL/CKNX Broadcasting Limited, Compusearch
Market and Social Research Limited, and Netmar Inc. In early
1987 the title of President was added to that of chairman of The
Blackburn Group Inc.

The relatively unknown sport of dressage held a special
interest for Blackburn's younger daughter. Her training in the
sport had begun in earnest in 1977. By 1982, her commitment
was more evident by her decision to look for a piece of property

of her own in the country. She recalled her father's interest in farming: "[He] was a gentleman farmer and I grew up around animals and grew to love horses. . . . We had a little bratty pony [called 'Princess']who used to dump us off regularly, and a nice old quarter horse [called 'Buckles']."[1]

In July 1983, a seventy-five hectare piece of land just outside of Thorndale, north-east of London, was purchased and named Kilbyrne Farm. The first assignment to be undertaken that year was a complete renovation of the house (circa 1880) on the property, that became the family home in June 1984, less than a year later. At the same time, construction was begun on a modern equestrian facility on the site, a former cornfield. In under two years, the stables with twelve horse stalls, an office, staff lounge and large indoor arena were completed as the multi-million dollar project began to take shape. As well, plans were developed for outdoor facilities, and a main competition ring, cross-country course and stadium jumping fences were built. The ground was also laid for a future steeplechase course; dozens of trees and shrubberies were planted.

In 1985, Blackburn organized two horse shows to start the process of bringing recognition to the farm name: additional staff were hired. Kilbyrne Farm was officially christened at a private celebration attended only by the farm staff, members of the planning team and the family in May, 1985. The determination she brought to the sport of dressage, her farm project and her community fund-raising activities for such organizations as Theatre London, the Memorial Boys and Girls Club of London, the London Regional Art Gallery and World Wildlife Fund (Canada) was now to be applied to the newspaper business.

She was confident about assuming the publisher's chair and welcomed the challenge: "My thinking is always, how can I do this better. I have always thought that way. . . . The struggle I went through with dressage, the challenge, the constant work and the commitment every single day, until finally so many good things happen." The same approach was taken to her role as publisher of *The Free Press*: "It's a moving ahead process and you can move ahead as fast as the effort you are willing to put into it, your daily commitment."[2] Her first dressage coach, Gaye Johnson said that

202

Ms. Blackburn had shown the determination, application, and the patience to propel herself to the international level of competition if she had not [had] her considerable responsibilities as a daily newspaper publisher.

The fourth generation publisher hoped to continue her father's tradition of treating the business as a family company. The Employees' Association was to remain an important element in day-to-day operations. Still her own activity would be different from Walter Blackburn's. She would not be as directly involved in daily management. Her role would be to deal with what she described as the ethical side of the newspaper, overseeing the general and editorial content and philosophy.

As chairman of the board of directors of The London Free Press Holdings, her first announcement in 1984 was the appointment to the board of Richard Brock, president and chief operating officer of the Matthews Group Ltd., a London, Ontario, construction company. Brock was the second recent appointment of a director to be made from outside the family. A year earlier, J. Bruce Pearson, a founding partner of the Toronto firm of May, Pearson & Associates Ltd., management consultants, joined the board of directors. Pearson had considerable experience with the intricacies of family-owned businesses. An external opinion, it was felt, could assist Walter Blackburn with the important question of succession within the family business, a topic uppermost on his mind at the time. The Blackburn Group had been alerted to Pearson through contacts in the Young Presidents Organization in New York.

The new publisher also announced in August 1984 a name change in the company to commemorate her father's accomplishments. The London Free Press Holdings Limited became The Blackburn Group Inc. By including the Blackburn name in the corporate identity, the company recognized Walter J. Blackburn's contribution to the community and the industry and his impact on the success of the existing companies. The suggestion for the name change came from the company's senior administrative advisory committee comprised of Peter White, "Sandy" Green, William Porter, Mike Walker, Bob Elsden, Bob Turnbull and Ross Hamilton.

A Man for All Media

At the same time, a managerial realignment had been made to take the Blackburn enterprise into the fourth generation. Peter White, president of The London Free Press Holdings, assumed the position of chief executive officer and chairman of the subsidiary operating companies. He headed a team that included William Porter, who had replaced B.E. "Bev" Lanning as vice-president of finance; Mike Walker, vice-president of personnel and human resources; and the presidents of the four operating companies. Bob Elsden had succeeded Murray Brown who had retired as president of CFPL Broadcasting Limited. The new president and associate publisher of *The Free Press* was Bob Turnbull. R.A. "Sandy" Green maintained the presidency of the Pennysaver division. Ross Hamilton became president of CKNX Broadcasting in Wingham.

The new manager of CFPL radio was Bill Brady, who had replaced C.N. "Bud" Knight. Jim Plant, former director of operations for CFPL-TV, became station manager. Subsequent changes included the appointment of William Morley as editor-in-chief of *The London Free Press* following William Heine's retirement in May 1984. The next year James Armitage, a management consultant from Vancouver, was named president and associate publisher of the newspaper following Turnbull's retirement.

The London Free Press Holdings Limited had spent "several thousand hours of work" preparing new strategies to deal with changing developments in print and broadcast during the 1980s. In November 1983 the board of directors had approved a five-year strategic plan that covered the period between 1 September 1983 and 1 August 1988. Peter White, chairman of the eight-member Strategic Planning Committee (SPC), explained in February 1984 that the plan called for 11 million dollars to be reinvested in the newspaper and broadcasting companies with 1½ million dollars in the Pennysaver Publications. The shareholders of the company were also prepared to divest themselves of one or more of the properties, if such action was warranted. However, White said that divestiture was not a present consideration and added that it did not seem necessary.

Mike Walker, now Group vice-president, human resources

and personnel services, noted that Walter Blackburn's management style and philosophy were reflected in the strategic plan: "There were some standards and still are that come out of the Blackburn philosophy that are carried on today. . . . He certainly was . . . a person who was . . . forward looking."[3] The strategic plan called for the strengthening of a style of management that included "the pursuit of excellence, a strongly ethical approach to all aspects of the businesses, encouragement of innovation and the acceptance of making mistakes. . . . Consistent with these characteristics and as an essential foundation of its style, the Group [of companies] intends to maintain and further the far-sighted company philosophy . . . [of] W.J. Blackburn."[4]

This managerial blueprint for the future also drew attention to the humane philosophy that Blackburn had enunciated in the late 1950s. The memorable Blackburn addresses before dinner dances of the Employees' Association in 1957 and 1959 had stressed the notion of the corporation and staff as a family unit, a belief in the fundamental rights of man including freedom of association, and the concept of self-help. A good day's pay was required for a good day's work. This manifesto has continued to serve as the definitive statement on the philosophy of The Blackburn Group Inc.

Walter Blackburn's legacy was reflected in other endeavours. To enhance its position in the information field, The Blackburn Group Inc. acquired Compusearch Market and Social Research Ltd. in October 1984. This company, a demographic research and market information firm, holds a large, computerized Canadian market data base that includes site location data, census information and household and income figures. Compusearch has an extensive client list in both Canada and the United States. In 1986, Compusearch established the institute for Market and Social Analysis to aid in the development of innovative research methodologies and analytical techniques. The firm, founded by McGill geography student William Goldstein in 1974, now has offices in Montreal, Toronto, London and Vancouver. Goldstein said that the BGI has given him operating independence, financial backing and a range of administrative services: "The working relationship has been nothing short of superb."

Although he died prior to the purchase of Compusearch, Blackburn would likely have endorsed the acquisition — it would have appealed to his interest in new technologies. Mike Walker explained, "The acquisition of Compusearch would be his style because it is a sophisticated, technical kind of firm that he liked."

Until the fall of 1985 The Blackburn Group Inc. had its characteristic, quiet air of confidence and seemed prepared to meet the challenges that lay ahead. With the managerial changes that had taken place, the company appeared well organized as it entered a new generation of family ownership. But in September 1985 an uneasy mood gripped the staff when they learned that the fourth-generation publisher and her husband, Peter White, had decided to separate. One year later, in September 1986, White left the company. The Blackburn Group's board of directors said in a brief statement that White had resigned "for personal reasons." White described his move as "a reluctant resignation, not something I had actively pursued."[5] In July 1986 the Whites' separation agreement was signed. Their divorce was official in February 1987.

Ontario's Premier David Peterson announced in July 1987 that Peter White had been appointed a director and chairman of the Ontario Development Corp., a government body aimed at the encouragement of new industrial enterprises. White later became Managing Partner of Herman Smith International Inc., an international executive search firm, and subsequently joined a Montreal company. Peterson, a London native, had introduced the couple when the trio attended the University of Western Ontario.

The first public indication that *The Free Press* publisher had reverted to her maiden name came on 18 July 1986; "Martha Grace Blackburn" joined the names of the other family publishers — her father, Walter Juxon; great uncle, Walter Josiah; grandfather, Arthur Stephen; and great-grandfather, Josiah — atop the editorial page of *The London Free Press*.

Martha Blackburn was reluctant to talk about the reasons for her marital problems: "That is personal. . . . [Peter] had the office next to mine and there was obvious tension. . . . It wasn't going to work for him to stay on here." She praised White as a good manager and recalled the unsettled aura that surrounded the companies at the time: "It was a terrible time for everyone and I just don't say for myself and Peter personally. It was [difficult] for all the staff because of the uncertainty."

Ms. Blackburn sought to dispel the state of unrest throughout the print and broadcast companies in her address to the forty-third annual dinner dance of The Blackburn Group Employees' Association on 18 October 1986. Her speech was punctuated with nautical terms, a throwback to her father's love of boating: "We have been through turbulent times during the past three years and, as a result, the winds and the waves of change have tossed us about more than is usual. My father, who was affectionately known, as 'The Great White Chief', died nearly three years ago in December of 1983 and I, an unknown quantity to many of you, came on deck as the new owner/publisher."[6] She noted White's departure from the company: "There have been retirements and new staff hired — and more recently we absorbed the news of the resignation of our Chief Executive Officer, Peter White. All these represent change in our lives. Some more disturbing than others."

The Free Press publisher recalled her father's business philosophy to which she steadfastly promised to adhere: "Our company philosophy makes a very powerful statement. My father wrote it and expressed it publicly . . . at an evening such as this. His life and his career was the embodiment of excellence and his concept of his relations with his staff were based on the notion that 'mutual understanding brings mutual benefits.'" She drew attention to her lengthy family history in London and reminded staff of the 133 years of Blackburn media ownership: "It explains why our family and our companies, despite the storms and differences and difficulties which have beset us from time to time, have survived for such a long time. We have survived, too, through four generations of Blackburns because we have your warmth and loyal support."

After White's departure in September 1986, Martha Blackburn determined that no more sudden changes should occur in the organization. No hurried attempt would be made to name a new Chief Executive Officer (CEO). Still staff members, who had shown deference to "The Great White Chief," remained unsettled. They had perceived Peter White as another of W.J.'s protégés, someone who would hold to Blackburn's established practices. Eventually the new publisher, advised by Bruce Pearson and after lengthy discussions with the Group's presidents and vice-presidents, decided that no CEO would be hired. Instead, they created the office of the chairman. Martha Blackburn became chairman and president of The Blackburn Group Inc.; Pearson was named deputy-chairman. "It was Bruce who talked to all the operating presidents after a couple of months to give everyone time to sort of settle down," Ms. Blackburn recalled. "It seemed very apparent that most of the presidents . . . wanted to operate their own companies."

Martha Blackburn's time is devoted mainly to her role as chairman of The Blackburn Group Inc. She meets with her board members; Pearson, Richard Brock and Murray Brown, and more recently, John T. Myser, former president of 3M Canada Inc. Blackburn has enjoyed this role to the fullest: "I think it is fascinating because there are not too many people who have that overview. . . . We have been very satisfied with keeping The Blackburn Group Inc. board small [because] we can make decisions quickly." In her capacity as chairman, she is involved in such areas as strategic planning, executive compensation and the assessment of recommendations from the operating presidents.

As her father did as publisher of *The London Free Press*, she must listen to complaints and receive phone calls from community residents who may question the newspaper's coverage or performance: "I know [Dad] would mention that people who had concerns about the paper would put their hand on his shoulder at a cocktail party and express them there. . . . I get a few digs when I'm out publicly, but I certainly take them to heart, as much as he did, and look into them and get back to the people with an answer."

The more decentralized and autonomous structure that resulted when the office of the chairman was created does represent a sharp break with the past. The reorganization has allowed presidents James Armitage, Robert Elsden and R.A. "Sandy" Green, who head the newspaper, broadcasting and the Pennysaver operations respectively, to have a managerial latitude unknown during Walter Blackburn's era. "It was starting in Walter's time and he was aware ... that we [were] now dealing beyond southwestern Ontario," Bruce Pearson explained. "You can't walk out in the morning and see all your enterprises. ... In Walter's day, the companies were run as divisions of a single entity. Now they are run basically as separate companies."[7]

Clearly a cultural change within The Blackburn Group Inc. is evident. The greater autonomy given to the presidents of the operating companies and group decision making at all levels are the cornerstones of this modern, corporate philosophy. Greater staff participation has replaced the one-man dominance of the forty-eight-year era that Walter Blackburn dominated. For several generations, employees looked to "W.J." as the concerned patriarch, who would issue the instructions to senior management. The managers responded dutifully. Staff members remained comfortable knowing that the head of the company was a strong, hands-on, responsible owner. This managerial style nurtured a high level of deference.

Armitage sensed the need for greater staff participation in the decision-making process to achieve technical, organizational efficiency. He stressed a team effort instead of continually looking to the man at the top for direction. Armitage felt that Martha Blackburn, as head of BGI, had emerged as a forthright owner-publisher who was not to be taken for granted. She had a lot of learning to do but had learned very quickly.

The reorganization has placed the holding company, The Blackburn Group Inc., in a somewhat different context. While the financial function of the enterprise is heavily co-ordinated, the operating companies have greater autonomy that takes into account their difference in markets and personnel. Walter Blackburn was a hands-on manager who could grow with the business he inherited ecause of its smaller size. Martha, his daughter, does not have that advantage.

The generational difference is now apparent in the day-to-day operations of the enterprise. Pearson explained: "It is very common where other generations have to take over a business of complexity that they can't have that same privilege of knowing it from the ground up. . . . Martha is one who sees the need for more independence on the part of the operating heads of her company." At the same time the new publisher recognizes that there is no substitute for the owner's footsteps. Hence she travels frequently across the country, talks to management and employ-ees and does a great deal of listening. The process is designed to reinforce her management.

Like her father, Martha Blackburn holds a group of media properties that have always tempted prospective purchasers. When Peter White departed, the probing phone calls about a possible sale of either the print or broadcast entities that she owned intensified for a period and then began to wane. "A lot of the time, people don't ask me directly," she said. "They do it by a circuitous process, but the answer as always is no, no need to sell." In earlier years the Southam company clearly had shown an interest in the acquisition of *The Free Press*. The other major newspaper chain in Canada, Thomson Newspapers Limited, had made no serious overtures to Walter Blackburn when he was publisher. Ken Thomson, chairman and president of the company, maintained that his company was interested in acquiring *The Free Press*, but he knew "W.J." would never sell to his organization. "When it came to the prospect of Thomson newspapers even coming anywhere near possessing the London paper there was just no way. We knew it, we felt it." Thomson knew that Blackburn had reservations about newspaper chains: "I think he rather felt that group ownership and higher profit-ability probably was synonymous with lower quality. . . . We wouldn't agree with that, but Walter felt that way and if he felt that way bless his heart . . . Walter's heart was in his newspaper."[8]

The broadcast division of the Blackburn media enterprise drew inquiries even in the year that preceded Walter Black-burn's death. H.T. McCurdy, president of Standard Broadcasting Corporation Limited, wrote to Blackburn: "Even though I understand that you have no specific plans for divestiture, may I say that if and when you do, we would appreciate the opportunity of entering into discussions." McCurdy underlined "W.J.'s" business philosophy: "We, along with others in the Industry, have always held your operations in the highest regard, and I would like to think that Standard may have a comparable image in the broadcast community, with a reputation for ethical business standards, community service and good personnel relations. It follows that, if given the opportunity, Standard would maintain the high principles to which you have adhered over the years."[9]

Martha Blackburn keeps on file a list of names of possible purchasers should the day ever come when the company considers divestiture. But her objective is to buy and not to sell. Unlike her father, she has no reservations about presiding over a business organization that functions on a broad scale beyond southwestern Ontario: "I am a risk-taker but I also look very carefully around me. . . . We are outward thinking, we are pursuing and negotiating quite aggressively to acquire other properties in almost all of our businesses. . . . The goal is to move forward and move ahead but recognizing what our strengths are and sticking with the businesses that we have now." She is also a realist: "We are as competitive as other companies, but there is a certain point beyond which one has to say no and turn one's back. I learned that buying and selling horses. You set a value for something and there has got to be a cutting off point."

While Ms. Blackburn has a similar approach to her father's in the operation of the family business, she remains her own person. "I think for a while when I became publisher . . . people were keeping a pretty watchful eye on me wondering just how I was going to shape up," she said. "Some people perhaps thought that I was not just going to follow my father's footsteps but to do things exactly the way he did. I have to do things my own way." Bruce Pearson, on whom Blackburn relied in her early years as publisher, saw a parallel in the third and fourth family generations: "I don't think that there is any way Martha would tolerate going into a situation or a venture where people or employees were not treated in a way that they had been around *The Free*

Press. . . . [Walter Blackburn] was always concerned that there be [a public] understanding of both the business and the family. Martha is very concerned about that relationship."

Unlike her father who represented the company at meetings of the General Committee of the Employees' Association, Martha Blackburn left that role initially to Peter White. After White's departure, Mike Walker attended the GC meetings as the BGI board representative. She has chosen to keep an arm's length relationship with the association, although she endorses its role to the fullest. Ms. Blackburn was also supportive of a General Committee initiative that saw it undertake its own strategic plan. "[Members] were beginning to question what the role of GC was," she noted. "The GC has put together its own strategic plan . . . and I don't know of any other example in Canada, with a privately owned company, where that has happened."

The GC's initiative was undertaken after its members approached Mike Walker, the vice-president of human resources. The GC found itself growing irrelevant. Employee matters would arrive on its agenda when they should have been handled in either the Newspaper or CFPL Broadcasting committees, or the BGI committee for head-office staff, three offshoots of the General Committee. The meetings of the newspaper and broadcasting committees consisted of the appropriate GC representatives in session with their respective presidents and other managers to discuss operational matters. As Walker explained, "They [GC] said, look, we are not as an employees' association in tune with the organizational structure of the company."[10]

Walker arranged for an external facilitator, a senior corporate executive, to meet with GC representatives and to develop a plan for the GC's future. After two days of planning with the facilitator, the GC made formal presentations to the presidents of the operating companies to outline the thrust of the strategic plan. Essentially the GC strategic plan formalized the role and function of the operating companies' committees. The central GC deals with major, long-range policy items. The operating committees, in all divisions of The Blackburn Group Inc., handle the day-to-day complaints, suggestions and operational questions.

Each of the operating companies in The Blackburn Group Inc. devises a five-year strategic plan that is updated annually. However, the newspaper and broadcasting committees of the Employees' Association only have access to strategic planning information relevant to their particular areas. As Mike Walker explained, "The newspaper's strategic plan for instance was covered in great detail in the newspaper committee, but the newspaper would not communicate its strategic plan in any group that had a broadcaster in it . . . and the same with broad-casting."

The affairs of the Employees' Association are thus more formalized since the days of Walter Blackburn. But although the BGI has become a larger enterprise, "W.J.'s" philosophy could not help but influence senior managers. Blackburn had a tall order for his management group; if there was a need for third-party intervention between the company and staff, manage-ment was not doing the job properly. This demanding edict dictated that a rigid test of fairness was applied to all staff policies. Mike Walker remembered Blackburn's insistence on this method of operation: "One of the first things he would say if we were going to do something that related to staff . . . [was] 'is it fair?'"

Bob Elsden, president of CFPL Broadcasting, remembered a discussion on the notion of maternity benefits in the early 1950s, a time when such a topic was a novel issue. The older employees did not understand why they should pay for such schemes when their families had grown up. They had already provided for their children and now were called upon to sup-port younger staff who were starting families. Blackburn, in his characteristic contemplative manner, listened to the discussion while puffing on his pipe. Then he remarked: "I can understand what the older employees are saying. You know, I've shot my bolt too."[11]

Elsden recalled the shock on people's faces at the plain language coming from the regal looking gentleman. Blackburn then drew employees' attention to the act that the younger staff obviously put money into peoples' pensions. The fairness of maternity benefits then registered more clearly on the older staff. "He didn't give his opinion first," said Elsden. "It was always a measured opinion after everyone else had spoken. I am sure he sat there many times thinking this is ridiculous, it's petty and so forth but he never let that on. . . . That was really the strength of the staff council which is still there."

When Walter Blackburn made decisions single-handedly that involved the Employees' Association, his senior managers were often taken aback. Mike Walker remembered how on-the-spot policy suddenly emerged, much to the chagrin of his senior managers who would not hear about new developments until after the GC meetings. Such an issue arose when Blackburn decided in front of a GC meeting to provide cars for members of the newspaper's circulation department. Mike Walker recalled: "We didn't have company cars at the time and he came back to the next meeting and said; 'I am sorry. I have to retract what I said. . . . Our managers have told me this is a major problem [and] that we would have inequities within the company if I did that. . . . I can't provide cars to the newspaper circulation department.'" Blackburn was forced to curtail his generosity.

Despite Martha Blackburn's commitment to her father's principles, there were indications of the emergence of a more demanding corporate environment. Employees had seldom been fired in recent years, but Bill Morley, *The Free Press* editor-in-chief was summarily dismissed in May 1987. There was no attempt to couch this surprising development in comforting language. The stark newspaper headline read: "Free Press fires editor-in-chief."[12]

James Armitage, the president of *The Free Press*, had decided that a new editor was needed. Armitage brought a scientific approach to the operation of the daily newspaper in September 1985. A graduate of Stanford University where he received his master's degree in business administration, Armitage had specialized in media issues as a consultant. Shortly after he became president of the newspaper, he hired a Boston consulting firm, Urban and Associates, to undertake a readership study of the London newspaper to determine the attitudes of readers and non-readers.

The survey showed that *The Free Press* was viewed as a competent, workmanlike newspaper. The findings revealed further that some Londoners perceived the paper as dull and parochial, and that they wanted more information that related to current lifestyles and news that was more people than institution related.

Armitage presented the results of a new five-year strategic plan for *The London Free Press* to the employees' Newspaper Committee on 28 May 1987. *The Fourth Estate* noted in its June 1987 edition that the five-year plan had three important goals: "To raise the newspaper's household penetration in the key London market from the current 61 percent to a range of 65-70 percent; to achieve significant growth in advertising revenues; and to bring the newspaper's profitability in line with industry averages." Armitage noted the changing nature of the London newspaper market, the increased competition from radio and television, and the need to provide stories with a strong regional thrust to keep *The Free Press* as the dominant newspaper in London and Middlesex County.

As a result, a new entertainment section, "On The Scene," appeared in *The Free Press* for the first time on 11 September 1987. The paper was also redesigned to provide a brighter look and to enable readers to find the material they wanted faster. On 31 October 1988 *The Free Press* was relaunched with a fresh look that was aimed at making the newspaper easier to read by presenting information in clearer form. The relaunching called for a new sectionalized format that was to be introduced in stages: "Our Times", a section on fashion and life-styles was introduced on 31 October 1988; redesigned "Sports" and "Business" sections were presented on 5 December 1988; new "London and Region" pages on 16 January 1989; and finally, a new-looking front "Section A" arrived on 30 January 1989.

A new direction for the newspaper was in the offing. Institutional news, such as city hall developments, board of education and the courts, would be de-emphasized. Greater attention would be given to issue backgrounders, and a concerted effort would be made to relate important issues to the community and to Londoners. Reporters would try to find out how major issues affected city residents rather than simply report the outcome of decisions made at meetings. Instead of the institutions setting the agenda for the newspaper, *The Free Press* would be more adventuresome in its approach. Reporters were expected to get behind the leading community issues and explain why they had arrived on the city council agenda in the first place. *The Free Press* traditionally had been viewed as a writer's newspaper where stories could get full treatment. Reporters now were instructed to tighten their copy drastically and practise economy of language.

Armitage discovered that *The Free Press* ran the risk of losing market position if they did not adapt. "We reached only about 60 per cent of the households in London on an average day," he said. "With no real growth on the revenue side beyond the rate of inflation, our costs were mounting very rapidly. We had an expensive production operation. We . . . still tend to be more heavily staffed as a newspaper than many other newspapers."[13] These were the kinds of concerns St. Clair Balfour used to raise with Walter Blackburn before "W.J." purchased the Southam interest in *The Free Press*.

When he arrived in London Armitage had expected to take over a newspaper that essentially was a licence to print money. He saw that this reputation of *The Free Press* was false: "In terms of its overall profitability, the newspaper [had] been running at about half of the industry average in Canada. We always have been very close with our financial information . . . yet I can tell you that when I look at this and started to understand, it really surprised me."

The surprising dismissal of Bill Morley was seen as a forerunner of changes at the newspaper. A twenty-eight-year employee with the company, Morley had worked his way from reporter to editor-in-chief. He had held the positions of assistant city editor, assistant news editor, news editor and assistant managing editor — production. Morley largely agreed with the findings of the readership survey that Armitage had commissioned. However, he was concerned that the greater emphasis that Armitage had given to profitability might result in a loss of editorial integrity: "I think in the three years I was editor we

216

built a pretty good team based on editorial integrity which parlayed certainly into the credibility of the newspaper, something you know . . . Walter Blackburn firmly believed in. I just hope for those who are going to continue on that they are going to keep up that fight for editorial integrity."[14]

Armitage wanted to move *The Free Press* into a new era in which the newspaper would be marketing-driven rather than production-driven: "By marketing I don't just mean advertisers. I mean readers. Readers come first and, if the readers are there, then the advertisers will be obtainable and . . . we figure out how we are going to produce it, not the other way around." He along with the publisher was concerned about the developments that led to Morley's dismissal: "I feel badly about the Bill Morley situation . . . Bill was not the right man for the job and I don't think that was Bill's fault. . . . I realized that we needed an editor who was what I call 'the content leader' of *The Free Press*."

Morley's replacement was Philip R. McLeod, the senior deputy managing editor of the *Toronto Star*. McLeod commented at the time of his hiring: "What you have is a very fine newspaper that's looking for a slight bit of new blood, a slight new direction to it. I'm looking forward to having some fun running the place."[15]

Matters related to the production of *The Free Press* historically received strong emphasis, especially under the presidency of Robert Turnbull. The accent on improved production hardware was an outgrowth of Walter Blackburn's determination to keep pace with the lastest technological developments. The result today is that the London newspaper boasts a plant that is well equipped and in superb condition. Although he never met "W.J." personally, Armitage recognized that the newspaper had always been an early adopter of new technology: "Having Walter Blackburn's influence as the owner and having had Bob Turnbull precede me is much to my advantage. . . . From a production point of view, the place really does function like clockwork. compared to most other newspapers, it is very well set up."

While some aspects of Walter Blackburn's legacy, such as the role of the Employees' Association, are still apparent, there has been a shift in emphasis in the family business. The Blackburn

Group Inc. is larger and therefore less personal. Profitability has been given even higher priority. "W.J." ranked his three corporate objectives in the following order: the production of strong newspaper and broadcasting entities, the promotion of harmonious staff relations and the support of worthwhile community projects. Blackburn argued that a profitable enterprise would result from the achievement of these three goals. Armitage sees the newspaper at a new stage: "People used to trust that one way or another Walter Blackburn would look after them and he did, no question. . . . Ensuring the long-term viability of this newspaper is going to require us, in some ways, to be tougher and more organized than the newspaper had to be [in the past]."

"W.J.'s" legacy is also manifested in the company's electronic media. Two years after his death a new extension to the CFPL-TV building in London opened on 9 October 1985, coincidentally the date of his daughter Martha's forty-first birthday. When the new premises were under construction, the design plans could not allow for windows to be located in both the executive board room and the employee lounge and lunchroom. In the original plans, the staff lounge was to be situated at the basement level of the building. In the end the employees received first consideration: at Martha's urging, the plans were altered to include the lounge on the first level where windows could be provided.[16]

Blackburn would have approved. His nineteenth-century, paternalistic outlook dictated that the workplace should have the proper accoutrements. Twenty years earlier he had been critical of the initial construction plans for the York Street premises that housed *The Free Press* and AM-FM radio stations. He felt the design did not give proper consideration to the general working conditions: "I do not like [the] the proposed staff entrance to the east," he wrote. "It does not provide sufficient dignity to staff and too mixed up with our trucks and vehicles delivering supplies. Along [the] same line I want staff washrooms, living rooms if any and cafeteria to be comfortable and attractive."[17] The handsome surroundings of the new building serve as a testimony to Blackburn's desire for technological efficiency and a people-oriented working environment.

The CFPL-TV newsroom boasts the most up-to-date technology including Newstar, a computer system that collates material from wire services, displays program run-sheets and supplies hard copy print-out for scripts and teleprompter. CFPL officials described the innovation as the first installation of such a system in a Canadian television newsroom. Adjacent to the newsroom are editing suites, audio booths and a news packaging room. TV's director of news and information, George Clark, explained: "Gone are the reams of script for the teleprompter; gone too are the piles of scripts for the archives, and the noise of a dozen typewriters clacking away as deadlines approach."[18]

Bob Elsden, president of CFPL Broadcasting Limited, could not help but be influenced by the man who started it all. He recalled Blackburn's introduction of retraining programs for staff whose positions were affected by technological change: "He was so far ahead of his time in that sort of thing. He was wise enough to see that there were going to be changes in the workplace." From the beginning Blackburn insisted that the company exploit television's distinctiveness from radio. "We got into the development of film right off the bat," Elsden remembered from his early days with the company. "Walter's idea was he didn't want newscasts to be talking heads. He didn't want it to be radio with pictures. He wanted film."

As president of the entire broadcasting division (CFPL/ CKNX), Elsden faced the challenge of taking the stations on an independent course. Effective 4 September 1988, CFPL/CKNX went on air for the first time as independent stations. CFPL-TV held a gala celebration with Canadian film director Norman Jewison as guest of honour to usher in the new era of independence. The move to disaffiliate from the Canadian Broadcasting Corporation had been contemplated for many years. The company had undergone a similar experience in radio. By August 1973 all CBC programming was removed from CFPL-FM. CFPL-AM (Radio 98) disaffiliated from the CBC network in 1978.

Prior to his hospitalization for cancer, Blackburn had discussed with Elsden the options for CFPL-TV. The CBC planned to become a more vigorous public broadcaster with a heavier schedule of Canadian programming. Elsden saw the corporation eventually resembling the Public Broadcasting System in the United States, a sort of "PBS of the North." Affiliates would find themselves forced to provide more reserved time for such programming and forego commercial revenue in the process. "The move of The National to ten o'clock and the Journal was a great move for the CBC," said Elsden. But: "If you look at the other side of the coin, it took five hours [per week] of prime-time programming and revenue right out of the affiliates' pocket."

Blackburn had always taken seriously his stations' relations with the CBC in both radio and television. "Walter liked a lot of the CBC programming," said Elsden, so it was a difficult decision. "He never said to me, 'I think that is the wrong direction to go, I think we should stay with the CBC.'" Elsden maintained that the corporation did not encourage CFPL to remain as a CBC affiliate: "It was a question of take it or leave it. . . . People don't understand that the only revenue that we receive from the network is the share of the commercial revenue that they sell on the station . . . we [were] getting less of that. So anything they put on which is deemed to be a public service, there is no payment for that." In the end the station decided it should be master of its own fate as it looked to the 1990s.

The move to disaffiliate did not come without a price. CFPL-TV had to generate 50 per cent more programming after withdrawal from the network. When CFPL-TV applied to the CRTC, the station projected its revenue in the first year following disaffiliation at $16.9 million. Of this amount, $2.4 million would be from local sales. The London station lost network revenues, the network news service and news feeds. CFPL Broadcasting Limited estimated the replacement cost of these three items to be $4.5 million.

Despite the price to be paid, Elsden explained to the commission on 1 December 1986 the central reason for CFPL wishing to disaffiliate: "In the early years, we had in our affiliations with the CBC a carefully balanced sharing of time, programming and revenue. The last eight to ten years has seen this balance change towards more CBC control of time, without recognition by the CBC of the financial requirements to its private affiliates."

Walter Blackburn's pragmatism would probably have triumphed despite his interest in public broadcasting. He would have recognized that disaffiliation was an economic imperative. Blackburn also would have recognized that CFPL/CKNX might even provide a better service to viewers as disaffiliated stations, since managers would now have greater control over their future in markets they knew well. Still, his admiration for the public broadcaster was undeniable. Blackburn felt both broadcasting sectors could make contributions and provide alternative services. For these reasons he enjoyed a long period of co-operation with such CBC notables as Davidson Dunton, Alphonse Ouimet and Pierre Juneau. Elsden recalled the part-public, part-private nature of the early days of CBC television in Canada: "The pioneers, the people like Walter Blackburn who started this business off ... literally took the CBC from two stations in Montreal and Toronto and extended that service right across the country without one nickel of cost to the taxpayer. They did a good job of it."

One of The Blackburn Group's boldest moves was the recent bid by CFPL Broadcasting Limited to open a new independent television station in Ottawa. In March 1987 The Blackburn Group Inc., in a joint venture with Montreal-based Radio-Nord Inc., lost out to Baton Broadcasting Inc., the largest member of the CTV television network. The awarding of the licence to Baton sparked a furor in the industry. Standard Broadcasting Corp., the owner of CJOH television in Ottawa, a CTV affiliate, questioned the CRTC's decision in awarding the licence to Baton. In July 1987 Baton purchased CJOH-TV and in the process turned back to the CRTC the disputed licence for the independent station. The CRTC reopened the licence application process in the latter part of 1988; however, CFPL Broadcasting Limited decided not to reapply for a licence for the Ottawa station.

The Blackburn Group Inc. has examined a number of markets in Canada for possible acquisitions of TV and radio stations. Martha Blackburn is eager to expand, assuming the circumstances are right: "There are ... ways in which you can acquire properties without our group of companies putting up all the dollars; seek partners or 50-50 deals, slow buy-outs. There is great range." An illustration of her interest in the expansion of the company is the BGI's joint venture with Comac Communications Ltd. of Toronto. The companies teamed up to publish a London edition of the magazine *Ontario Living*. The first issue was published in September 1987. In September 1988, however, BGI bought out the Toronto company and is now the sole publisher of the London edition. *Ontario Living* has a circulation of about 50,000 across the province.

The new publisher took over The Blackburn Group Inc. at a volatile period and is fortunate that her father left the company debt free. Never in its history has the company been involved in so many business ventures. Bob Elsden observed that Martha's style of management is still reminiscent of her father's: "She has the same inquisitiveness as her Dad. She doesn't want to know *that* something has happened, buy *why* and *how* did it happen and so forth in an informative way. . . . [Martha] has the same touch with staff. She likes to come in the building here which is great, walk anywhere and talk to people. They enjoy it [because] it's refreshing."

Netmar Inc., the wholly owned subsidiary of The Blackburn Group Inc. that operates a network of weekly publications including Pennysavers and weeklies, has been most active in the field of joint ventures, especially in western Canada. It recently purchased a half interest in Infobag Inc. of Calgary. This distribution system, operated by Ed and Alvin Brower, was a division of North Hill News, a commerical printing operation. R.A. "Sandy" Green, head of Netmar, explained the nature of the joint ventures: "We were able to put together an agreement whereby we provided our systems and expertise and so on, and some cash, and they [included] their operations. . . . we basically went about developing the business between us."[19] The agreement allowed Netmar to buy out the other half of the operation that it eventually will own in full.

An agreement similar to that with Infobag was reached with Quebecor Inc., a major newspaper chain that owns the *Winnipeg Sun*. Netmar developed a distribution company in that city with the Montreal based publishing company. The Winnipeg newspaper had a direct distribution system, Globe Distributors, in which Netmar purchased a 50 per cent interest.

A third joint agreement was reached with an Edmonton based group. Netmar had purchased *The West Edmonton Examiner* from Terry Clements, owner of "Westweb Inc.," a commercial printing operation. Netmar merged that paper with *The Times* in south Edmonton, which the London company had also purchased. *The Times* was then renamed *The Examiner*. Netmar and Clements formed Netweb Inc. located in London. Netweb was responsible for the printing and production of Pennysavers between Windsor and Toronto.

Netmar teamed up also with a Courtenay, British Columbia firm, E.W. Bickle Limited, a second-generation, family-owned publishing business similar to the Blackburn enterprise. Bickle published three weekly newspapers in and around the Comox Valley on northern Vancouver Island. "E.W. Bickle had started the *Duncan Citizen* newspaper just ... north of Victoria," said Green. "We set up our own distribution system there to distribute it [with a] circulation of about 25,000 weekly ... we ultimately decided to merge the distribution and the publication into one and we ... [joint ventured] that."

Netmar Inc. purchased an equity interest in Woodroe Nicholson Publishing in August 1987. This firm has published the weekly *Peterborough Sun* and three shopper publications in the Ontario centres of Peterborough, Lindsay and Belleville. Green described these joint ventures as consistent with the practices of The Blackburn Group Inc.: "there tend to be participants in our industry ... who perhaps are missing some elements. We are able to provide those, but we ... don't wish to go in and start competing head-on-head with them and having a terrible confrontation and a very, very expensive one. ... it seems to make good sense for both sides." Netmar initially held a 50 percent interest in Woodroe Nicholson; the London company purchased the other half of the Peterborough firm effective 3 January 1989, giving it 100 percent ownership.

Green reflected recently upon Blackburn's steady concern over the need to keep his media operations in southwestern Ontario. One conversation that took place around Blackburn's large oval-shaped teak table in his spacious office at *The Free Press* stands out in his mind: "It became very, very clear that here was a chap that was committed beyond any business purposes to an area of the country that he really loved. It was . . . important to him to . . . look after southwestern Ontario, the people within it, and to make sure the family name was kept intact in so doing."

Like many businessmen, "W.J." had grown more conservative with age. As a younger businessman he had been more adventuresome. Green recognized that Blackburn was not in a risk-taking mood when he arrived in 1976, the year after the Southam purchase. He had attempted to consolidate his operations. Surprisingly he did not reject outright the entry into Netmar: "He took a flyer on [television] and he lived with the problems in FM radio for the longest time. . . . The whole business of Netmar and the purchase of Compusearch and the kinds of things we are doing, it's all taking chances." Green described as "a breath of fresh air" the new autonomy and responsibility Martha Blackburn has given to the operating presidents: "There are certain checks and balances and we have to make absolutely certain that we operate within them. . . . The responsibility is, in fact, greater because it is no longer shouldered by the boss as it were."

Besides his influence on the present senior managers, "W.J.'s" legacy is also to be found in the various social benefits programs that employees now enjoy. His eye for detail and painstaking approach have left The Blackburn Group Inc. with a precise set of policies in such areas as vacations, hours of work, holidays and so on. He had insisted that employees should be fully aware of their terms of conditions of employment.

The overtime policy of *The London Free Press* served to illustrate Blackburn's determination to leave nothing to chance in the formulation of benefits for staff. Staff policy number 10, which the General Committee of the Employees' Association endorsed on 24 February 1987, contained a detailed set of equations that "W.J." introduced. Overtime pay for staff working day-shifts is one-and-one-half times the staff member's basic hourly (day) rate.

"For staff on day shift: OP (Overtime Pay) = OHW (Overtime Hours Worked) × BHDR (Basic Hourly Day Rate) × 1.5. For day staff when overtime extends into night differential hours: OP = (OHW × BHDR × 1.5) + (hours worked in night differential period × Hourly Night Differential × 1.5)."[20] Mike Walker, vice-president of human resources, recalled Blackburn's exact methods: "[The overtime] policy is detailed down to the last letter. . . . I doubt if we will ever change it. He spent a lot of his time on these things."

Two buzz phrases, "standard of excellence" and "the test of fairness," were Blackburn call-signs. "I think [W.J.] would be very pleased if he knew that we were . . . considered to be one of the 100 best companies [in Canada] and I hope we can continue to be," said Walker. "We were expected to be among the leaders in our field and the senior level people were expected to contribute to the [broadcast and print] industries at that level. . . . It wasn't just his personal organization. He was interested in the [industries] as well."

Blackburn expressed concern about employees in the Netmar operation and how their interests would be represented. At his urging, the various branches of Netmar have adopted the same management style as The Blackburn Group. "If we have a person who is in a branch in Vancouver who is troubled in a financial sense or in a personal sense, we give him the same support as we do in London or Wingham," Walker explained. "We still lend money to people, [to] staff who had a disaster or something. I think there was a wondering . . . [among] staff after ["W.J."] died if this would continue, but we still do."

Blackburn's community contribution was commemorated in April 1986 when Ontario's Premier David Peterson, a native Londoner, proposed that a new transplant unit at University Hospital, heavily financed by the province, be named after *The Free Press* publisher. The unit, first of its kind, brought together all transplant patients in one hospital area. Patients previously had been placed in different hospital areas after recovering from operations. The Walter J. Blackburn Multi-Organ Transplant Unit, which featured computerized hospital technology, raised the level of post-operative care. "He was very interested in . . . [this] care and very aware the hospital was lacking in that respect," his wife Marjorie explained. "This kind of planning . . . would be very dear to his heart. I'm sure he would be absolutely delighted."[21] Since then, his wife Marjorie and two daughters have contributed jointly to a redesign of the garden area of the unit, which is to be completed in 1989.

Premier Peterson opened the $5.3 million transplant unit on 31 August 1987 in the midst of a provincial election campaign. Peterson described Blackburn as "a decent, kind man who gave much to the local health care community" as a fundraiser and hospital board chairman.[22] Blackburn's wife, Marjorie, and her daughter, Martha, attended the official opening along with medical officials and a heart transplant recipient, Fred Caswell of Regina. The fourth-generation publisher expressed pride in the naming of the transplant unit after her father. She saw the medical monument as testimony to the fact that in death there is life.

Like her father, Martha Blackburn has frozen her estate and has prepared to take the family business into the fifth generation. No heir has been designated because the timing of that decision has not arrived. Her son, Richard, turned twenty-two years old in January 1989. Two years before she described her daughter, Sarah, as "a wonderful 17-year-old going on 25," and Annabelle, who had turned 15 in October, was "a bit more of a contemplative individual, more like her grandfather . . . but very much herself."

Martha Blackburn is the embodiment of the family spirit that has taken The Blackburn Group Inc. into four generations and made the organization a lasting media dynasty. She showed a burst of enthusiasm as she looked to the future with an eye on the past: "I can't imagine selling this newspaper or selling [radio] or television, [entities] that are very close to our . . . family base. But that doesn't mean to say that I don't think in somewhat similar terms with Netmar and Compusearch."

Like her father, she recognized that the ownership of media is essentially a people-oriented business: "I see, as I sit at the board level, the intricacies and the ups and downs of management and developing a business . . . seeing it grow and the entrepreneurialism. [There is] the taking of risks and that is something the operating presidents assume. They are responsible for their companies. But in the long run it's always people, people, people", and it is I who am ultimately responsible for everything either directly or indirectly related to the companies.

After five years as publisher, Martha Blackburn confronted her first major management-employees dispute. The considerable changes introduced to the style and format of *The London Free Press* had created an unsettled environment that culminated in a move by some editorial department members to seek certification with the Southern Ontario Newspaper Guild. On 27 January 1989, the Ontario Labor Relations Board certified the Guild as bargaining agent for some 150 editorial employees. Martha Blackburn's reaction was, like her father's would have been, that it was a regrettable situation. She was disappointed and concerned. Now as before she supported the role of the Employees Association.

The Blackburn Media Employees Association adopted a neutral stance in the unionization drive, because its membership included both staff and management. The Association, which Walter Blackburn established in 1943, intended to stay in existence.

At the same time, Martha Blackburn was obviously excited at the end of 1988; she expanded the broadcast wing of the company with a major transaction. The Blackburn Group's purchase of CHCH–TV, Hamilton, from Maclean Hunter Ltd. for 68.5 million dollars (subject to CRTC approval), the largest acquisition ever in the company's history, was completed on 30 December 1988. She described the deal as a very important acquisition, because it would allow the television operation to compete more vigorously for advertising and programming which were so important to stations that do not have a network affiliation. The BGI had been examining, with other owners of independent TV stations, the possible development of a consortium or co-operative to help it attain more effective buying power; the costs of productions could also be spread over a number of different stations.

The CHCH purchase was to be financed through bank loans

which would be repaid initially out of the earnings of the existing broadcast operations. Bruce Pearson, deputy chairman of The Blackburn Group Inc., noted that beyond broadcasting, the acquisition did not have a heavy impact on the other divisions of the media enterprise. CFPL/CKNX Broadcasting and CHCH television eventually would be merged into one company, Blackburn Broadcasting Inc., which would not necessarily be a wholly-owned operation. It could be open to outside investors who would help to finance the long-term debt the company had assumed.

The CHCH purchase re-emphasized the regional to national shift in The Blackburn Group Inc. from the third to fourth family generations; this transition had started in 1978 with the growth of what eventually became Netmar Inc. in 1985. Walter Blackburn preferred London and southwestern Ontario as his sole base of operation. As chairman of the BGI, a company now estimated at worth more than $200 million, Martha Blackburn has remained eager to expand to remain competitive in a changing and challenging media environment.

EPILOGUE

◇————————————◇

WALTER JUXON BLACKBURN left a permanent imprint on the Canadian broadcasting and newspaper industries. He combined a humanitarian approach in business affairs with a belief in the need for technological advancement and adaptation. Blackburn strove to keep his media holdings modern and competititve on the technological side. At the same time he was progressive in his managerial approach towards employees. He saw the growth of his media holdings to be inextricably linked with the evolution of London and southwestern Ontario.

Blackburn's career from 1936 until 1983 can be divided conveniently into three distinct periods that related to the innovation, consolidation and acquisition stages of his enterprise. From the mid-1930s until the introduction of television to southwestern Ontario in 1953, he was preoccupied with streamlining the technological and financial aspects of the newspaper. He rebuilt a rustic AM radio station and financed the beginning of television, a medium that few individuals, including officialdom in Ottawa, understood at the time.

Blackburn's decision to close *The Advertiser* was clear evidence that London, like many other Canadian cities, could not support two newspapers. He also recognized an expansive business philosophy that involved heavy expenditures if *The Free Press* were to meet the requirements of the publisher-capitalist age. His monopoly position in London neither inhibited him nor fostered a conservative business approach. Rather Blackburn responded to the social responsibilities faced by owners in single newspaper cities. Similarly, he recognized that holding a broadcasting licence, a public property, carried with it a concomitant responsibility for media owners to provide a credible level of service.

Radio came of age in the depression years and experienced its golden years throughout the Second World War. But the AM station owned by *The Free Press* began to make financial headway only in the post-war period. The FM station, established in 1948, lost money for almost 30 years.

When television arrived in the early 1950s, the sharp reluctance on the part of advertisers towards the medium did not ensure overnight success for high-risk entrepreneurs. Yet Blackburn eagerly embraced television. He viewed it as another form of communications in which his company should be involved. Rather than holding to the status quo and controlling expenditures, Blackburn insisted on the early development of FM radio and television, even though they did not immediately pay their own way.

The period between 1953 and 1970 was one of consolidation for Blackburn and his regional media. When television arrived, the radio and to a lesser extent the newspaper had to realign themselves to cope with this powerful electronic instrument. The number of radio sets in use in the evening hours declined, but CFPL found new success among morning listeners. *The Free Press* also expanded its service to readers.

CFPL radio began to adjust to the changed electronic media environment through the adoption of new programming formats that featured local radio personalities and improved community service. Heavy emphasis was placed on daytime programming, especially during the mornings. Blackburn recognized that radio's future role essentially would be as a local and regional medium, leaving TV to hold the national stage. Thus he set out to modernize the sound of CFPL-AM and provide an alternative source of programming through FM radio.

In the midst of these changes, *The Free Press* realigned its editorial division and improved its news gathering facilities outside of the immediate London area. At the end of the consolidation stage, the special Senate committee on Mass Media in 1970 gave Blackburn an overwhelming endorsement for the level of service his media enterprise provided to southwestern Ontario.

During the next thirteen years Blackburn expanded and solidified his empire still further with a series of acquisitions. He went beyond London for the first time as the sole purchaser of CKNX radio and television in Wingham, Ontario. He repurchased the Southam shares in the family business and approved the development of a network of shopper publications in numerous Canadian cities.

By the time Blackburn died in 1983, The London Free Press Holdings had grown from roughly a million dollar business, shortly after World War II, to a multi-million dollar enterprise. By 1989, five years after Walter J. Blackburn's death, the family enterprise included print-broadcast operations in London; radio-TV in Wingham, TV in Hamilton, Compusearch, and Netmar Inc., whose weekly distribution system delivers flyers and advertising material to over 3 million Canadian households. The Blackburn Group Inc., employs some 2200 people.

Blackburn had a deep sense of family history and an elitist outlook that had to be reconciled with economic pragmatism. He was often hesitant to break with the past, as in his reluctance to cancel the evening edition of *The Free Press*. He also believed that his radio operation should be able to provide a loftier form of music and programming for cultural enthusiasts, and not simply be concerned with the mass audience.

Still he was a pragmatist and insisted on a reasonable profit. When he ultimately realized that advertising revenue demanded a sizable audience, which could not be attained by catering to the interests of a minority, his elitism gave way to the dictates of the market place. Similarly, when faced with the prospect that the newspaper could not remain sufficiently profitable by providing an evening edition, he reluctantly endorsed its cancellation.

His shyness, austere demeanour, conservative dress, white hair and measured speaking manner often gave him the appearance of a remote individual. Those who knew him on a close

personal level would argue otherwise. Underneath the Edward-
ian exterior was a warm, humane individual who could be
touched by people and events. In his later years he was moved
deeply by the poverty and squalor he saw on a trip to India. He
was equally concerned abut the plight of employees who worked
for him.

The Free Press Employees' Association was formed in direct
response to the labour strife at the newspaper in the mid-1930s.
Blackburn's outlook was decidedly anti-union. Still there is no
discounting the accomplishments of the Association or Blackburn's contribution through his thoughtful introduction of
numerous company benefits and social measures. Clearly he
was responsible for bringing the family enterprise into the mid-
twentieth century. His social commitment and philanthropic
qualities showed that Blackburn paid more than lip-service to
individual employees and community organizations.

Though a successful businessman, Blackburn's life was not
without its personal disappointments. His son's death and his
failure to gain the presidency of the Canadian Press were his
greatest setbacks on both the personal and professional levels.
Nevertheless, he responded to both incidents positively. He displayed a high level of leadership and community spirit in the
health care field through the time, energy and financial support
he devoted to the construction of University Hospital. After his
defeat as a CP director, he returned to the national news agency
to help reform the assessment structure for member newspapers, a controversial issue that placed small papers against
larger dailies.

"Walter was never president of the Canadian Press," said I.
Norman Smith. "But there was only one Walter Blackburn in my
recollection of CP. ... He made a tremendous contribution
.... with that quiet graciousness of his."[2] Throughout his career
Blackburn had attempted to set noble objectives for both his
print and broadcast entities. This "man of all media," as Dr. D.
Carlton Williams, a former Western president, once described
him, had "never been known to be dissatisfied with the best."[3]

◇——————————◇

CHAPTER ONE

1. Walter J. Blackburn Papers (London), "The Aunts" to Walter Blackburn, n.d.

2. Ibid., Constance Blackburn to Walter Blackburn, 3 June 1936.

3. The quotations and material in the preceding paragraph of the text on pp. 2-3 are drawn from this source. Elwood Jones, "Josiah Blackburn," *Dictionary of Canadian Biography*, XI, 1881-1890 (Toronto, Buffalo, London, 1982), 80.

4. *National Encyclopedia of Canadian Biography* (Toronto, 1935), 332.

5. Albert Peel, *The Congregational Two Hundred* (London, England, 1948), 138-139.

6. *The London Free Press*, interview between Walter J. Blackburn and George Hutchison, 29 June 1979. Unless otherwise noted, this interview and undated interviews conducted by George Hutchison, as part of a series, are the sources of quotations in this chapter attributed to Walter J. Blackburn.

7. Elwood H. Jones, Introduction to "Fan-Fan's Poetry, The Collected Poetical Works of Victoria Grace Blackburn," *Western Ontario History Nuggets*, No. 33, iii, London Public Library and Museum.

8. Violet M. Cunningham, *London in the Bush: 1826-1976* (London, 1976), 1.

9. W. A. and C. L. Goodspeed, *The History of the County of Middlesex*, rev. ed. (Belleville, 1972), 168.

10. Jones, "Josiah Blackburn," 80. After 1872 the daily became *The London Free Press*.

11. Geo. P. Rowell & Co.'s *American Newspaper Directory* (New York, 1873), 229 as cited in Stevens Wild, *A Short History of the London Advertiser* (M.A. Essay in Journalism, Western School of Journalism, 1985), 8. Much of the material and related quotations on *The Advertiser's* competition with *The Free Press* and the Blackburn family's purchase of *The Advertiser* is drawn from the unpublished paper of Stevens Wild. See also Orlo Miller, *A Century of Western Ontario: The*

Story of London, The Free Press, and Western Ontario. 1849-1949 (Toronto, 1949), 197.

12. Elwood Hugh Jones, *Political Aspects of the London Free Press: 1858-1867* (M.A. Thesis, University of Western Ontario, 1964), 2, 6, 16.

13. Ibid., 57, 63, 127. *The Free Press* views on the double shuffle on p.8 in the preceding paragraph are from the Jones thesis.

14. Charles M. Segal, *Conversations with Lincoln* (New York, 1961), 335, 336, 423. See also Miller, *A Century*, 152.

15. *Strathroy Age*, 14 July 1871.

16. For a fuller history of the Southam empire, see Charles Bruce, *News and the Southams* (Toronto, 1968).

17. *The London Free Press*, 5 August 1905.

18. BGI, Board minutes of The London Free Press Printing Company, 7 January 1890, 47.

19. Jones, "Josiah Blackburn," 82.

20. *The London Free Press*, 28 June 1924.

21. Jones, "Josiah Blackburn," 82.

22. BGI, Josiah Blackburn Last Will and Testament, 18 July 1888.

23. Walter Josiah and Arthur Stephen Blackburn Papers (London), Free Press advertising figures 1902-1920, and Wild, *Short History*, 25.

24. *The Fourth Estate* Supplement, December 1979.

25. Interview, Ernie Agnew, 19 June 1984.

26. Interview, Cedric Tanner, 6 June 1984. The following quotations from Cedric Tanner in the text are from this interview.

27. Interview, Fred Jenkins, 24 May 1984.

28. Interview, Mark Inman, 25 May 1984.

29. Interview, Mel Pryce, 11 June 1984.

30. Interview, Larry Dampier, 27 September 1984.

31. University of Western Ontario (UWO), D.B. Weldon Library, Regional Collection, *The London Free Press* files, "A History of *The London Free Press*," by Walter J. Blackburn, 3 December 1935, 6. The following quotation in the text is from this essay.

32. Walter J. Blackburn, "The Merchandising Activities of a Typical Canadian Daily Newspaper" (B.A. Thesis, University of Western Ontario, 1936), 1, 41, 47.

33. Ross Harkness, *J.E. Atkinson of the Star* (Toronto, 1963), 204–5. Hark-

ness has noted the amount paid by *The Free Press* for *The Advertiser* and the circulation problems *The Advertiser* faced in London after supporting the Laurier Liberals. See also Wild, *A Short History*, 29-30, 40.

34. BGI, Board minutes of The London Free Press Printing Company, 15 February 1926, 331.

35. W.H. Kesterton, *A History of Journalism in Canada* (Toronto, 1970), 73.

36. Canadian Radio Television and Telecommunications Commission (Hull), CKLW Radio, examination file, Raymond Morand to Colonel W.A. Steel, 10 July 1934.

37. Arthur Blackburn Papers (London), Arthur Blackburn to F.I. Ker, 23 September 1927. The other letters referred to in the text were exchanged between F.I. Ker and Arthur Blackburn on 30 September 1927; between F.N. Southam and Arthur Blackburn on 28 June 1932 and 7 July 1932; and between F.N. Southam and J.F. MacKay Esq., on 20 November 1934.

38. Interview, Eleanor Robarts, 11 July 1984.

39. *Typographical Journal*, April 1934, 374.

40. University of Western Ontario, D.B. Weldon Library, Regional Collection, Compiled by Margaret Gahlinger, Box 4982, File No. 17, London Labour 1931-40: Strikes and Disputes, "London Free Press and Advertiser Strike, 1934-35," 6.

CHAPTER TWO

1. *The London Free Press*, interview between Walter J. Blackburn and George Hutchison, June 29 1979. Unless otherwise noted, this interview and undated interviews conducted by George Hutchison, as part of a series, are the sources of quotations in this chapter attributed to Walter J. Blackburn.

2. *The London Free Press*, 17 December 1983.

3. Thomas Goldwasser, *Family Pride: Profiles of America's Best-Run Family Businesses* (New York, 1986), 2.

4. Russ Waide Papers (London), "The History and Philosophy: London Free Press Printing Company Limited," July 1963, 8. The following four quotations in the text are from this booklet on the company.

5. *The Fourth Estate* Supplement, December 1979.

6. Interview, Jack Schenck, 17 June 1987.

7. Interview, Bruce Pearson, 16 June 1987.

8. Interview Russ Waide, 24 May 1984.

9. Stevens Wild, *A Short History of the London Advertiser* (M.A. Essay in Journalism, University of Western Ontario, 1985), 44.

10. Ibid., 45.

11. Arthur Blackburn Papers (London), Memorandum to Mr. [F.N.] Southam, "Combined Earnings of London, Ontario Newspapers," 19 May 1932.

12. *The London Advertiser*, 30 October 1936.

13. Charles Thomas Papers (London), Charles Thomas to Susan Blackburn, 4 July 1944. The quotations or remarks attributed to Charles Thomas are from this letter.

14. *The Fourth Estate*, 9 December 1944.

15. Interview, Marjorie Blackburn, 6 July 1987. The following six quotations in the text attributed to Marjorie Blackburn are from this interview.

16. Interview, Marjorie Blackburn, 15 July 1985.

17. Interview, Tom Lawson, 27 March 1985.

18. Interview, Doug Trowell, 20 February 1985.

19. Interview, Joseph Jeffery, 15 April 1986.

20. Interview between George Hutchison and Walter J. Blackburn and Marjorie Blackburn, n.d.

21. Interview, Marjorie Blackburn, 6 July 1987.

22. Interview, Martha Blackburn White, 22 August 1984.

23. Interview, Susan Toledo, 30 August 1984.

24. *The Fourth Estate* Supplement, December 1979.

25. *The London Free Press*, 27 April 1942.

26. Ibid., 28 April 1942.

27. BGI, Board of Directors Report to the annual shareholders meeting of The London Free Press Printing Company, 5 December 1944, 12.

28. Ibid.

CHAPTER THREE

1. Interview, Murray Brown, 15 May 1984.

2. *The London Free Press*, interview between George Hutchison and Walter J. Blackburn, 29 June 1979. Unless otherwise noted, this interview and undated interviews conducted by George Hutchison, as part of a series, are the sources of quotations in this chapter attributed to Walter J. Blackburn.

3. BGI, CFPL brief submitted to the Canadian Broadcasting Corporation, "Comments Regarding London Licence Application Submitted by CFPL, London to the Canadian Broadcasting Corporation, [1944], n.d. The following three quotations in the text are from this CFPL brief.

4. Canadian Radio Television and Telecommunications Commission (CRTC), CFPL Radio AM, vol. 1, Examination File, W.J. Blackburn to Walter A. Rush, 23 October 1944.

5. Ibid., W.J. Blackburn to Davidson Dunton, 21 September 1946.

6. Interview, Murray Brown, 15 May 1984.

7. CRTC, Blackburn to Dunton, 21 September 1946.

8. Ibid., Blackburn to Dunton, 8 July 1947.

9. Ibid., Blackburn to Dunton, 22 July 1947.

10. Ibid., H.S. Walker to Blackburn, 15 November 1945.

11. Ibid., Blackburn to Dunton, 14 September 1947.

12. *The London Free Press*, 27 December 1945.

13. BGI, Walter Blackburn's annual report to the shareholders of The London Free Press Printing Company for the fiscal year ended 31 October 1944, 3.

14. *The Uncertain Mirror: Report of the Special Senate Committee on Mass Media*, vol. 1 (Ottawa, 1970), 47.

15. Interview, Doug Trowell, 20 February 1985.

16. Max Ferguson, *And Now Here's Max: A Funny Kind of Autobiography* (Toronto, 1967), 4-6.

17. Letter from Jim Bowes to the author, 21 October 1985. The following four quotations in the text are from the Bowes letter. The Toronto Sun Publishing Company acquired a sixty per cent interest in Bowes Publishers Ltd. in April 1988.

18. Walter J. Blackburn papers (London), John McHugh to W.C. Heine, 27 January 1982. A memo entitled "UWO Journalism School - Its History and Relationship with the *London Free Press*," is attached to the 27 January 1982 memo.

19. Interview, St. Clair McCabe, 13 November 1984.

20. BGI, Minutes of the Free Press Printing Company's board of directors meeting, 24 August 1946, 24.

21. *London Echo*, 20 March 1957.

22. McCabe interview.

23. Public Archives of Canada (PAC), Victor Odlum papers, vol. 4, Ford Arthur R. 1940-66 file, Arthur R. Ford to General Victor W. Odlum, 13 October 1948.

24. BGI, Annual Report of the London Free Press Printing Company for the fiscal year ended 31 October 1949, 1-2.

25. Ibid.

26. Ibid., 3.

27. Ibid.

28. Ibid., 5-6.

29. *The Fourth Estate*, 13 April 1946, September 1947, November 1947, and April 1950.

CHAPTER FOUR

1. *The London Free Press*, interview between George Hutchison and Walter J. Blackburn and Marjorie Blackburn, n.d.

2. *The London Free Press*, 17 December 1983.

3. Interview, Helen Daly, 1 November 1985.

4. Canadian Radio Television and Telecommunications Commission (CRTC), CFPL Radio AM, vol. 1, examination file, R.J. Cudney to R.E. Keddy, 17 October 1950.

5. Ibid., W.J. Blackburn to Davidson Dunton, 11 November 1950.

6. Interview, Ken Lemon, 4 March 1986.

7. House of Commons, Special Committee on the Canadian Radio Commission, *Minutes of Proceedings and Evidence* (Ottawa, 1936), No. 3, 7 April 1936, 74.

8. Canadian Press records (Toronto), "Report of the Radio Relations Committee to the Executive Committee," 8 April 1952, 1, 2, 6, 7-8. The following four quotations in the text are from this report.

9. Carman Cumming, Mario Cardinal and Peter Johansen, *Canadian News Services*, Research Studies on the Newspaper Industry for the Royal Commission on Newspapers, vol. 6, (Hull, 1981), 8.

10. Interview, Charles Peters, 27 June 1984.

11. *News Services*, 33.

12. Interview, I. Norman Smith, 15 August 1984.

13. Llewellyn White, *The American Radio: A Report on the Broadcasting Industry in the United States from the Commission on Freedom of the Press* (Chicago, 1947), 176-177.

14. David Ellis, *Evolution of the Canadian Broadcasting System: Objectives and Realities, 1928-1968* (Ottawa, 1979), 34.

15. CRTC, CFPL Radio AM, vol. 1, examination file, "London Free Press Printing Company Limited Balance Sheet," 1 November 1950.

16. The Blackburn Group Inc., (BGI), Annual Report of the President and Directors of the London Free Press Holdings Limited for the year ended 31 October 1954, 9.

17. BGI, London Free Press Printing Company Limited application to the CBC, "A Brief Supporting Application for Authority to Establish a Private Commercial Television Broadcasting Station," 16 March 1953, 2.

18. Interview, Bruce Pearson, 16 June 1987.

19. BGI, Annual Report of the President and Directors of The London Free Press Printing Company for the year ended 31 October 1950, 1-2.

20. Ibid., Annual Report of the President and Directors of The London Free Press Holdings Limited for the year ended 31 October 1951, 11.

21. Interview between George Hutchison and Walter J. Blackburn, n.d.

22. Interview, Glen Robitaille, 19 May 1984.

23. BGI, *Communications in the Community* (London, 1966), 82. This book was published by the Special Printing Unit of *The London Free Press* when the company moved to its present headquarters at 369 York Street in London.

24. Interview, Davidson Dunton, 16 August 1984. The following two quotations are from this interview.

25. Interview, Murray Brown, 15 May 1984.

26. Interview, Bob Elsden, 28 September 1987.

27. *Communications in the Community*, 85.

28. BGI, Annual Report of the President and Directors of The London Free Press Holdings Limited for the year ended 31 October 1954, 9-10. The following two quotations in the text are from this report.

29. Interview between George Hutchison and Walter J. Blackburn, n.d.

30. Jon Ruddy, "Foxhounds and Tea Cosies in London, (Ontario)," *Maclean's*, (June 1968), 34.

31. Interview, Joseph Jeffery, 15 April 1986.

32. Frederick C. Whitney, *Mass Media and Mass Communications in Society* (Dubuque, Iowa), 236-237.

33. Jeffery interview.

34. Brown interview.

35. Cited in E. Austin Weir, *The Struggle for National Broadcasting in Canada* (Toronto, 1965), 298.

36. *The Fourth Estate*, March 1979, 13. The following quotation attributed to Walter J. Blackburn in the text is from this issue of *The Fourth Estate*.

37. BGI, Annual Report of the President and Directors of The London Free Press Holdings Limited for the year ended 31 October 1955, 2.

38. Martha Grace Blackburn's address to the 43rd Annual Dinner Dance of The Blackburn Media Employees' Association, 18 October 1986, 9.

CHAPTER FIVE

1. Interview, Bruce Pearson, 16 June 1987.

2. Canadian Radio Television and Telecommunications Commission (CRTC), vol. 1, Examination, CFPL Radio AM file, "Memorandum outlining proposed reorganization and change of shareholdings of London Free Press Printing Company Limited," n.d., 1.

3. Interview, Ken Lemon, 20 February 1985 and 4 March 1986.

4. BGI, The London Free Press Holdings Limited and London Free Press Printing Company Limited, Annual Report of the President and Directors for the year ended 31 October 1958, 4.

5. Lemon interview, 4 March 1986.

6. Interview, Marjorie Blackburn, 15 July 1985.

7. Public Archives of Canada (PAC), National Personnel Records Centre, Minister's Office, Department of National Defence, HQ 2502-Blackburn WJ, "Memorandum," J.D.B. Smith to the Minister, 8 May 1959.

8. Ibid., F.A. Clift to Lieutenant Colonel W.J. Blackburn, 10 July 1959.

9. *The London Free Press*, 14 July 1959.

10. Interview, Tom Lawson, 27 March 1985.

11. Cited in J.M. Beck, *Pendulum of Power* (Scarborough, 1968), 352.

12. Interview, Norm Ibsen, 4 February 1986.

13. *The Fourth Estate* Supplement, December 1979.

14. *The London Free Press*, interview between George Hutchison and John Elliott, "notes on conversation with John Elliott re Blackburn", n.d.

15. Cited in Beck, *Power*, 351.

16. *The Fourth Estate* Supplement, December 1979.

17. (PAC), Victor Odlum papers, vol. 4 Ford Arthur R. 1940-1966 file, Ford to General Victor Odlum, 31 December 1964.

18. Interview, William Heine, 25 June 1984.

19. PAC, Odlum papers, Ford to Odlum, 31 December 1964.

20. *The London Free Press*, 20 March 1964. The following two quotations in the text are from this *Free Press* article.

21. William B. Forbes, "How London Free Press put a plant around a plan for easy production," *Canadian Printer & Publisher* (March 1966), 39, 44.

22. Ibid., 40.

23. BGI, *Communications in the Community* (London, 1966), 28. This publication by the Special Printing Unit of *The London Free Press* is not paginated. A page number was assigned to each page. All numbering follows this method of pagination. The following quotation in the text is also from this publication on page 6.

24. Walter Blackburn papers (London), Walter J. Blackburn to R.M. Fowler, 10 June 1965.

25. E. Austin Weir, *The Struggle for National Broadcasting in Canada* (Toronto, 1965), 455.

26. Andrew D. Cameron and John A. Hannigan, "Mass Communications in a Canadian City," in Benjamin D. Singer, ed., *Communications in Canadian Society*, 2nd ed. rev. (Toronto, 1975), 84-85.

27. Interview, Peter G. White, 30 August 1984.

28. Interview, Ross Munro, 23 August 1984.

29. BGI, Minutes of the directors' meeting of London Free Press Printing Company Limited, 29 June 1967, 162.

30. Ibid., Annual Report of London Free Press Printing Company Limited, 31 October 1967, 2. The following two quotations in the text are from this report on page one.

31. Orlo Miller, *A Century of Western Ontario: The Story of London, The Free Press and Western Ontario, 1849-1949* (Toronto, 1949), 282.

32. Interview, William Carradine, 13 November 1984.

33. *The Fourth Estate* Supplement, December 1979.

34. Interview, Murray Brown, 15 May 1984.

35. Carman Cumming, Mario Cardinal and Peter Johansen, *Canadian News Services*, vol. 6, Research studies on the newspaper industry, *Royal Commission on Newspapers* (1981), 22.

36. Interview, Stuart Keate, 25 July 1984.

37. *News Services*, 22.

38. Interview, St. Clair McCabe, 13 November 1984.

39. Interview, Kenneth R. Thomson, 24 August 1984.

40. Interview, Beland Honderich, 25 July 1985.

41. Interview, St. Clair Balfour, 28 June 1984.

42. Canadian Press records (Toronto), Canadian Press Annual Report, Annual Meeting of Members, 14 April 1964, 27.

43. Interview, Robert Turnbull, 5 May 1986.

44. Interview between George Hutchison and Walter J. Blackburn, (Tape marked Walter, Jr.), n.d.

45. Interview, Judith Millsap Helliwell, 24 July 1984.

46. Interview, Jack Schenck, 17 June 1987.

47. Interview between George Hutchison and Walter Blackburn, n.d.

48. Judith Millsap Helliwell interview.

49. Interview, Marjorie Blackburn, 17 July 1984.

50. Carradine interview.

51. *The Fourth Estate* Supplement, December 1979.

52. *The London Free Press*, 21 January 1970.

53. Ibid., 22 January 1970.

54. Ibid.

55. *The Uncertain Mirror, Report of the Special Senate Committee on Mass Media*, vol. 1 (Ottawa, 1970), 66-67. The following four quotations in the text are from this report, pages 67 and 71.

CHAPTER SIX

1. *The London Free Press*, interview between George Hutchison and Walter J. Blackburn, n.d.

2. Memo from Stuart Keate to the author, 20 July 1984 and interview, 25 July 1984.

3. Interview, Douglas Trowell, 20 February 1985.

4. T.J. Allard, *Straight Up: Private Broadcasting in Canada 1918-1958* (Ottawa, 1979), 41.

5. Interview between George Hutchison and Walter J. Blackburn, n.d.

6. Ibid.

7. BGI, Annual Report of The London Free Press Holdings Limited for the year ended 31 August 1970, broadcasting section, 4.

8. BGI, Presentation by Murray T. Brown to hearing into application by the London Free Press Holdings Limited to purchase CKNX Radio and Television, 16 February 1971.

9. Walter J. Blackburn papers (London), Walter J. Blackburn to John Dauphinee, 26 March 1971.

10. Ibid., Walter J. Blackburn to M.T. Brown, 30 March 1971.

11. Ibid., Blackburn to Dauphinee, 30 March 1971.

12. Ibid., Charlie Edwards to Walter J. Blackburn, 8 April 1971.

13. Ibid., Norman Smith to Walter Blackburn, 8 April 1971.

14. Ibid., Don Covey to Walter J. Blackburn, 24 September 1971. The resolution passed at the Victoria meeting was attached to the letter from Covey.

15. Interview, William Carradine, 13 November 1984.

16. Interview, Marjorie Blackburn, 17 July 1984.

17. Citation read by President D. Carlton Williams at University of Western Ontario Convocation, 6 June 1977.

18. Interview between George Hutchison and Walter J. Blackburn, n.d. The following two quotations in the text are from this interview.

19. *The London Free Press*, 20 June 1980.

20. Interview, J. Allyn Taylor, 14 May 1984.

21. *The London Free Press*, 24 January 1967.

22. Interview, Dr. O.H. Warwick, 13 March 1986.

23. Ibid.

24. University Hospital Archives (UHA), Annual Report of the

London Health Association, 4 May 1967, 5.

25. Interview, Diane Stewart, 14 March 1986.

26. Interview, Patrick Blewett, 14 March 1986.

27. UHA, Annual Report of the Board of Directors of the London Health Association, 29 May 1973, 4.

28. Blewett interview.

29. Interview, Bill Brady, 9 June 1987.

30. *The London Free Press*, 22 September 1972.

31. Warwick interview.

32. UHA, Annual Report of the London Health Association, 29 May 1973, 8.

33. Interview, Millard McBain, 17 May 1984. The following three quotations in the text are from this interview.

34. Interview, Libby Murray, 5 June 1984. The following quotation in the text is also from this interview.

35. Interview, Marjorie Blackburn, 6 July 1987.

36. Interview, Norm Ibsen, 4 February 1986.

37. Interview, Huron Davidson, 5 February 1985.

38. Interview, Fred Jenkins, 24 May 1984.

CHAPTER SEVEN

1. Interview, J.J. Robinette, 29 May 1984.

2. *The London Free Press*, interview between George Hutchison and Walter J. Blackburn, n.d.

3. Ibid.

4. Gordon Donaldson, *Eighteen Men: Canada's Prime Ministers from Macdonald to Trudeau* rev. 2nd edition (Toronto, 1975), 239.

5. Interview, Norm Ibsen, 4 February 1986.

6. Carman Cumming, Mario Cardinal and Peter Johansen, *Canadian News Services*, vol. 6, Research studies on the newspaper industry, *Royal Commission on Newspapers* (1981), 14-15.

7. *The London Free Press*, 5 July 1974.

8. CFPL AM radio records, editorial files, 1974 election editorial, 5 July 1984.

9. *Royal Commission on Newspapers*, Kent Commission (Hull, 1981), 9.

10. Interview between George Hutchison and Walter J. Blackburn, n.d.

11. Interview, Peter White, 30 August 1984 and Walter J. Blackburn papers (London), For discussion with Mr. St. Clair Balfour file, "Notes Re: May 1975 Proposal to eliminate the Southam 25% interest in The Free Press Holdings Operations", 12 May 1975, 2.

12. Interview, St. Clair Balfour, 28 June 1984.

13. Interview between George Hutchison and Walter J. Blackburn, n.d.

14. Interview, Fred Auger, 24 July 1984.

15. Interview, William Carradine, 13 November 1984.

16. Balfour interview.

17. Interview between George Hutchison and Walter J. Blackburn, n.d.

18. Walter J. Blackburn papers, For discussion with Mr. St. Clair Balfour file, "*The London Free Press Holdings Limited*, Memorandum setting out certain information in connection with a determination of the fair market value of the common shares," 5 May 1975, 4.

19. Interview, Ken Lemon, 29 May 1986.

20. Balfour interview.

21. Walter J. Blackburn papers, For discussion with Mr. St. Clair Balfour file, "Notes Re: May 1975 Proposal to eliminate the Southam 25% interest in the Free Press Holdings operations," B.E. Lanning to W.J. Blackburn, 12 May 1975, 2.

22. Ibid., For discussion with Mr. St. Clair Balfour file, Ken Lemon, Bev Lanning, WJB meeting notes, 20 May 1975.

23. Ibid., For discussion with Mr. St. Clair Balfour file, "Notes Re June 1975 Verbal Agreement with Southam to eliminate their 25 per cent interest in The Free Press Holdings Operation," B.E. Lanning to W.J. Blackburn, 20 June 1975, 1. Fisher is quoted in Lanning's note to Blackburn.

24. Ibid., For discussion with Mr. St. Clair Balfour file, Gordon N. Fisher to W.J. Blackburn, 3 June 1975.

25. Ibid., For discussion with Mr. St. Clair Balfour file, "Memorandum Re Purchase for cancellation by London Free Press Holdings Limited of 300 of its outstanding common shares," 7 July 1975, 1.

26. Lemon interview, 29 May 1986.

27. Interview, John Ralph, 29 January 1985.

28. Interview, C.N. Knight, 25 June 1987.

29. BGI, Annual Report of The London Free Press Holdings Limited

and its subsidiary companies for the year ended 31 August 1975, 1.

30. Interview, Martha Blackburn White, 22 August 1984.

CHAPTER EIGHT

1. *The London Free Press*, interview between George Hutchison and Walter J. Blackburn, 29 June 1979.

2. Interview, Norm Ibsen, 4 February 1986.

3. *The Fourth Estate*, October 1979.

4. Interview, Peter White, 30 August 1984.

5. Interview between George Hutchison and Walter J. Blackburn, n.d.

6. Ibid.

7. Interview, Martha Blackburn White, 22 August 1984.

8. Walter Blackburn papers, William C. Heine to A.J. Briglia, 24 November 1978.

9. *The London Free Press*, 12 February 1979.

10. Blackburn papers, Heine to Briglia, 24 November 1978.

11. Ibid.

12. Ibsen interview.

13. Blackburn papers, W.J. Blackburn to W.C. Heine, 11 January 1979.

14. *The London Free Press*, 12 February 1979. The following quotation in the text is from this *Free Press* story.

15. Walter J. Blackburn papers, Canadian Press records, "Third Report of Assessment Committee," 7 August 1963.

16. Carman Cumming, Mario Cardinal and Peter Johansen, *Canadian News Services*, Research studies on the newspaper industry, vol. 6, *Royal Commission on Newspapers* (Hull, 1981), 14.

17. Interview, Glen Witherspoon, 24 July 1985.

18. Blackburn papers, CP-Assessment Committee file, Paddy Sherman to Walter Blackburn, 23 January 1979.

19. Ibid., Blackburn to Sherman, 4 February 1979.

20. Ibid., Ross Munro to Blackburn, 1 February 1979.

21. Witherspoon interview.

22. Interview, Ross Munro, 23 August 1984.

23. Canadian Press records (Toronto), Minutes of the fall meeting of the board of directors, 18 September 1979, 12.

24. *Canadian News Services*, 23.

25. Interview, R.A. Green, 3 September 1987.

26. Ibid.

27. Interview between George Hutchison and Walter Blackburn, n.d.

28. White interview.

29. Eva Innes, Robert L. Perry, & Jim Lyon, *The Financial Post selects the 100 Best Companies to work for in Canada* (Toronto, 1986), 150.

30. Canadian Radio Television and Telecommunications Commission, Notice of Public Hearing (Ottawa, 9 February 1979), 7.

31. BGI, Michael Nolan, "Presentation for the Canadian Radio— Television and Telecommunications Commission with respect to the concentration of ownership in private broadcasting and the question of cross-ownership," 25 April 1979, 2.

32. Report of the *Royal Commission on Newspapers* (Hull, 1981), 237.

33. BGI, Walter J. Blackburn's opening statement to the Royal Commission on Newspapers, 3 February 1981, 3. The following five quotations in the text are from Blackburn's brief to the Commission.

34. *Royal Commission on Newspapers*, Transcript of Proceedings, vol. VIII, 3 February 1981, p.1923. The following five quotations in the text are from these proceedings: pp. 1903-1904; 1916-1917; 1933-1934.

35. Report of the *Royal Commission on Newspapers*, 239.

36. *The London Free Press*, 19 August 1981.

37. Ibsen interview.

38. White interview.

39. Innes, Perry & Lyon, *100 Best Companies*, 150. The London Free Press Holdings Limited became The Blackburn Group Inc. in August 1984.

40. *The London Free Press*, 2 October 1981. The following three quotations in the text are from this issue of *The Free Press*.

41. *The Fourth Estate*, December 1981.

42. Ibid., April 1982.

43. Ibid., September/October 1982.

44. Interview, Martha Blackburn, 12 August 1987.

45. Interview, Susan Toledo, 30 August 1984.

46. Interview, Ken Lemon, 29 May 1986.

47. BGI, The London Free Press Holdings Limited intervention in

media-cross ownership and renewal of licenses for CFPL-AM and CKNX-AM, 1 March 1983, 3. The following quotation in the text is from the submission by LFPH, page 23.

48. *The Fourth Estate*, October 1983. The following two quotations in the text are from this issue of *The Fourth Estate*.

49. Interview, Dr. O.H. Warwick, 13 March 1986.

50. Interview, Martha Blackburn White, 22 August 1984.

51. Interview, Marjorie Blackburn, 6 July 1987.

52. Interview, J. Allyn Taylor, 14 May 1984.

53. Interview, William Heine, 25 June 1984.

54. *The London Free Press*, 17 December 1983. The following three quotations in the text are from this issue of *The Free Press*.

55. Ibid., 19 December 1983.

56. Ibid., 21 December 1983.

57. Ibid., 17 December 1983.

CHAPTER NINE

1. *Encounter, Sunday News Magazine of The London Free Press*, 9 June 1985.

2. Interview, Martha Blackburn, 12 August 1987. Unless otherwise indicated, all subsequent quotations attributed to Martha Blackburn are from this interview.

3. Interview, Mike Walker, 2 September 1987. This interview is cited throughout the chapter.

4. *The Fourth Estate*, March 1984, 10.

5. *The London Free Press*, 23 September 1986.

6. Martha G. Blackburn's address to the 43rd Annual Dinner Dance of The Blackburn Media Employees' Association, 18 October 1986, 2-3, 8. The quotations in this and the next paragraph are from this address to the association.

7. Interview, Bruce Pearson, 16 June 1987. The following quotation in the text is also from this interview.

8. Interview, Ken Thomson, 24 August 1984.

9. Walter Blackburn papers, H.T. McCurdy to Walter Blackburn, 2 February 1982.

10. Walker interview. The Newspaper-Holdings Committee has been

248

split into two groups: one for newspaper and the other for BGI head office staff. There are now BGI, CFPL Broadcasting and Newspaper committees.

11. Interview, Bob Elsden, 28 September 1987. Subsequent remarks attributed to him are from this interview.

12. *The London Free Press*, 20 May 1987, A3.

13. Interview, James Armitage, 25 August 1987. The following quotation on the newspaper's profitability is from this interview.

14. *The London Free Press*, 20 May 1987, A3.

15. *The London Free Press*, 15 October 1987.

16. Eva Innes, Robert L. Perry & Jim Lyon, *The Financial Post selects the 100 Best Companies to work for in Canada* (Toronto, 1986), 148.

17. Walter Blackburn papers, Personal notes, "Our plans," 19 September 1962.

18. George Clark, "Canada's First Computerized Newsroom: Core of CFPL-TV London expansion," *Broadcast Technology*, (March/April 1986), 18.

19. Interview, R.A. Green, 7 September 1987. The following quotations in the text attributed to Green are from this interview.

20. BGI, London Free Press Printing Company Limited, Staff Policy #10, "Overtime," 24 February 1987, 2.

21. *The London Free Press*, 8 April 1986.

22. Ibid., 1 September 1987.

EPILOGUE

1. BGI, Annual Report of The London Free Press Holdings Limited for the year ended 31 October 1954, 5.

2. Interview, I. Norman Smith, 15 August 1984.

3. Citation read by Dr. D. Carlton Williams at the University of Western Ontario convocation, 6 June 1977.

A NOTE ON SOURCES

◇ ———————————— ◇

THE MAIN PRIMARY SOURCES for this book were the personal papers of
Walter J. Blackburn and the financial records of The Blackburn Group
Inc.

A series of taped interviews that former *Free Press* reporter George
Hutchison conducted with Walter Blackburn and his wife Marjorie, for
an article entitled "Commitment To a Legacy" in a supplement to *The
Fourth Estate*, December 1979 were also of great assistance. In these
thoughtful interviews, Walter Blackburn spoke about both his professional and personal lives. The tapes were specifically made in order to
assist a future biographer; they have been invaluable.

In addition, many individuals generously granted me interviews. I
would like to thank the following:

Ernie Agnew	Sandy Green	Mel Pryce
James Armitage	William C. Heine	Gil Purcell
Fred Auger	Judith Millsap Helliwell	John Ralph
St. Clair Balfour	Beland Honderich	Eleanor Robarts
Marjorie Blackburn	Harold Hunter	J.J. Robinette
Martha Grace Blackburn	Mark Inman	Glen Robitaille
Pat Blewett	Joseph Jeffery	Jack Schenck
Bill Brady	Fred Jenkins	I. Norman Smith
L.N. Bronson	Stuart Keate	Diane Stewart
Murray Brown	Keith Kincaid	Cedric Tanner
Ernie Bushnell	C.N. "Bud" Knight	J. Allyn Taylor
William Carradine	Tom Lawson	Walter Thompson
Randolph Churchill	Ken Lemon	Ken Thomson
Helen Daly	Garnett Moore	Susan Toledo
Larry Dampier	Bill Morley	Doug Trowell
Huron Davidson	Ross Munro	Bob Turnbull
Tony Dumoulin	Libby Murray	Russell Waide
Davidson Dunton	Mac McBain	Mike Walker
Rudy Eberhard	St. Clair McCabe	Harold Warwick
Emilie Elliott	Bruce Pearson	Peter White
Bob Elsden	Charles H. Peters	Carlton Williams
Chuck Fenn	Ed Phelps	Glen Witherspoon

Advertiser, The, 11-12, 23, 29
advertising revenues, 53-4; CFPL and CKNX, 136; prior to First World War, 11-12
Advisory Committee on broadcasting, 117
Affleck, Donald, 186
Agnew, Ernie, 13
Alltrans Group Canada Limited, 180
Aluminum Company of Canada, 139
American Newspaper Guild, 90
American Newspaper Publishers Association, 82
Archbishop of Canterbury, 3
Armitage, James, 204, 209, 214, 216, 218
Armstrong, Major Edwin, pioneer in FM radio, 62
"As the World Wags On," 70
Atex computer system, 190
Auger, Fred S., 158
"aunts," 44; influence on Walter Juxon, 4, 12, 22, 45-6

Baird, J.L., 16
Balfour, Helen, 167, 197
Balfour, St. Clair, 121, 125, 158-65, 159, 167, 171, 197
Bambrick, Kenneth, 175
Banff Centre School of Fine Arts, financial support of, 151
Bank of Canada, 169
Bank of Montreal, 107, 117; financing for Southam purchase, 161, 164
Bassett, John, 96
Baton Broadcasting Inc., 221

Beck, Sir Adam, 14, 51
Bell, Del, 190
Beltempo Farm, 193
Betts, Peter V.V., 172
Bickle, E.W., 223
Big Creek Muskrat Farms Limited, 13
Billingham, Marion, wife of Josiah Blackburn, 11
Bishop Strachan School, 127
Blackburn Group Inc., The, 89, 189; and bid for Ottawa TV station, 221; Martha named chairman, 208, 209; name change to, 203; and prospective purchasers, 210-11;
Blackburn Holdings Limited, 107-8, 192, 193
Blackburn Media Employees Association, 227
Blackburn, Arthur Stephen, 5-7, 11-13, 28; family life, 14; and health, 2, 12, 17
Blackburn, Constance Margaret, 1-2, 12. See also Constance Margaret Orr
Blackburn, Eleanor Lucy, 1, 4, 174
Blackburn, Etta Irene, 14
Blackburn, Henry Stephen, 11
Blackburn, Reverend John, 2-3
Blackburn, Josiah, 2-3, 5-11, 71, 141, 158
Blackburn, Margaret Rose, 1, 4, 39
Blackburn, Marjorie, 110, 128, 140, 191-2; arts and travel, 149-50, 152; the house and farm, 48, 167;

life in London, 49-50; and Walter's illness, 196
Blackburn, Martha Grace, 48, 79, 102-3, 128, 139; and CRTC hearings, 194; executive positions, 161, 166, 171, 191-3, 201, 208; financial trusts, 107; management style, 182, 188-9, 210, 214, 221-2, 224, 226-7; marriage and children, 172, 206-7; relationship with father, 49, 196
Blackburn, Mary Charlotte, 3
Blackburn, Miriam Irene, 1-2, 12. See also Miriam Irene Smith
Blackburn, Sarah Emma, 3
Blackburn, Stephen, 9
Blackburn, Susan May, 1, 4-5, 39, 44, 74.
Blackburn, Susan Marjorie, 46, 49, 107
Blackburn, Victoria Grace, 4, 12, 74
Blackburn, Walter Josiah See Josiah Blackburn
Blackburn, Walter Juxon, 1, 3, 31, 42-4, 44, 155; at regulatory hearings, 99, 184-7; attitude towards women, 79-80; business philosophy and management style, 31-3, 35, 114, 131-2, 139, 166, 170, 218; character of, 33-4, 49, 77-80, 187; CKNX purchase, 134-5; construction of house, 167; and cultural support, 148, 150, 151; death of, 197-8;

and Canadian Press, 82, 124, 139; early years, 12, 14-22; and election coverage, 154-55, 174; enmity between newspapers and radio, 83; and family matters, 1, 32, 45, 48-9, 78-9, 126, 172, 191, 195-7; holdings in LFPH, 107; honors 110, 141; independent newspapers, voice for, 153; and Murray Brown, 64; negotiations with Southam, 158-65; personal interests, 15, 16, 102, 152; and radio frequency allocation, 59-62; television station opening, 93; and unions, 27-8, 34, 36; and University Hospital, 128, 140-1, 143-8; and World War II, 46-8

Blackburn, Walter Juxon, Jr., 48, 106, 107, 123, 126-8

Blahout, Arthur, 72

Blewett, Patrick, 146

Board of Broadcast Governors, 58, 99, 118; and CKNX, 136

Boon, Graham, 198

Border Cities Star, 23, 25

Boundy, Martin, 148

Bowes, Bill, 67

Bowes, Jim, 66-8

Bowes Publishers Limited, 66-8

10BP, 134

Brady, Bill, 146-7, 204

Bremner, Hugh, 85, 86

Bridgman, L.G., 63

Briglia, Jack, 68, 173

Broadcast News Limited, 82, 84, 136-7

Brock, Richard, 203, 208

Bronson, L.N., 189

Brower, Alvin, 222

Brower, Ed, 222

Brown, George, 7

Brown, Murray, 57, 60-1, 64, 72, 91, 118, 123, 135-6, 137, 171, 204, 208; board, role on 65, 159; Fowler Commission, 98-9; Senate Committee on Mass Media, 129

Buchanan, E.V., 52, 143, 150

Bucke, Harold, 45

Bucke, Richard Maurice, 45

Bureau of Broadcast Measurement, 97

Burgoyne, Bill, 137

BX 93 London, 119

Cable television, 119-20

Cableshare Inc., and videotex, 190

Cameron, John, 6-7

Canada Trust, 172

Canadian Association of Broadcasters, 87, 99

Canadian Brotherhood of Locomotive Engineers, 58

Canadian Cablesystems Limited, 170

Canadian Contemporary News Service, 136

Canadian content (Cancon), 100

Canadian Daily Newspaper Publishers Association, 158, 179

Canadian Diabetic Association, financial support of, 151

Canadian Free Press, The, 2, 5-6

Canadian Fusilers, 47

Canadian magazine, 120

Canadian Mental Health Association, 151

Canadian Power Squadron course, 102

Canadian Press, 82, 83-4; Advisory Committee, 179; assessment issue, 172, 175-8; elections to Board of, 106, 123-4, 125, 126, 179, 186; and electronic journalism, 85-6

Canadian Printer & Publisher, 116

Canadian Radio Broadcasting Commission, 24

Canadian Radio Television Commission, 164, 166

Canadian Radio-Television and Telecommunications Commission, 80, 194-5

Cardinal, Mario, 124

Carling Brewing and Malting Company, 11, 13

Carradine, William J., 122-3, 127, 129, 139-40, 159

Caswell, Fred, 226

CBC, 56-7, 58, 87, 98, 184

CBFT Montreal, 87

CBLT Toronto, 87

Central Collegiate high school, 127

Century of Western Ontario: The Story of London, The Free Press, and Western Ontario, 1849-1949, 71

CF-101B Voodoo interceptors, 111-2

CFPL London, 85, 86, 105-6; audience surveys and competition, 97, 118, 184, 219; and election coverage, 154-6; staff and programming

56, 96-7; and regulatory hearings, 194, 195
CFPL-AM London, 25, 55, 62, 65
CFPL-FM London, 62-3
CFPL-TV London, 87, 93-4, 218-9, 219-20
CFPL Broadcasting Limited, 122, 160
CFRB Toronto, 60, 85-6
Chamber of Commerce, 148
Charles I, 3
Chase, Howard, B., 58
Chatham Cable TV Limited, 120, 134, 160, 170
CHCH-TV Hamilton, purchase of, 227-8
CHLO St. Thomas, 92-3
CHML Hamilton, 85
CHOK-AM Sarnia, 119
Church of St. John the Evangelist, 198
Churchill, Randolph, 39
circulation statistics, 39
Citizen, The, and shopper publications, 182
CJBK London, 119
CJCH Halifax, 99
CJGC radio, 13-4, 24-5, 57, 155
CJOE London, 118-9
CKLW Windsor, 24
CKNX Wingham, 134-5, 160, 194, 219
CKOK Windsor, 24
CKSL London, 95-6, 137
CKSO Sudbury, 87
CKVL Verdun, 99
Clare, John Kingsley, 9
Clark, George, 219
Clarke, Sylvia, 143
Clarkson Gordon, 81, 161
Clements, Terry, 223
Clift, Brigadier F.A., 110

colour television, 95, 98, 119
Comac Communications Ltd., 222
Commonwealth Press Union, 82, 167
Communications in the Community, 116
Compusearch Market and Social Research Ltd., 205, 224
computerized typesetting, 121
computers: Atex, 190; DEC, 140
Congregational Union of England and Wales, 3
Congress of Europe, 70
conscription crisis, 53
Conservative Party, 7
Controlled circulation, 180
Cornell, Ward, 85
Crippled Children's Centre, 127
Cronyn, V.P., 52
cross-media, 130, 153
cross-ownership in the media, 92, 117, 129, 183-4, 187, 194
CRTC, 182-3 and CKNX, 135
Cruickshank, W.T. "Doc", 134-6
CT scanner, 146
CTV, and Owen Sound area, 135
Cumming, Carman, 124

Daly, Helen, 78, 106, 150
Dampier, Edward, 45
Dampier, Helen, 45
Dampier, Lawrence, 19, 45
Dampier, Lawrence Henry, 45
Dampier, Marjorie Ludwell, marriage to Walter Juxon Blackburn, 17, 45-6

See also Marjorie Blackburn
Dampier, Mary, 45
Dampier, Virginia, 45
Daniell, James, 2
Dauphinee, John, 137-8
Davey, Senator Keith, 106, 129, 130, 154
Davey Committee, 187
Davidson, Huron, 107
Davies, Michael, 179
Davis, T.C., 70
Davis, William, 146-7, 197
Dawe, Harding, 180
Delamore, Emma Jane, 3
Delta Upsilon, 18-9
Department of Public Printing and Stationery 1886, 10
Department of Transport: and colour television; 98 and radio frequencies, 60
Diefenbaker, John, 53, 99, 105, 111
Digital Equipment Corporation, 140
Dominion Network CBC, 94-5
Don Wright Chorus, 94
Donaldson, Gordon, 155
double majority principle, 8
"Double Shuffle", 7-8
Dresden Times, 67
dressage, 201-3
Duncan Citizen, 223
Dunton, Davidson, 60-2, 81, 92-3, 221

E. W. Bickle Limited, 223
Earle Terry Singer, 94
Edwards, Charlie, 85, 137-8
electronic editing, 166
electronic media, 32, 54, 94, 218
Elliott-Haynes survey, 97

Elliott, John Campbell, 114
Elliott, John K., 39, 113-4
Elsden, Robert, 93, 203, 204, 209, 213-4, 219
Emco Limited, 144
Employees' Association, and Martha Blackburn, 203, 207
English, Edith Isabella, 45
Essex Broadcasters Limited, 24-5
Examiner, The, 223

Family Pride, 32
Famous Players Canadian Corporation, 119-20
"Fan-Fan", 4
Farmers Advocate, 10
Farquharson, Bob, 38
Farrell, Reverend R.K., 198
Federal Communications Commission, 86
Fenn, Charles, G., 69, 120
Ferguson, Max, 65-6
Financial Post, The, 189
First Hussars, C Squadron, 46
Fisher, Gordon N., 163-4
Fletcher, Frederick E., 116
Ford, Arthur, 7, 39, 41, 42, 50-3, 107, 114; chancellor of UWO, 68; editor-in-chief, *The Free Press*, 68, 70; and the 1963 election, 111-14
Forest City Shopper, The, 180
Fort William Times-Journal, 124
Foulds, Nora, 72
Fourth Estate, The, 36, 172, 191, 215
Fowler Commission, 98-100, 118

Fowler, Robert, 98, 117
Free Press, The: administrative changes, 8, 72, 187-90, 215; attempts to buy Southam interest, 26-7, 157-65; building expansion, 105-6, 115-16, 117; centennial year, 70-1; editorial positions, 52-3, 112, 155, 172-5; job printing and lithographic departments 10; redesign, 215; World War II, coverage of, 50-1
Free Press Employees' Benefit Society, 34, 74, 195
Free Press Sick and Funeral Benefit Society 1886, 34
frequency modulation (FM), 54, 55, 62-3
Frigon, Dr. Augustin, 58

Galt Evening Reporter, 68
Gazette, The, 17-18
General Committee, London Free Press Employees' Association, 74, 100, 170, 212-13
Geneva Committee on World Information, 70
Georgian Bay retreat, 102
Globe, The, 7, 38
Globe Distributors, 223
Globe and Mail, competition for *Free Press*, 38
Goldstein, William, 205
Goldwasser, Thomas, 32
Goodman, Martin, 177

Gordon S. Adamson & Associates, 116
Gorman, Harry, 6
Goss Headliner Press, 117
Great Coalition, 8
Green, Howard, 112
Green, R.A. "Sandy", 179-81, 188, 203, 204, 209, 222
Group of Seven, 4
Grover, Lt. Col. Basil, 110
Gunn, Walter, 41-2, 53

Hall, Dr. G.E., 142
ham radio station, 16
Hamilton Spectator, 9, 25, 123
Hamilton, Margaret, 179
Hamilton, Ross, 203-4
Hansford, Lt. Col. D.F., 111
Harkness, Doulas, 112
Harry Smith affair, 173-5
Harte Hanks pennysaver, 180
Harvard Business School case method, 19-20
Havana conference 1947, 61
Havana Treaty 1937, 58
Heine, William, 31, 68, 78, 114, 173, 188-9, 197, 204
Henderson, Etta Irene, 12
Herman Smith International Inc., 206
Herman, W.F., 23
Hill, Dave, 198
Hoe press, 40
Holy Trinity Ukrainian Greek Orthodox church, 150
Honderich, Beland, 121, 124-5
horse shows, 202
hot metal, 166
House of Commons

Broadcasting Com-
mittee, 82
Howe, C.D., 91
Howes, Fred, 62
Hunt Club. *See* Lon-
don Hunt and
Country Club
Hunter, Charles G., 25
Hutchinson, George,
33

Ibsen, Norm, 68, 112,
150, 155, 169-70,
174, 187
Infobag Inc., 222
Inman, Mark, 17-18
Institute for Market
and social Analysis,
205
International Printing
Pressmen and
Assistants Union,
Local 173, 100
International Service
CBC, 94
International Typo-
graphical Union,
Local 133, 27
Investors' Club, 50,
149, 152
Ives Commission, 81

J.D. Woods and Gor-
don, 89-90
Jarmain Teleservices
Limited, 120
Jarmain, Edwin, 119
Jedicke, Peter, 175
Jeffery, Capt. Joseph,
47, 96, 98
Jenkins, Fred, 50, 152
Jenkins, Sally, 152
Jewison, Norman, 219
Johansen, Peter, 124
John P. Robarts
Research Institute,
172
Johnson, Gaye, 202-3
JOKE, 134
Juneau, Pierre, 135,
198, 221
Juxon, Bishop, 3
Juxon, Grandmother
of Josiah, 3

Keate, Stuart, 124, 133
Kent Commission,
183-7, 194
Kent, Thomas, 157,
183-4
Ker, F.I., 25-6, 82
Kilbyrne Farm, 193,
202
Kincaid, Keith, 178
Kingspark Crescent,
191, 196
Knight, C.N. "Bud",
80, 137-8, 164, 195,
204
Kostecki, Ted, 198

Labatt, John S., 52
labour relations, 27-8,
34-7, 90, 100, 227
Lamb, James B., 124
Lamb, Wilf, 144
Lanning, B.E. "Bev",
121, 123, 161-2, 204
Lawson, Ray, 52
Lawson, Col. Tom, 47,
111
LeCapelain, Nev, 68
Lemon, Ken, 81,
109,161, 185, 192
Leonard, Col. Ibbot-
son, 51, 143
Lester, Elsie, 107, 151,
161
Lester, Thomas, 151
Liberal party, 53, 105
Lincoln, President
Abraham, 8
London Advertiser
Company Limited,
88
London Advertiser, The,
22-4
London Board of
Education, 173
London Broadcasters
Limited, 96
London Camera Club,
16
London Civic Sym-
phony, 148. *See also*
Orchestra London
London Club, 46
London Echo Lim-
ited, 88

London Echo, The, 69,
72
*London Evening Adver-
tiser, The,* 6-7
*London Free Press, The
See Free Press, The*
*London Free Press and
Daily Western Adver-
tiser, The,* 6
London Free Press
Holdings Limited,
81, 87-8, 90, 100,
108, 151, 160-1, 203
London Free Press
Printing Company
Limited, 11, 31, 73,
80-1, 88, 107, 108-9,
160, 190
London Free Press
Printing and Pub-
lishing Company, 9
London Health Asso-
ciation, 51-2, 141,
143, 150, 172
London Hunt and
Country Club, 13,
46, 50, 152, 195
London Kiwanis Club,
148
London Life Insur-
ance Company, 47, 96
London Pennysaver, The,
182
London Regional Art
Gallery, 202
London Symphony
Orchestra, 141, 150
"Luke Worm," 189

3M Canada Inc., 208
McBain, Millard
"Mac", 148-9
McCabe, St. Clair, 68-
9, 125, 177
McConnell Advertis-
ing Agency, 41
McConnell, James, Jr.,
19-20
McCurdy, H.T., 210-11
Macdonald, Ed, 81
Macdonald, (Sir) John
A., 7
Macdonald, Sand-
field, 9

McElman, Charles, 131
MacFarlane, J. Doug, 123, 126
Macgillivray, G.B., 124
McInnes, Rex, 67
MacKay, J.F., 26
McKay, John B., 124
McKinstry, D.G., 63
Maclean Hunter Ltd., 227
McLeod, Philip R., 217
McLuhan, Marshall, 75
McManus, Joseph, 118-19
Mail and Empire, 38
Man Child, The, 4
Marketing Group, 120
Martin, Paul, 197-8
Massey Commission, 74, 87, 98
Massey, Denton, 82
Massey, Vincent, 74
Mathewson, Philippa, 38, 151
Mathewson, George, 37-8, 151
Mathewson, Henry, 9, 151
Matthews Group Ltd., 203
May, Pearson & Associates Ltd., 203
Mayflower Decision 1941, 86
media concentration, 54-6, 92, 154, 156, 182-4
Meighen, Arthur, 53
Memento ring, gift from Charles I, 3
Memorial Boys and Girls Club of London, 202
merchandising, thesis on, by Walter Blackburn, 21
microwave, 94
Middlesex Broadcasters, 119
Miller, Orlo, 71
Millsap, Jill, 127
Millsap, Judith, 127-8

Montreal Gazette, 84
Montreal Neurological Institute, 147
Montreal Standard Publishing Company, 120
Moore Business Forms, 64
Moose Jaw Times-Herald, 125
Morley, William, 204, 214, 216
Morris, Philip, 63
Munro, Ross, 120-1, 178
Murray, Libby, 149
Myser, John T., 208

Needham, Robert, 72
Netmar Inc., 69, 180, 222-5
Netmar Publications, 181
Netweb Inc., 223
Neville, K.P.R. interview, 18
New Western Electric, 63-4
New Yorker, The, 149-50
Newspaper Planning Report, 188
Newstar computer system, 219
Nichols, Tom, 123, 126
North American Regional Broadcasting Agreement (Havana Treaty) 1937, 58
North Hill News, 222
Northrup stop-cylinder press, 20
nuclear warhead issue, 112

Odlum, General Victor, 70, 115
O'Neail, Jim, 173
Ontario Development Corporation, 206
Ontario Hydro, 14
Ontario Labour Relations Board, 227
Ontario Living, 222

Ontario Ministry of Health, 146
Ontario Press Council, 139, 174-5
Orchestra London, 148
Orillia Packet and Times, 124
Orr, Alexander, 81
Orr, Constance, 81, 89, 192
Orr, estate of Constance, 107
Orr, Thomas, 10
Ottawa Journal, 85, 123
Ouimet, Alphonse, 221
overtime policy, 224-5

Parkinson, Bob, 41
Parkinson, Mel, 41, 42, 116
Parliamentary Press Gallery, 72
Parnell, F.E., 52
paternalism, 31-2
Payne, J. Lambert, 11
Pearkes, George, 110
Pearson, J. Bruce, 89, 106, 203, 208-9, 211, 228
Pearson, Lester, 105, 112
Peel, Albert, 3
Penfield, Dr. Wilder, 147
Pennysaver Publications, 180, 204
pennysavers, 69, 179, 222
personnel department, 37, 41
Peterborough Sun, 223
Peters, Charles, 84
Peterson, Premier David, 197, 206, 225-6
photo typesetting, 166
Picard, Laurent, 185-6
Plant, Jim, 204
Pointe-au-Baril, 102
politics: and *The Advertiser*, 22-3; and the *Free Press*, 25, 53

Porter, William, 203, 204
Press News, 83
Press Ownership Review Board, 186
Proctor and Gamble Company, 122
program performance standards, 118
Progressive Conservatives, 53, 105, 111
property holdings, 171
Pryce, Mel, 19, 152
Pryce, Ruth, 152
Purdom, Thomas, 22-3

Quebec referendum, 155
Quebecor Inc., 222
Quick, Gordon, 69

R.C.A. transmitter, 64
radio, as national network service, 94
radio frequency allocation, 59-62
Radio-Nord Inc., 221
Ralph, Dr. John, 12, 46, 164
Rasminsky, Louis, 169
Rathbun, John, 172
RCA Victor Company Limited, 62, 127
Red Cross committee, 14
Reform Party, 7
Regan, F. Vincent, 96
Regional War Labour Board, 54
Reinhart, Bob, 91
Renaud, Paul, 70
revenue, centennial year, 72
Richard Ivey Foundation, 147
Richardson, Ron, 198
Robarts, Premier John, 144
Robinette, J.J., 153-4
Robinson, George W., 50, 172
Robitaille, Glen, 91
Rossie, Melville, 22

Royal Canadian Regiment, 47
Royal Commission on Broadcasting, 98
Royal Commission (Kent Commission), 183-7
Royal Commission on National Development in the Arts, Letters and Sciences. *See* Massey Commission
Royal Commission on Newspapers, 157
Rush, Walter, 60
Ryerson Public School, 14

Sacramento Daily Union, 8
Safer, Morley, 190
salary administration plan, 89-90
Salvation Army, 141
Sanderson, Gordon, 190
Sarnia Observer, 124
Saskatoon Phoenix, 23
Schenck, Jack, 33-4, 127
School of Journalism, University of Western Ontario, 68
Schroeder, Bob, 198
Scott, Bill, 85
Sharpe, Bruce, 148
Shaw, Gerry, 198
Shaw-Wood, Anna Burgess, 14
Shearer, Robin, 196
Shelley, Brian, 163
Sherman, Paddy, 177
shopper publication business, 69, 179
9th Signal Regiment, Royal Canadian Corps of Signals, 110-11
Sinclair, Gordon, 86
Smith, Desmond, 81
Smith, Emilie, 173
Smith, Harry, 173-5
Smith, I. Norman, 85,

123-4, 126, 138, 232
Smith, Maj.-Gen. J.D.B., 110
Smith, Miriam Irene, 81, 89, 107, 192
Smith, Robert, 3
Smith, Sarah, 3
social welfare, 169
Southam Company Limited, 25-6, 107, 157-65
Southam, Fred, 26
Southam Press Limited, 120, 158-65
Southam, William, 9, 10, 158
Southam, William and Sons Limited, 38
Southern Ontario Newspaper Guild, 227
Southstar Publishers Limited, 120-1
Spears, Borden, 186
Special Senate Committee on Mass Media, ("the Davey Commission") 106, 128-32, 133, 154, 186
staff relations, Blackburn Group, 209, 224
Standard Broadcasting Corporation Limited, 210
standard of excellence, 225
Stanford University, 214
Star, Paris, 2
Stenben Sanitarium, 12
Stephanie, 126
"Stereo 96" FM, 184
Stevens, Jack, 144-5
Stewart, Diane, 145
Stiller, Dr. Cal, 196
Stovin, Horace, 58-9
Strategic Planning Committee, 204
St. Catharines Standard, 137
St. John the Evangelist Anglican Church, 46, 49

St. Paul's Cathedral,
11, 150, 198
Stuparik, Andrew, 85
Sutherland, William,
2, 71

Talbot, Alfred, 69
Talbot Street Baptist
Church, 150
Tanner, Cedric, 15
taxes, effect on broad-
cast policy, 106, 108-
9, 154
Taylor, J. Allyn, 143-4,
150, 197
technological change,
20, 40, 115
television, 54-5, 75, 88-
9, 91, 93; and CBC
requirements, 91-2;
and colour, 95, 98;
and political envi-
ronment, 86-7
test of fairness, 225
Theatre London, 141,
150, 202
32nd Regiment, Brit-
ish regulars, 5
Thomas, Charles, 12,
25, 27-8, 42-4
Thomson Newspapers
Limited, 124, 179,
210
Thomson, Kenneth
Roy, 125, 177-8, 210
Thomson, Roy, 64, 96,
181
Times, The, 223
Tingley, Merle, 189
Toledo, Antonio, 126
Toledo, Kate, 172
Toledo, Kyra, 172
Toledo, Susan, 126,
172, 191-3
Toledo, Tony, 172
Toronto Globe, 7
Toronto Star, 23, 120,
124, 125, 176-7, 217
Toronto Sun Publish-
ing Company, 68
Trans-Canada Net-
work CBC, 94

transistors, 97
Tremblay, Cal, 180
Trestain, W.G., 71, 116,
122
Trinity College
School, 127
Trowell, Douglas, 47,
65-6, 85, 134, 137
Trudeau, Prime Minis-
ter Pierre, 123, 155,
183, 191
Turnbull, Robert, 126-
7, 188, 203, 204, 217
Twigg Communica-
tions Limited, 119

Unions, 100, 185
University Hospital,
51, 140, 146-8
University of British
Columbia, 144
University of Western
Ontario, 16, 52, 68,
141-2, 151
Urban and Associates,
214

Vancouver Province,
158, 177; and the
strike, 185
Vancouver Sun, 133
Videopress, 190
videotex, 190

WAAB Boston, 86
Waide, Russell, 37, 72,
100
Walker, H.S., 62
Walker, Mike, 203-6,
212, 214, 225
Walter J. Blackburn
Multi-Organ Trans-
plant Unit, 225-6
Warner, Canon Quin-
ton, 46
Warwick, Dr. Harold,
144, 147, 195
Washington hand
press, 20
Washington printing
press, 172
Weekend magazine, 120

Weld, John, 10
Weldon, D.B., 52
*West Edmonton Exam-
iner, The,* 223
Western Ontario
Conservative Assi-
ciation, 25
Westweb Inc., 223
Whaley, John, 175
Whig-Standard, King-
ston, 179
Whitaker, Henry, 6
Whitaker, Susanna, 6
Whitaker's Almanac, 6
White, Annabelle, 172,
226
White, Martha. *See*
Martha Grace Black-
burn
White, Peter G., 120,
170-2, 185, 192, 194,
203-4; tenure as
executive, 139, 161,
166, 173, 179-81,
206-7
White, Richard, 172,
226
White, Sarah, 172, 226
Wild, Tom, 197
Williams, Dr. D.
Carlton, 141, 232
Wingham Investments
Limited, 135
Wingrove, Cliff, 85
Winnipeg Sun, 222-3
Winnipeg Telegram, 41
Witherspoon, Glen,
177-8
WJR Detroit, 59
Woodroe Nicholson
Publishing, 223
Woods, Gordon &
Company, 120-1
World Wildlife Fund
(Canada), 151, 202
Wright, Don, 63-5, 72

YM-YWCA, 141
Young Presidents
Organization, The,
192, 203